DIGITAL PAINTING

Made Simple

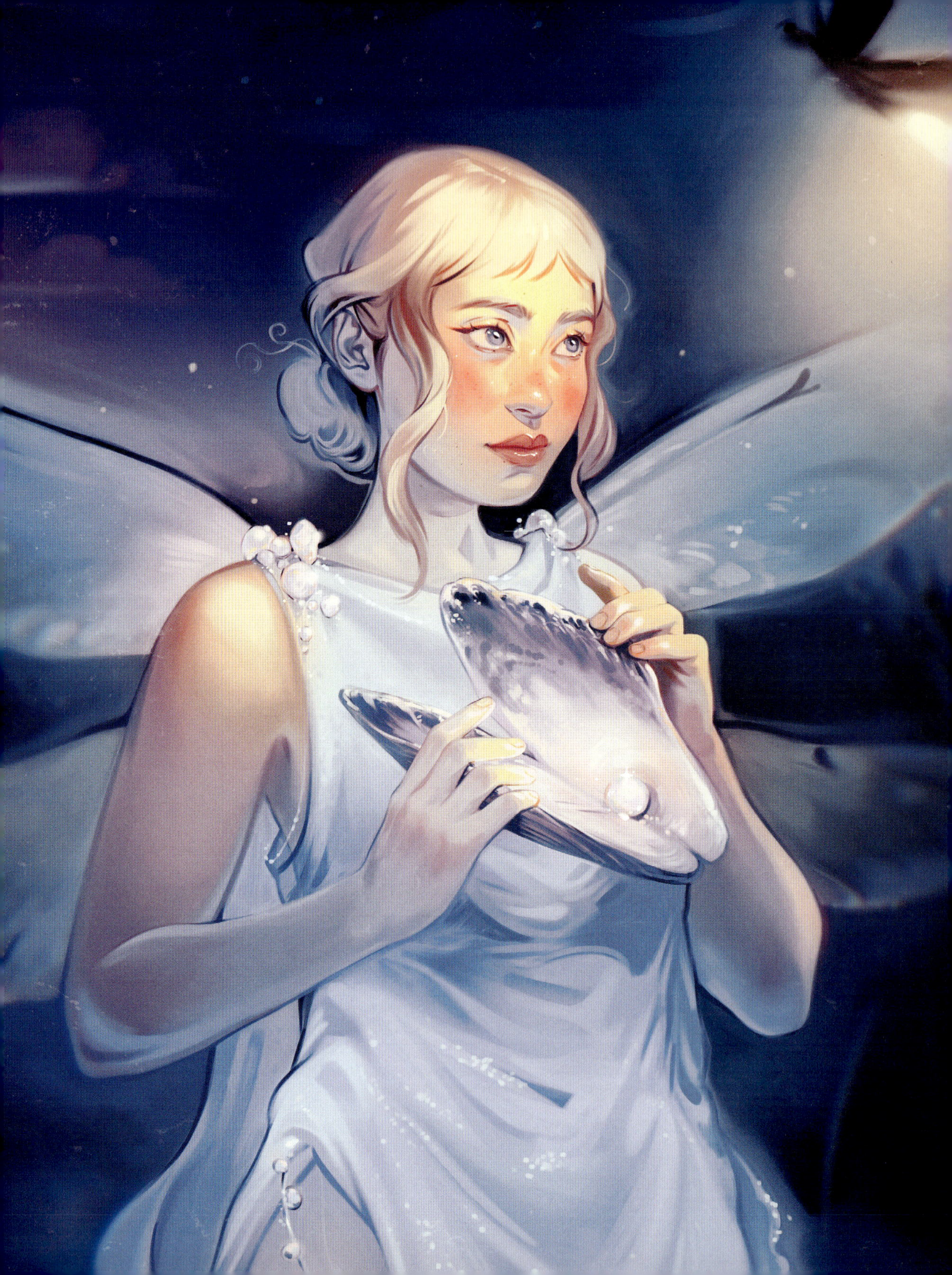

DIGITAL PAINTING
⋆ Made Simple ⋆

Create Captivating Portraits in Clip Studio Paint, Procreate®, Photoshop® & More

Sara Tepes

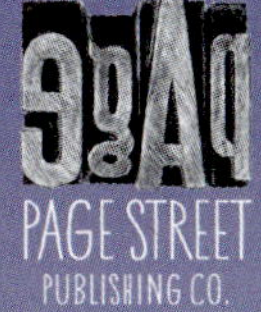

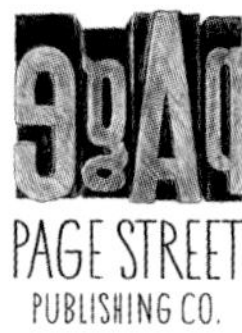

First published in 2025 by

Page Street Publishing Co.

27 Congress Street, Suite 1511

Salem, MA 01970

www.pagestreetpublishing.com

Distributed by Macmillan, sales in Canada by The Canadian Manda Group.

29 28 27 26 25 1 2 3 4 5

ISBN-13: 978-1-645-67552-5

Library of Congress Control Number: 2021938436

Edited by Sarah Monroe

Cover and book design by Laura Benton for Page Street Publishing Co.

Artwork by Sara Tepes

Printed and bound in the United States of America

Page Street Publishing protects our planet by donating to nonprofits like The Trustees, which focuses on local land conservation.

To you, the artist who
treasures the small
details—may this book
spark your imagination
and inspire you to create.

CONTENTS

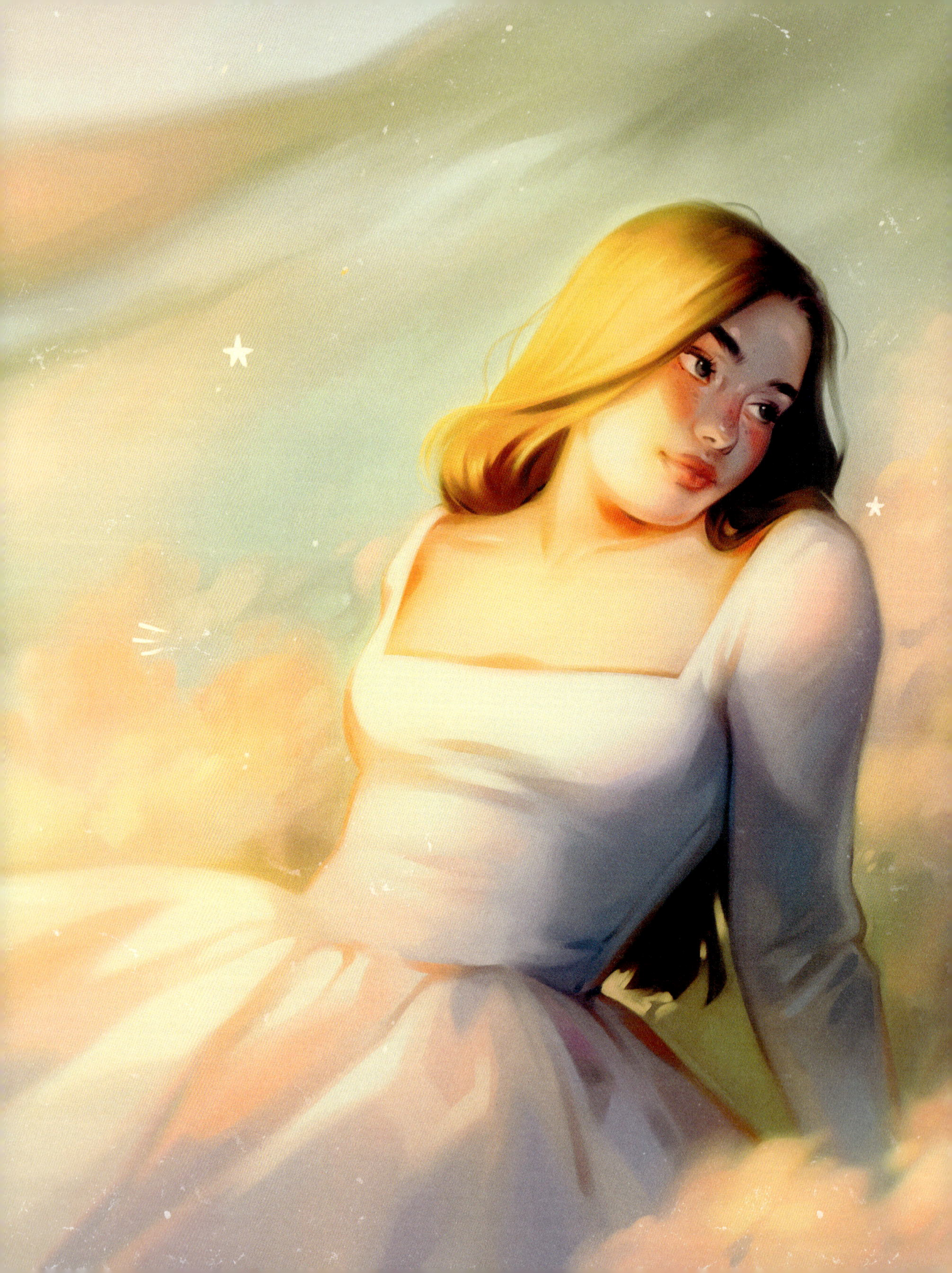

INTRODUCTION

Ever since I was little, drawing was my identity as an immigrant child who wasn't involved in sports, dance or music. I quickly learned that I was a notch better at drawing than the other kids in my grade, and so every day, I would work hard at learning how to be even better at it. My older brother and I would compete against each other, drawing different animals and people; he was naturally detail oriented and inclined to draw animals rather than people, while I loved drawing girls.

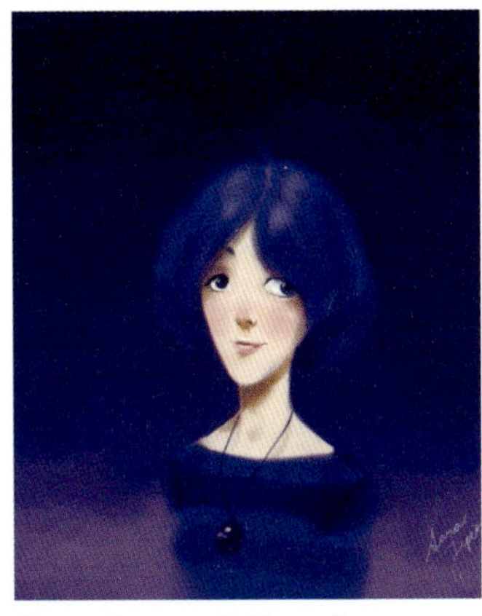

One of my paintings from 2012

I was homeschooled since the second grade, and growing up in a turbulent home, drawing was my escape. I poured myself into learning as much as I could, reading numerous books on anatomy, lighting, painting and digital art, as well as watching a multitude of YouTube videos on all these topics.

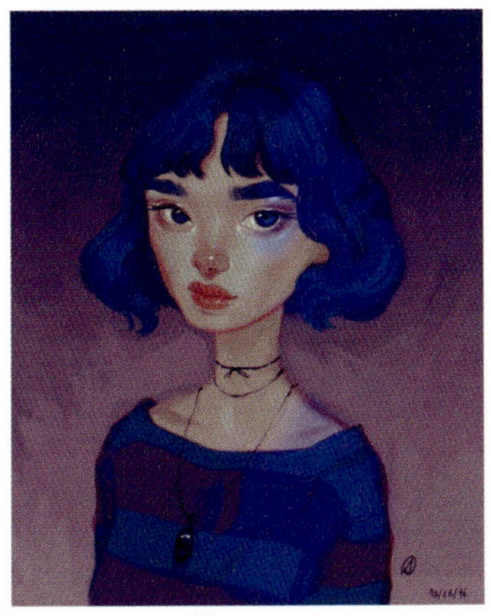

Reworking the same concept in 2016

I've now been digitally painting for over 13 years and have learned what specific techniques have helped me develop my skills and style in as streamlined a manner as possible. I want to share the tips and tools that I personally use and have learned in my own painting journey throughout the years. If you want to try out a different technique, brush, style, color palette, etc., go for it! I hope this book is a resource to you in creating semi-realistic portraits, in my case specifically of feminine subjects, and that you can add it to a collection of references, including books on realistic anatomy, comprehensive color theory and traditional media.

Nothing beats the joy of adding that one final touch that makes your painting pop, knowing how to use contrasting shades and values to bring definition to your subject or creating something exactly as you had it pictured in your imagination. I truly find so much joy in creating pieces inspired by classical fairy tales, literature or paintings, and I hope to share my thoughts and journey with you in a way that will inspire you to seek out your own personal style.

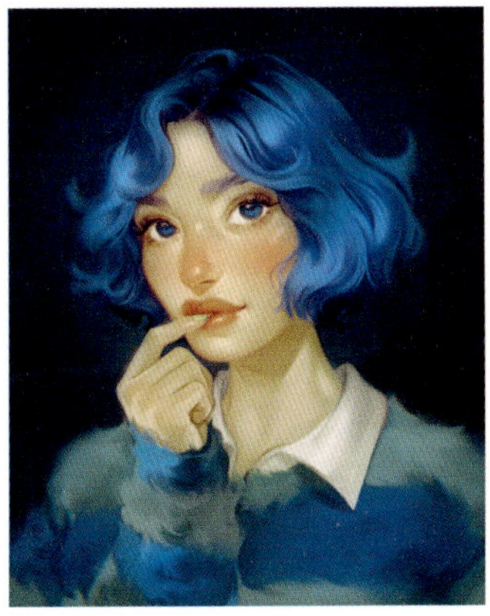

My progress in 2021

SARA TEPES

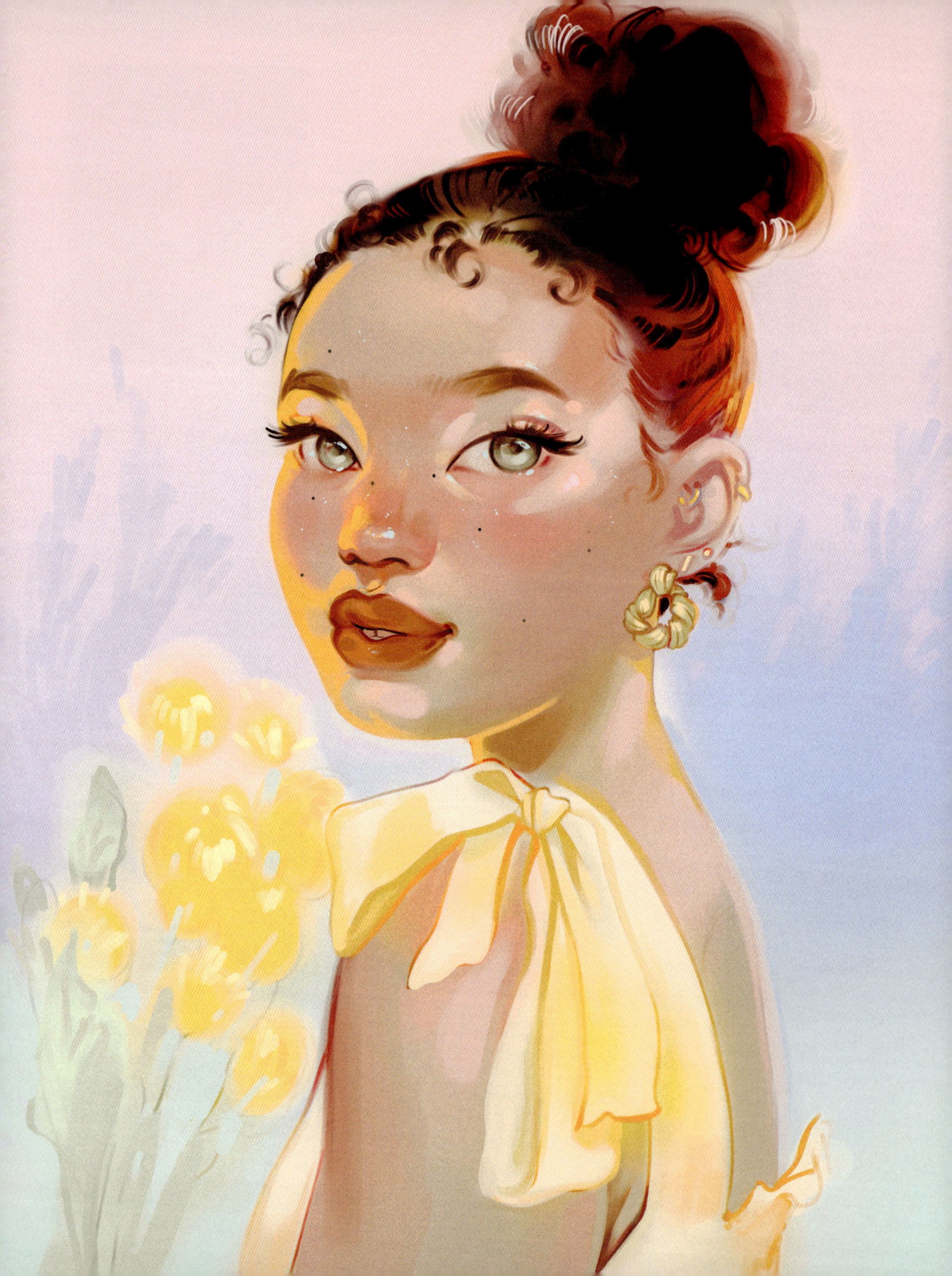

Chapter 1

GETTING STARTED DIGITAL PAINTING

For those new to digital art, this chapter will guide you in selecting the right painting software and drawing tablet to suit your needs. You'll also discover how to set the canvas size, choose color palettes and brushes, organize layers effectively and work with various adjustment layers and tools. Let's dive in!

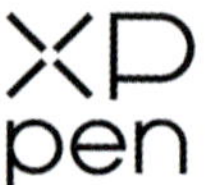

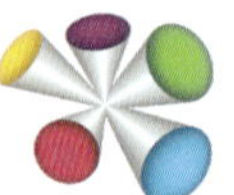
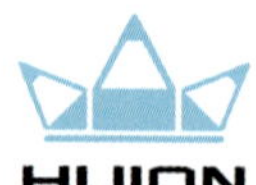

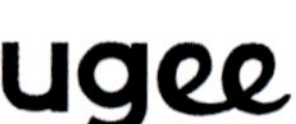

DIGITAL PAINTING PROGRAMS

I began digital painting when I was 11. First, I started with Gimp, a free digital painting program, and then switched over to Krita, another free program. I worked and learned digital painting primarily in Krita, using it from 2016 to 2020 until I switched over to Adobe Photoshop (or simply Photoshop), and then finally to Clip Studio Paint, the painting program I use and love now. If you are a beginner and cannot afford a monthly subscription to Photoshop or Clip Studio Paint, consider trying out a free digital painting software. There are many options out there for you to choose from and begin developing your skills, even if you don't have a high budget. You can also get a heavy discount on the Adobe Creative Suite if you are a student; don't forget to check if your school offers you a complimentary subscription.

For the sake of continuity in this book, I will be referencing Clip Studio Paint (or CSP) in its interface, shortcuts and features. If you are personally not using CSP, there is a more than likely chance that your program will have a similar feature. Most of the features I will be using in CSP have equivalents in Photoshop and Procreate. If you're using a slightly more obscure program, make use of a quick Google search and look up the equivalent feature for what I will be mentioning.

USING TABLETS

There are many great tablet companies to choose from and purchase. I have personally reviewed and tested dozens of tablets, large and small, in every price range. The most well-known brand used by professionals is Wacom Co., Ltd.; I have personally worked with Wacom in the past. I have had five Wacom® tablets over the years and can recommend them as a good company. However, I personally use a Huion® WH1409 V2 tablet and will always recommend Huion tablets to my followers. I've been sent multiple tablets for review by this company but have not accepted payment or an affiliate link for speaking about them. I've used this tablet for several years (starting out with the original model and then switching over to this second version). I love the feel of the pen; it is ergonomic and the best pen I've used for multiple-hour painting sessions and daily use. It is also highly affordable, making it a great tablet to recommend to you.

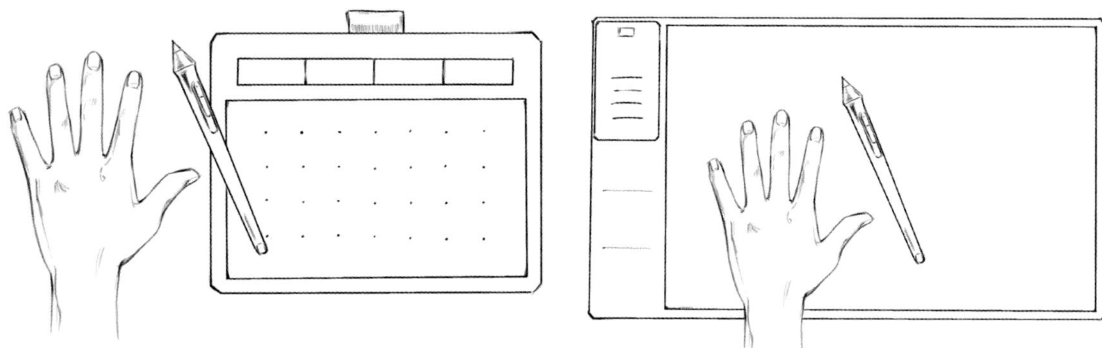

A smaller tablet size is convenient for travel, while a larger tablet size is better for your wrist's health. I recommend choosing the largest tablet size possible within your budget and travel constraints.

The most inexpensive and accessible way to begin digital painting is with a drawing tablet and desktop/laptop. A drawing tablet does not have a screen, so you will look forward at your monitor to see your painting process. Display tablets are slightly more expensive but feature a pressure sensitive screen that can display your program. Most display tablets must be connected to a desktop/laptop to run the painting software. Lastly, an iPad® works with the Apple Pencil® and Procreate. An iPad is the most expensive option but can be used independently from a desktop/laptop. I personally use a simple drawing tablet with no screen, but choose your desired tablet based on your budget.

When deciding on what tablet you would like to purchase, consider your needs. Do you need something lightweight for constant travel? If you are looking for something that can fit into your backpack for use during school, work or painting sessions at a coffee shop, look for a tablet on the smaller side. However, if you do not have the restriction of portability, I highly recommend looking for a large tablet, one that has a working size of over 9 x 12 inches (23 x 30 cm).

I started off using a Wacom Bamboo tablet (it had a working size of roughly 4 x 6 inches [10 x 15 cm]) for my digital art, and quickly realized that after continued use, I was straining my wrist horribly and developing backaches. A small working size is good for small tasks, like signing documents or quick handwriting. If you are serious about digital art, consider the long-term health effects that you might experience. Purchasing a larger tablet will ensure that you are using fewer wrist motions and more sweeping arm motions. This will help with avoiding carpal tunnel syndrome, maintaining good posture and supporting your back and spine health.

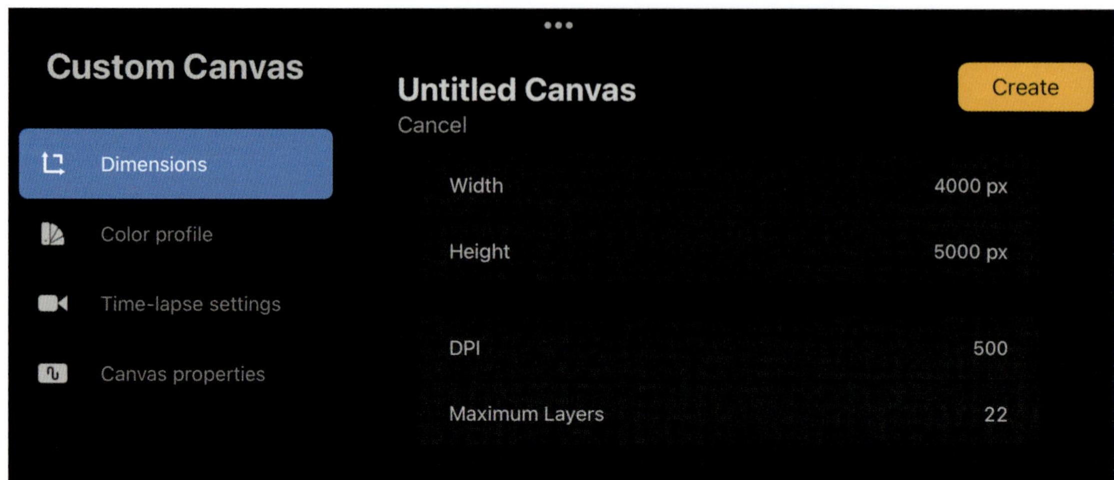

This is the general canvas size I use in Procreate when creating a portrait painting. I recommend not dropping your dimensions below 2500 x 2500 px.

SETTING UP A DOCUMENT

Once you have chosen your program and tablet, it's time to start a new painting! You can start a new canvas by opening up CSP and going to "File > New." In Procreate, go to the top right-hand corner, hit the "+" and create a custom canvas. One question I get often is, "What size should my canvas be?" I recommend first deciding where you want the piece to end up: Are you only posting to social media, or would you like to make prints of it?

Instagram's in-feed post ratio is 4:5, which works perfectly for me, as I like to have 8 x 10—inch (20 x 25—cm) prints in my shop. One of the most important aspects of determining a canvas size is knowing the appropriate "dots per inch" (dpi) and "pixels per inch" (ppi). Dpi refers to the number of dots per inch in printing, while ppi refers to the pixel density in a digital file. A good rule is to use a dpi/ppi of 72 or 150 for sharing on social media, a dpi/ppi of 300 for anything you want to print and a dpi/ppi of 600 if you want to enlarge the print.

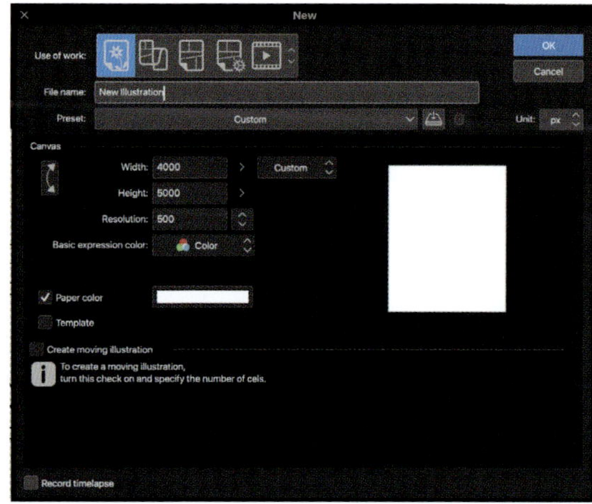

I use these dimensions when creating a new portrait painting in Clip Studio Paint. Make sure the resolution does not drop below 300 dpi/ppi if you plan on printing your work.

So, if I want to enlarge my 8 x 10—inch (20 x 25—cm) print to 11 x 14 inches (28 x 36 cm), I would set the dpi/ppi of the canvas to 600, just to make sure I'm not losing any quality or detail as I enlarge the print. I recommend creating at a minimum size of 300 dpi; you can always scale an image down.

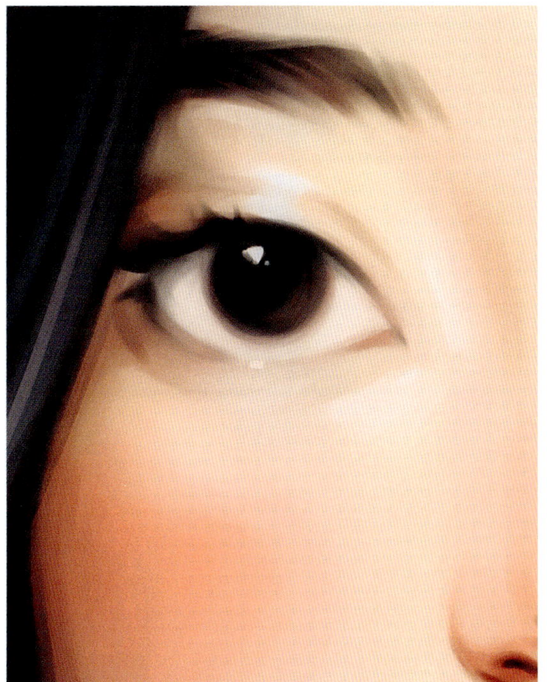

600 dpi

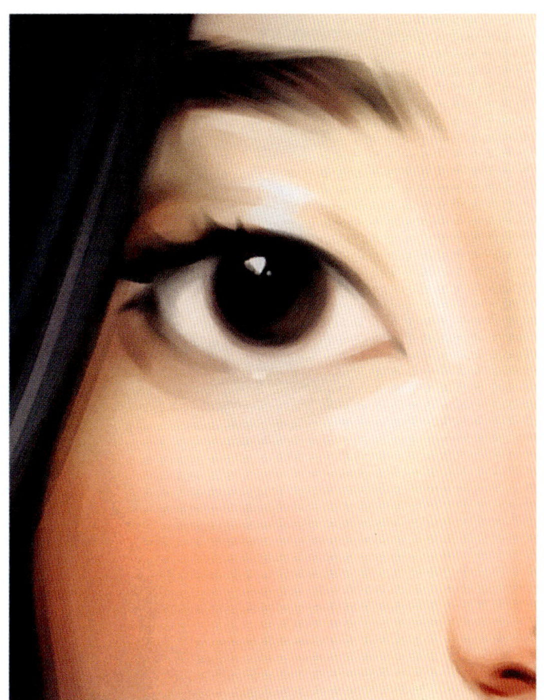

150 dpi

There is a "dpi" setting in the Procreate custom canvas, but for CSP, you can set this in your new canvas by changing the "Resolution" size or altering it later by going to "Edit > Canvas Properties > Resolution." The larger your file size, the more RAM will be used by your computer and the larger file size you will have in the end. Don't create a larger canvas than you need; it will just slow down your computer and your painting process. It's possible to slightly scale up lower-resolution files, but since you're working with a raster image rather than one that relies on mathematical vectors, you won't be able to scale up the details or sharpness, only create the possibility for those added details to be painted in once you've upscaled.

Note: A raster image is a digital picture composed of pixels, each containing specific color and tonal information that come together to create the final image.

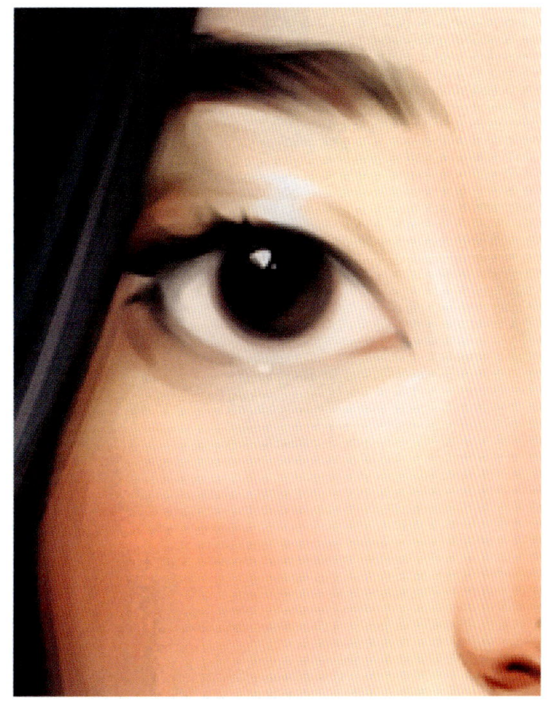

72 dpi

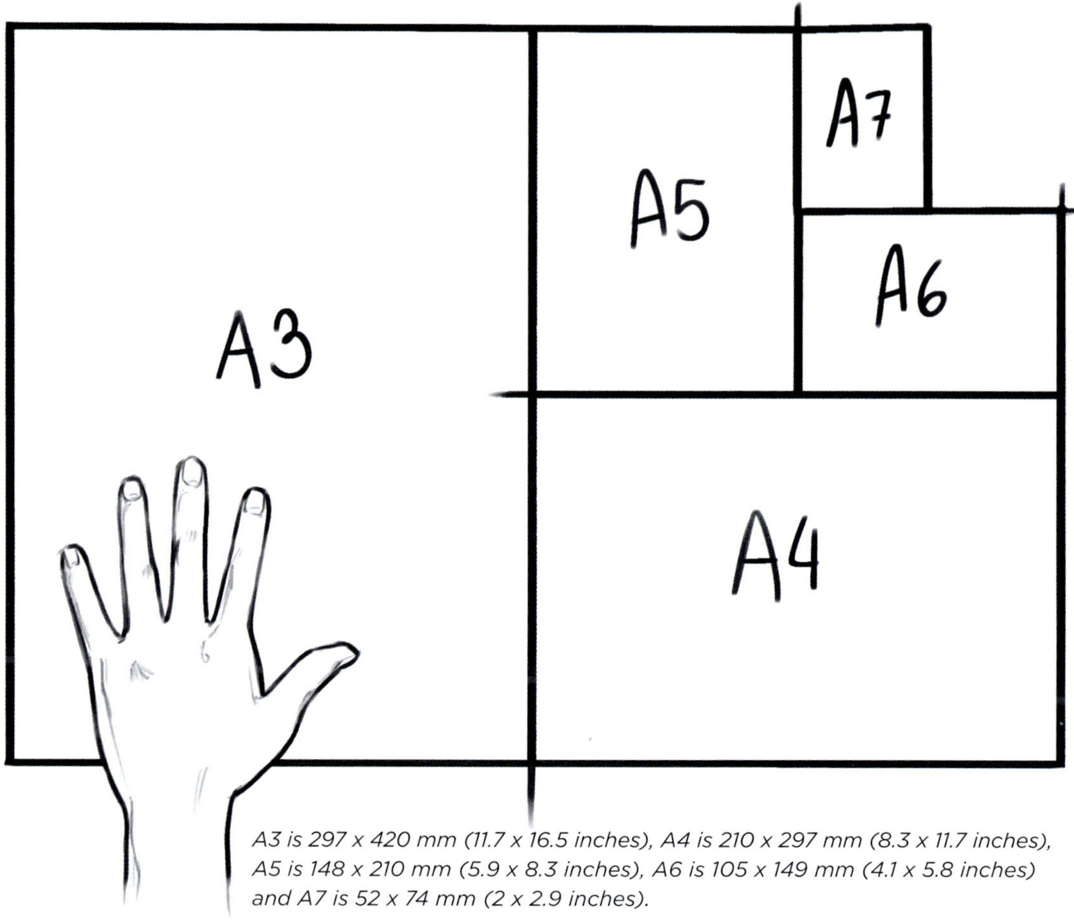

A3 is 297 x 420 mm (11.7 x 16.5 inches), A4 is 210 x 297 mm (8.3 x 11.7 inches), A5 is 148 x 210 mm (5.9 x 8.3 inches), A6 is 105 x 149 mm (4.1 x 5.8 inches) and A7 is 52 x 74 mm (2 x 2.9 inches).

Common canvas sizes are square, 4 x 6 inches (10 x 15 cm), 5 x 7 inches (13 x 18 cm), 8 x 10 inches (20 x 25 cm), 11 x 14 inches (28 x 36 cm), 13 x 19 inches (33 x 48 cm), A3, A4 and A5.

Once you've selected the dimensions of your canvas, set your color profile to RGB if you intend to post online only, and CMYK if you intend to print this piece. I personally always start with RGB and then change it to CMYK when I want to print. Since I post all my pieces to my social media first, I am comfortable painting in RGB. Translating your file from RGB to CMYK will result in slight shifts of color, which you might need to later adjust. For more on color theory in digital painting, see page 104.

Note: RGB stands for Red-Green-Blue. CMYK stands for Cyan-Magenta-Yellow-Key ("key" is used for black because B commonly refers to blue, as in RGB).

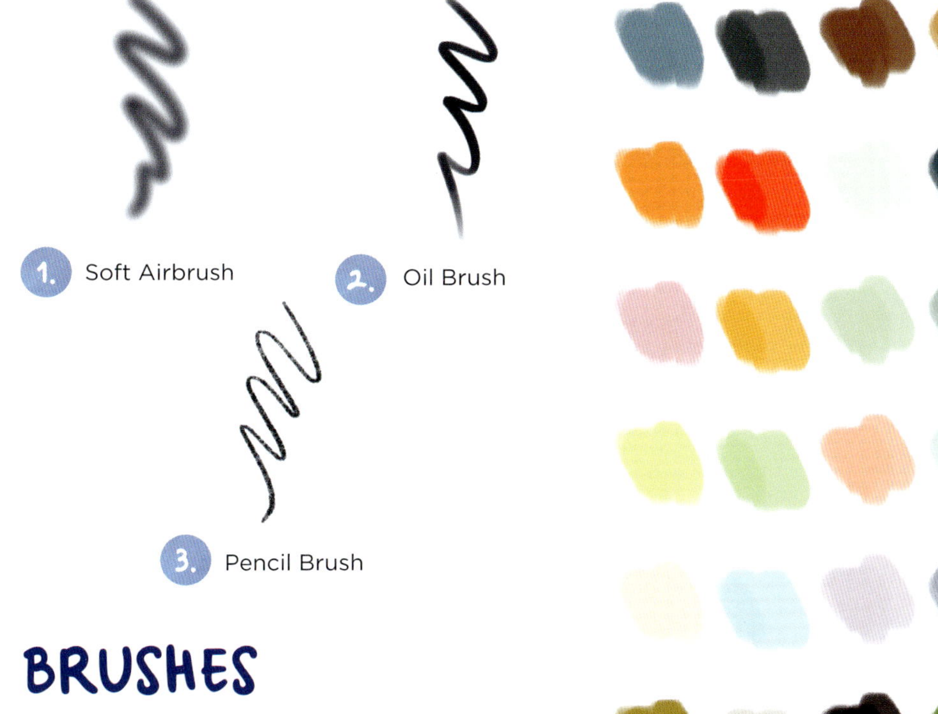

BRUSHES

Above are the brushes I use on a regular basis for my paintings. You can download them on my website (sarucatepes.com/resources) for free and install them in Photoshop, Clip Studio Paint or Procreate.

1. Soft Airbrush
2. Oil-type brush
3. A pencil-type brush for sketching

COLOR PALETTES

Here are some color palettes I recommend experimenting with if you find that you're unsure of what colors to pick for your piece: sarucatepes.com/resources. I've included a variety of natural and colorful swatches that you can download alongside the brush pack for easy color picking in Clip Studio Paint, Photoshop or Procreate.

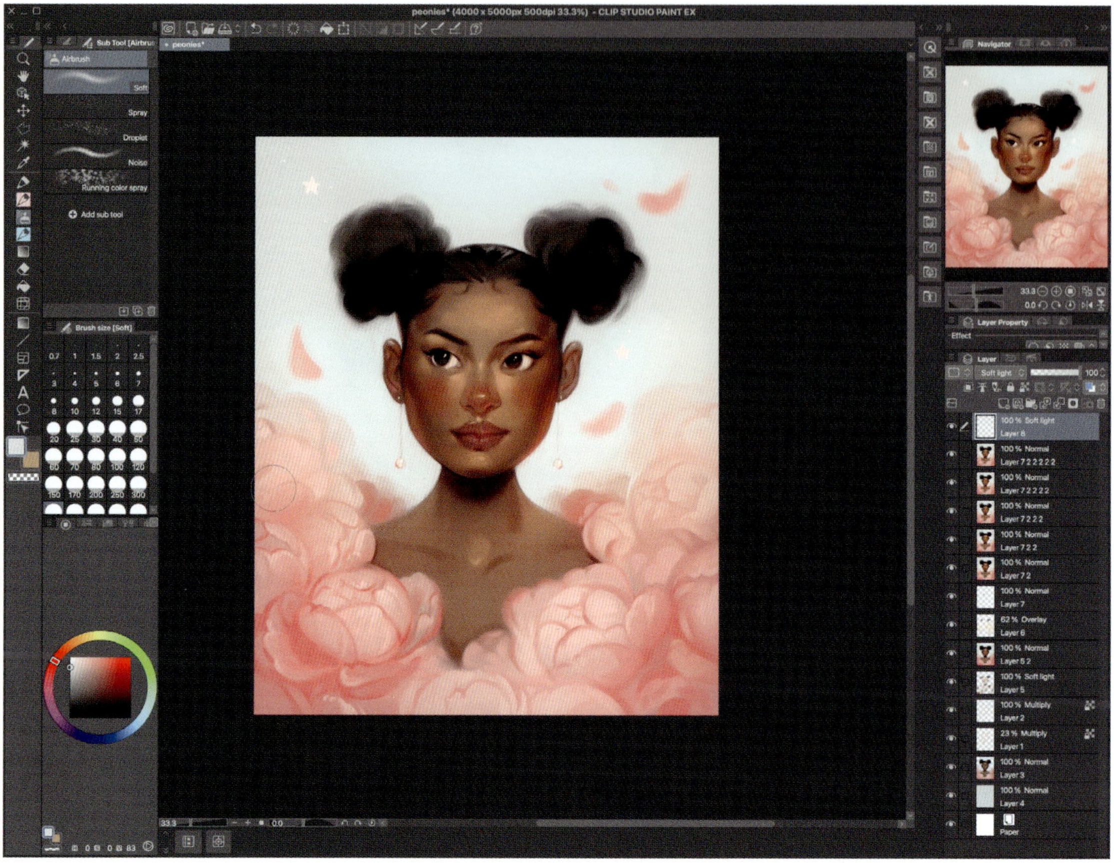

A finished painting in Clip Studio Paint generally has 10 to 15 layers.

CREATING LAYERS

Every digital artist will utilize layers in their own way. If you are like me, your layers will be highly disorganized, not labeled, sporadic and illogical. That's okay! It works for me, and it might work for you. On the other hand, you might be a very organized person by nature, with a penchant for labeling and color coding everything in your reach. Clip Studio Paint has you covered. Here are some of the basic tips I have for you if you aren't sure how to use layers in your paintings.

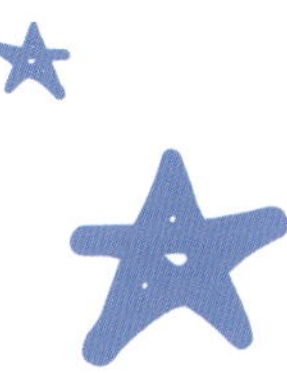

Tip #1: Create a new layer every time you want to try something new or are painting a new section of your piece.

If you're worried about disturbing the work you've already done, duplicate your current layer before starting a new section to preserve your progress. For example, if you want to make a drastic change to an area you have already spent a good amount of time detailing, duplicate that layer or start a layer on top of it to preserve the original. You can find layers in the "Layers" panel of CSP or in the top right-hand corner of Procreate. The joy of digital painting is the ability to save multiple versions of a file. Take advantage of this feature and play it safe.

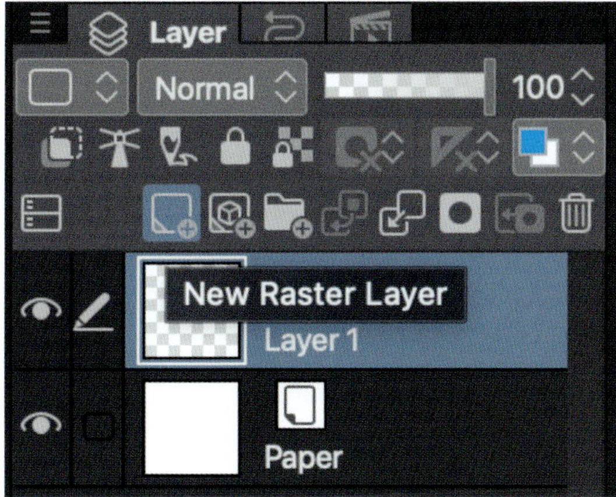

Click the "New Raster Layer" button to create a new layer.

Tip #2: Label each layer accurately.

This is especially helpful if you are working on a large project that will take you over ten hours to create, or if you're going to be sharing the editable file with someone else. If you have a specific pattern for creating layers, you probably won't personally need to label each layer, but organization is very important if you are working with a team or working on a project that will take multiple sessions spanning a long period of time. You can even put layers into their own groups; if you painted each individual facial feature on a separate layer, you can group all those into a group called "face" or "rendering." While this is the best practice, I personally rarely label each layer or keep my files organized.

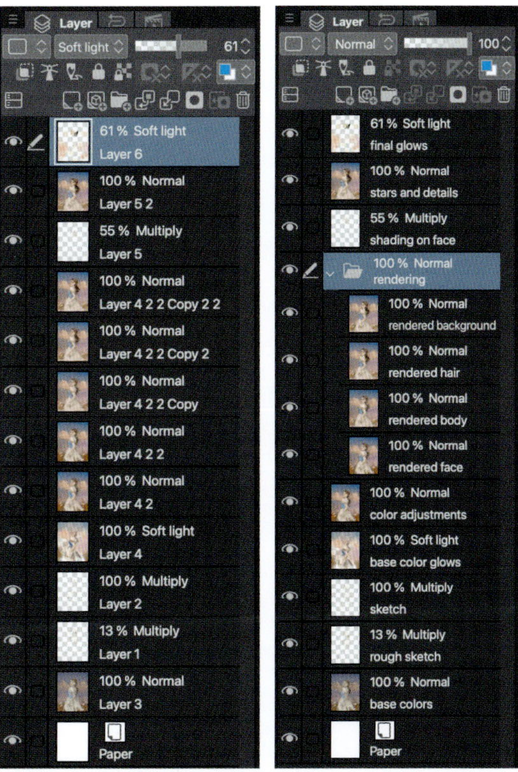

Naming and organizing your layers can be useful if you're working over an extended period or sharing the file.

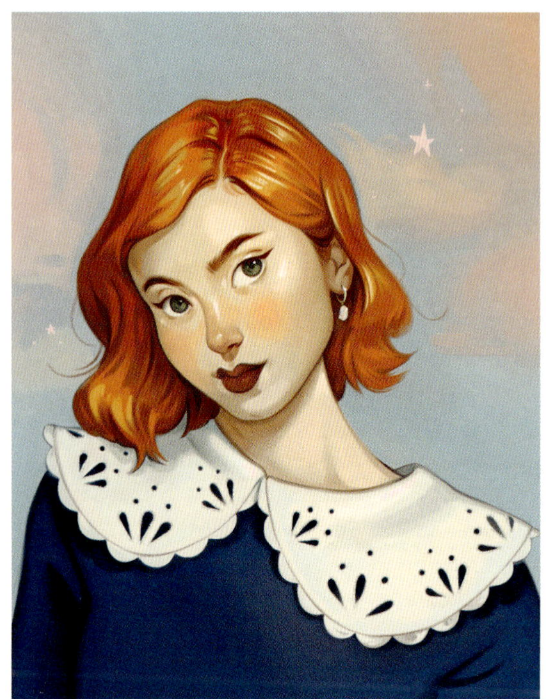

Without adjustment layers

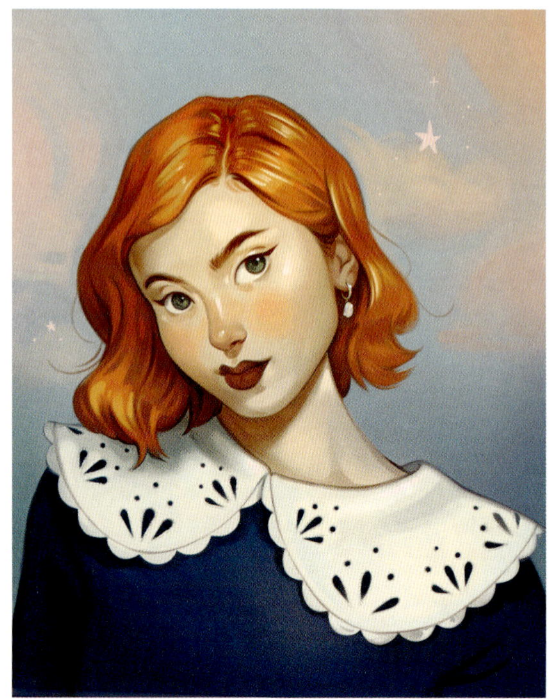

Multiply at 100%

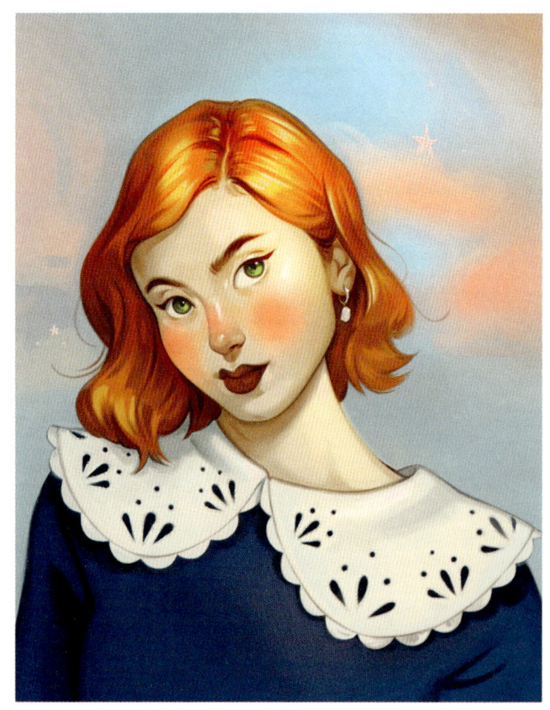

Overlay at 100%

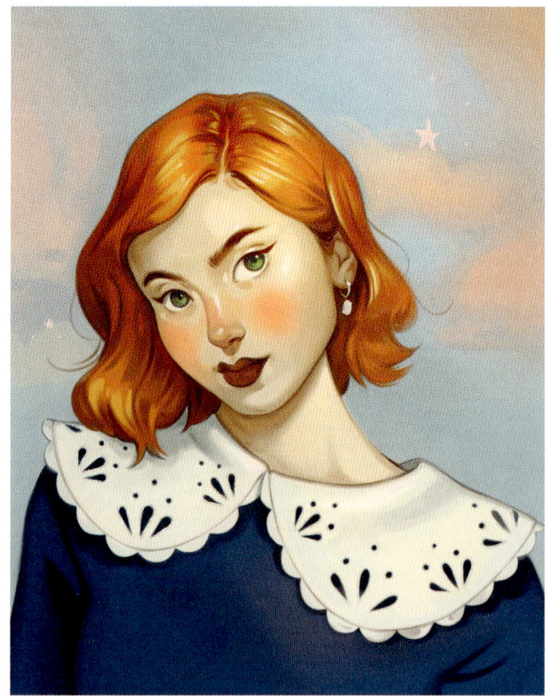

Soft Light at 100%

Tip #3: Use a combination of blending modes and adjustment layers to add life to your piece.

Here are some that I consistently use, but feel free to play around with other ones if you feel that they would mesh well with your personal style. With all of these layers and blending modes, I adjust the opacity to keep the colors and values from becoming too harsh. You can find Opacity on the Layers tab next to Blending Modes.

1. **Multiply:** This blending mode is useful for taking line art that has been drawn on a white canvas and melding it with base colors on a separate layer. It can also be used to darken an area without completely repainting over that section. I added a darkening gradient to the bottom of this painting using the Soft Airbrush.

2. **Overlay:** This blending mode is great for adding strong colors that modify your existing painting. I use this mode for drastically changing the vibrancy of a piece; you can add electric tones, flares and gradients to a piece without changing the integrity of the brushstrokes and detailing underneath. I often use an Overlay layer close to the end of a piece to add bright pops of color in areas I don't feel are vibrant enough. Here, I added a golden hue with the Soft Airbrush to illuminate the side of her face and hair.

3. **Soft Light:** This blending mode is good for intensifying colors and adding shadows and highlights. Soft Light is much more subtle than an Overlay layer; you can also deepen shadows or their vibrancy without adding too much saturated color to your piece. Using the same colors as with the Overlay layer, I used the Soft Airbrush to add highlights to the side of her face and hair. You can see how the colors are softer than the Overlay adjustment layer.

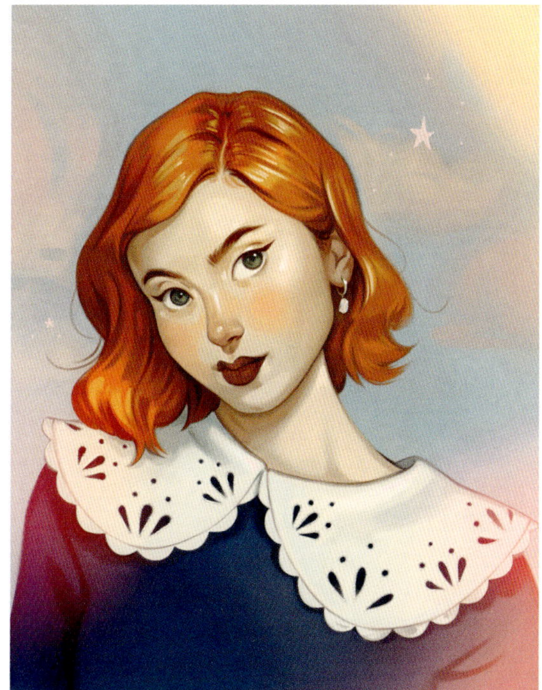

Hard Light at 100%

4. **Hard Light:** This blending mode adds a burnt effect with whatever color you lay down. I don't reach for this layer often, but it is good for adding rim lighting, strong flares or even individual dust scratches to a piece. Due to its intensity, it removes most, if not all, of the details you have placed down on a previous layer, so its uses are very specific. With the Soft Airbrush, I added pink and golden flares around the corners of the painting.

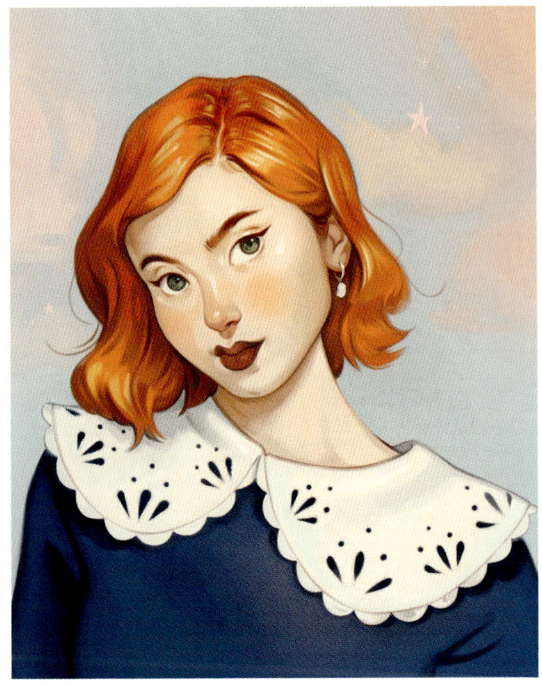

Curves at 100%

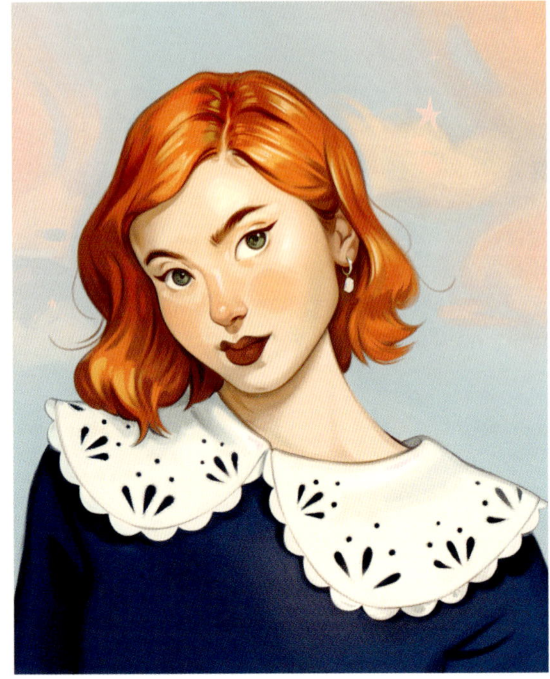

Levels at 100%

5. Curves: This adjustment layer is possibly my most used type of layer. A Curves layer will help modify and unify tones and values. I use multiple Curves layers in a piece; I edit the base colors with one and then edit the final piece with one or multiple of these adjustments. I used Curves to lighten the painting and to gently tint the shadows with a teal color.

6. Levels: This adjustment layer is good for solely adjusting values (for more on values, see page 112). You can use a Curves adjustment layer to adjust the values as well, but it is more streamlined than the Curves layer if you are only looking to adjust the brightness and values of your piece. I adjusted the Levels to add extra brightness and contrast to the painting.

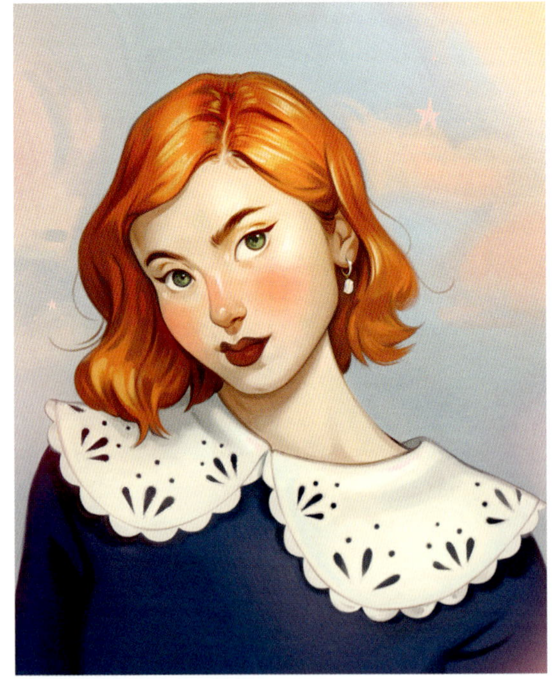

With Multiply at 25%, Overlay at 30%, Soft Light at 75%, Hard Light at 80%, Curves at 60% and Levels at 40%

BEST PRACTICES

If you are serious about digital painting, it is imperative to begin building good habits as quickly as possible; these good habits are what I like to call "best practices." While on the surface, digital painting might seem like a fun and painless hobby to learn, you can quickly become discouraged or overwhelmed if you are not keeping best practices in mind. While some of these tips might be boring or unexciting, or even seem too tedious and drawn out, I promise that they will save you so much frustration, anger and time in the long run. It took me years to build up these habits (since no one told me about them, I had to learn them myself), and I hope that you take them into consideration and integrate them into your workflow.

Saving Your Files

First and foremost, have autosave set to saving your file every five minutes. You can do this by going to "File > Preferences > File." In addition, make a conscious effort to save as often as possible; never make the *conscious* decision to NOT save a file! I have done this so many times before and have always regretted it. Inevitably, your computer or tablet will freeze or crash at some point, and you will likely lose hours of work, leaving you so discouraged. Since digital art is so physically taxing (taking a toll on your back and wrists), the loss of your time and painting is compounded with the added strain you will experience when having to start over on your piece.

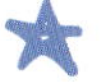

If you are painting in Photoshop, you can utilize the History tab whenever you plan to make a drastic or experimental change to your painting. Click on "Create a new snapshot," or the camera icon, under the History tab. Adding a snapshot is a way for you to be able to undo a large series of actions and brushstrokes even if you have reached the possible limit for undoing an action. This will give you freedom to experiment with your piece and come back to the original starting point if you are unhappy with the changes you made. At the near end of the painting process, I will sometimes choose to merge all of my layers into one single, flattened image. This makes for easier adjustments to the entire painting, as well as a reduced file size, provided that I am happy with the painting and don't wish to alter any of the layers. In this type of situation, I will add a snapshot in the case that I want to go back and make a change to the original layers. One thing to note is that CSP and Photoshop will not save the history after you've saved and closed out of your file, so save a copy of the file with all the layers still separated if you plan to edit those layers in the future.

Filing Your Documents

Keep all of the files and references for a particular painting in one labeled folder on your computer. Keeping everything in the same place will make it easier for you to access specific assets or to come back to a piece after a long time. You will start accumulating a crazy number of files in between saving multiple copies of your paintings and using color and model references, so having them in one specific folder will keep your desktop clean and organized.

My Favorite Shortcut: The Eyedropper

Use the Eyedropper tool to color pick often; using the Eyedropper should become second nature to you as you become comfortable with your program and tablet. You can find the Eyedropper tool in the left-hand tool bar in CSP, but I recommend using the shortcut below for easier toggling between the Eyedropper and your brush in Photoshop or CSP. You can hold down with one finger anywhere on the canvas to access the Eyedropper in Procreate, dragging your finger to the desired color and letting go once you've selected the color you like.

Color picking will save you so much time when blending two contrasting shades, as well as help you achieve subtle variations in the tones you lay down and tying shades from different areas of the painting together. If your model is wearing a blue dress, color picking that blue and adding a subtle reflection to the chin or jaw will make it look as if light is bouncing off the dress and hitting the subject's face. Small details like this will take your painting to the next level.

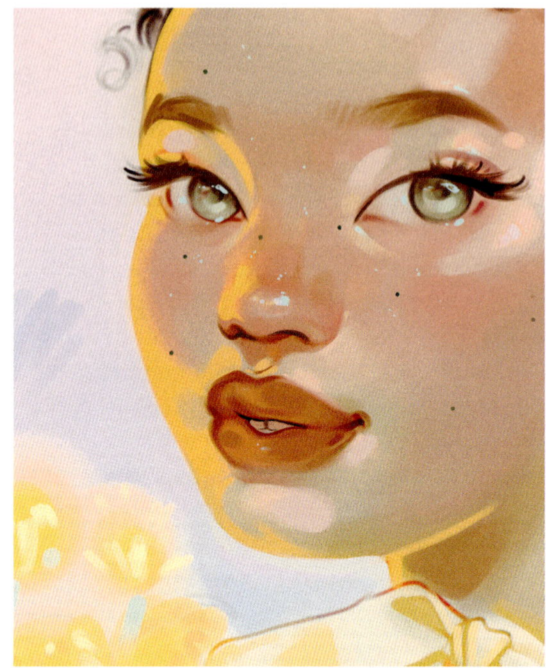

I color picked from the flowers to add the yellow glow across the side of the subject's face.

Utilize shortcuts to streamline the painting process! CSP/Photoshop shortcuts to know are:

1. **Free Transform:** Command+T (on Mac)/ Control+T (on PC)
2. **Color Picker/Eyedropper:** hold down Option (on Mac)/Alt (on PC)
3. **Decrease Brush Size:** [
4. **Increase Brush Size:**]
5. **Undo:** Command+Z (on Mac)/Control+Z (on PC)
6. **Redo:** Shift+Command+Z (on Mac)/ Shift+Control+Z (on PC)
7. **Save:** Command+S (on Mac)/Control+S (on PC)

Procreate shortcuts to know are:

1. **Color Picker/Eyedropper:** tap and hold down with one finger on the canvas
2. **Undo:** two finger tap
3. **Redo:** three finger tap
4. **Cut/Copy/Paste:** three finger swipe down

Taking Breaks

Step away from your painting if you're becoming tired, unhappy or rushing the process. Especially when it comes to deadlines, it might seem like the best idea to power through any discouragement or creative block you are having in order to complete a piece. However, straining your body is going to be more harmful in the long run than you think. Keeping yourself from falling into complete exhaustion is important. Take a break from your painting. Chances are, you have been sitting for hours and your body feels terrible. Ideally, sleep on the painting and come back to it in the morning with fresh eyes. If you have an imperative deadline and cannot afford the time, take a walk around your neighborhood, drink some water, stretch, do some chores and come back to the piece after 30 minutes or more.

Setting distance between yourself and the piece is important for coming up with creative solutions. You might be frustrated that you aren't able to paint a feature as well as you would like; this might be the result of wrist pain, exhaustion or prolonged exposure to the piece in a way where you cannot realize the mistakes or flaws in your process. Coming back with fresh eyes can quickly help you identify the problems and gives your body a chance to recover from the strain. Staying in tune with your body and what it is telling you is important in maintaining your overall workflow and inspiration.

Exporting Your Painting

You can export your painting in a variety of file types, with the most common being JPEG, which offers a good balance of quality compression and smaller file size. Export in PNG if you want to preserve any transparency in your artwork, or in TIFF if you want to preserve your details and image quality to the highest degree.

Breaking Rules: The Wrong and Right Ways

Lastly, break rules if you have a brilliant idea and know that you are breaking a rule. Making a deliberate decision to break away from the norm and experiment can lead you to developing a masterpiece or coming up with a unique and attractive personal style. However, it's silly to not understand or practice a rule or theory and then claim that your poorly executed piece is "just your style." You should have a valid reason for going against a rule or concept. If you are trying to paint a turbulent piece and don't use traditional rules to compose the character in their setting, that can help you create an unsettling look. On the other hand, if you are planning on painting a serene image, the same composition can be telling of your poor skills and knowledge as an artist. My advice is to learn traditional art techniques, study the work of the masters and then make your own informed decisions about where you want your art style to go.

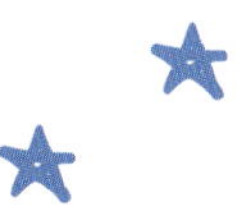

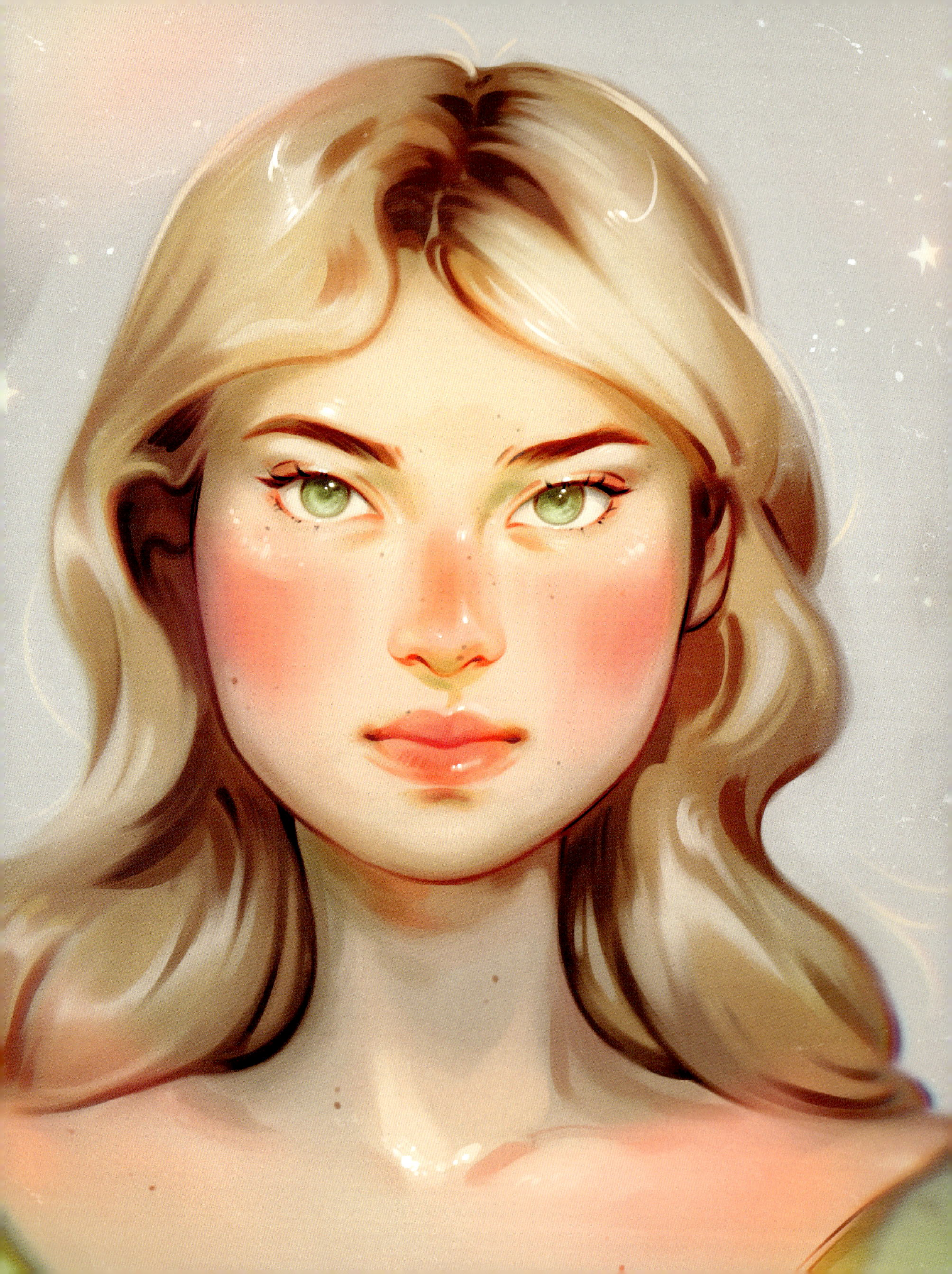

PROMPT: CREATE YOUR FIRST PAINTING

Now, let's put all that information into practice! I invite you to paint a portrait based on your favorite food, using the food as your color scheme.

Be mindful of what your thought process is when coming up with an idea, what techniques you use and are comfortable with, and what you struggle with and would like to improve on. Jot all these thoughts down for future reference. Regardless of your skill set and confidence in your art, I would love for you to paint something that resonates with where you are in your life and journey so far. This piece is meant to establish your grounding point, from which we will build and refine your skills throughout the rest of this book.

My painting was inspired by a Caesar salad. The color of the dress and eyes is a warm shade of green like that of romaine lettuce, while the golden hair is inspired by toasted croutons and Parmesan.

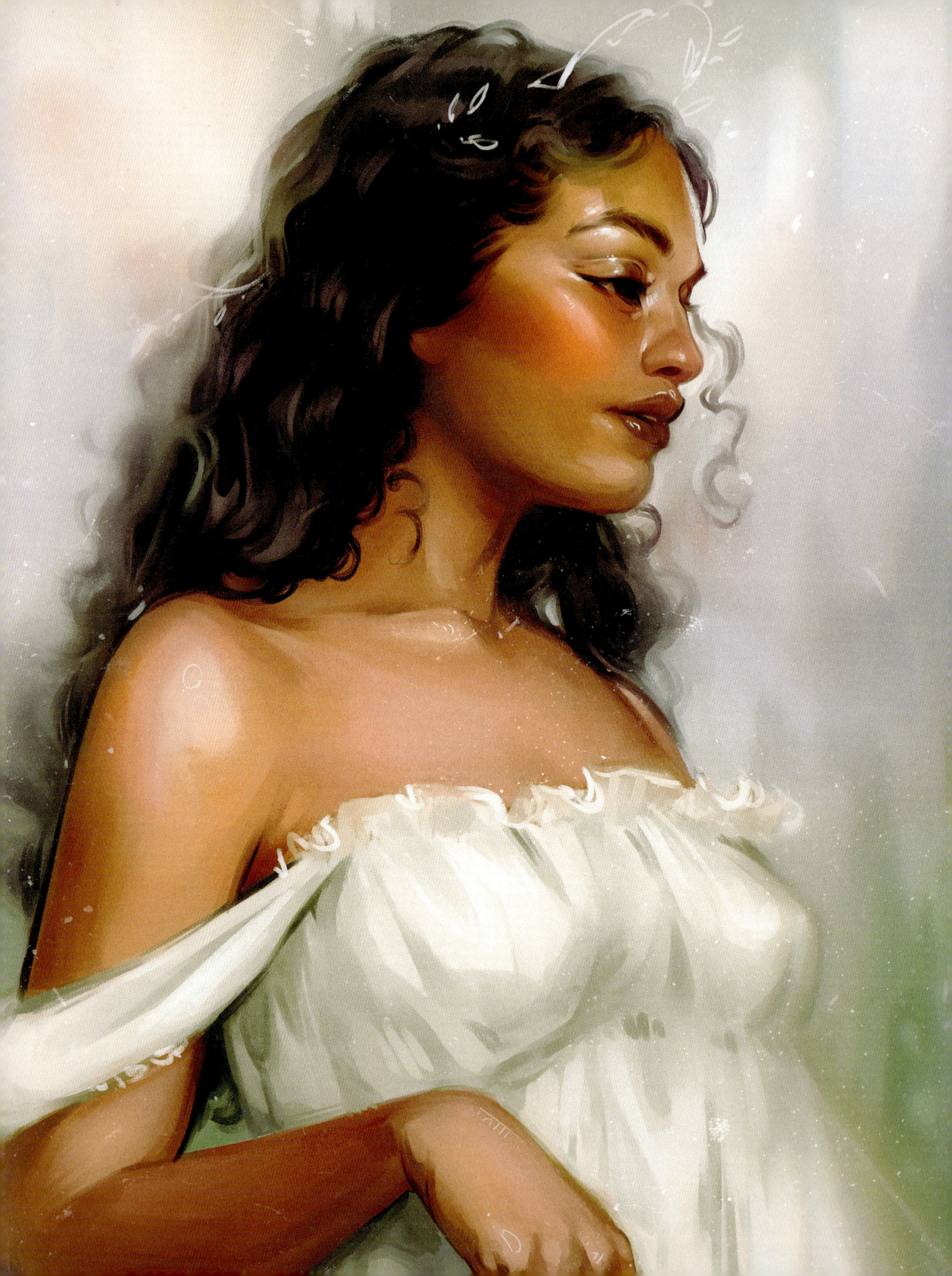

Chapter 2

PAINTING THE BODY

Digital painting has a unique learning curve when it comes to the universal concepts of mastering anatomy and fleshing out the human form. There are both helpful and challenging nuances to this medium, but practicing and growing your skills will be endlessly rewarding. In this section, you will learn to paint the features of the face, like eyes (page 35), noses (page 56) and lips (page 46), as well as the concepts of different skin tones (page 81), hair textures (page 64) and even a brief foray into full-body poses (page 30). While there is much to cover, you can and should take these walkthroughs at your own pace. Remember that no matter what your skill set is, everyone had to start from square one at some point, and that the defining factor in your success at painting the human form is the practice and dedication that you put into learning these concepts. While realism is daunting, take each feature one at a time instead of worrying about the whole just yet.

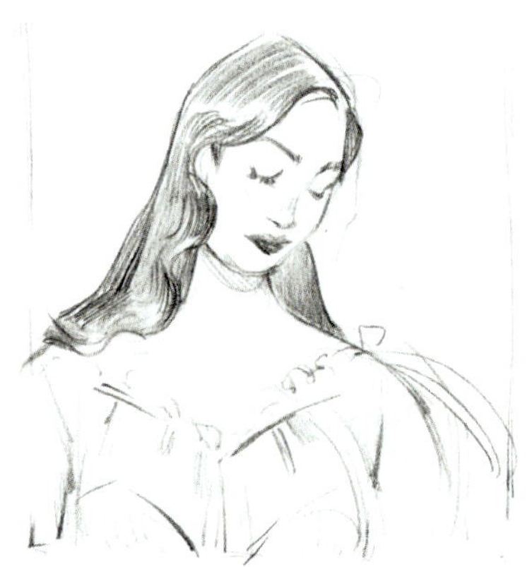

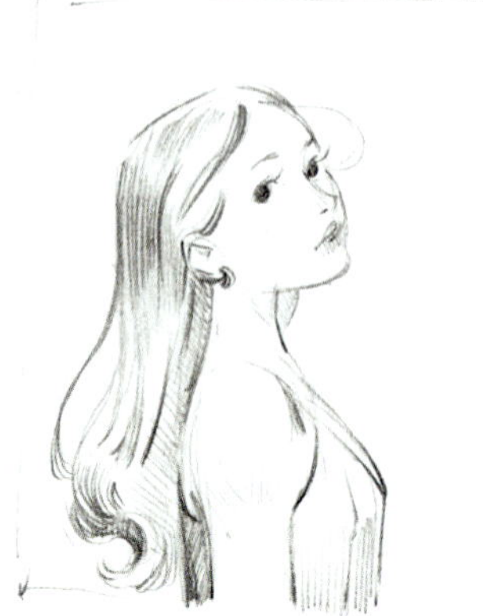

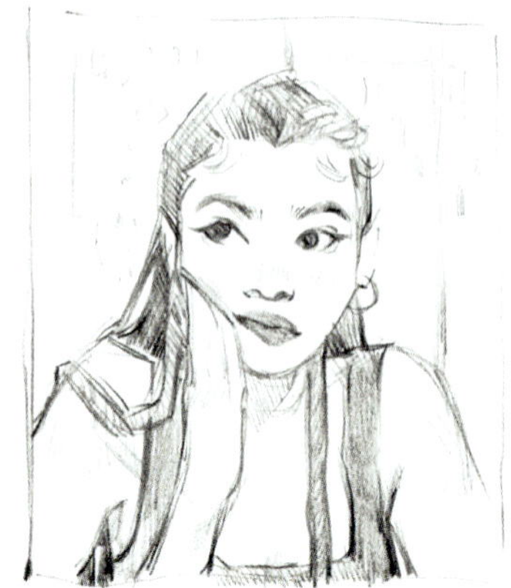

BASIC ANATOMY

In this section, I share my thought process when stylizing female anatomy. I'm sure your style is different than mine, but if you feel stuck when drawing a proportional face or body, these are the guidelines I use for every sketch and painting. Feel free to reference books or videos specifically about realistic human anatomy if you'd like to improve your character art further.

I also want to mention that, as an artist, you should be seeking to learn about and celebrate as diverse a selection of people, body types and cultures as you have time to learn about. It is not an excuse to exclude yourself from becoming well-rounded in drawing people of all shapes and sizes if you are serious about portraiture. There is a lot of power and encouragement in representing individuals not commonly celebrated by Western society's standards, and it is up to every artist to beautifully represent people from backgrounds other than their own.

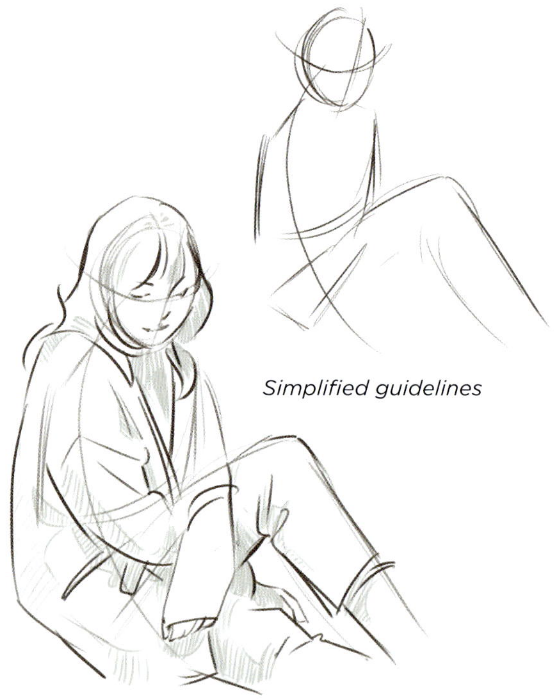

Simplified guidelines

Rough sketch using guidelines

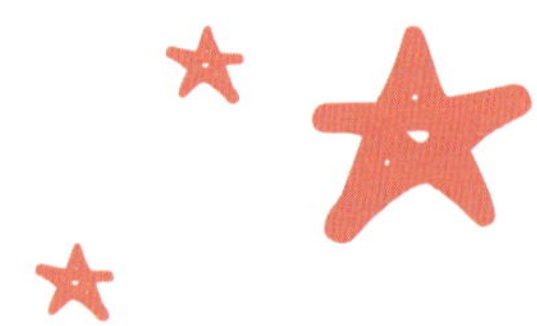

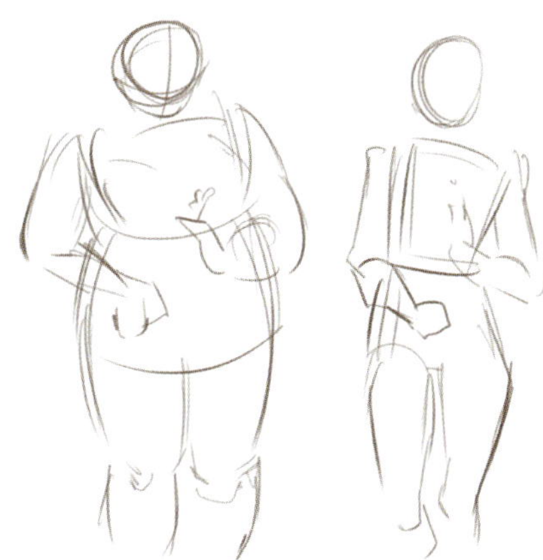

Draw the rough shapes of the body using simplified cylindrical lines. Focus on creating movement in your linework instead of worrying about anatomical accuracy.

When drawing the body, it is best to study the skeletal and muscular structure of human anatomy. Break down the shape of the body into the basic forms of the skeleton and muscles, and add detail to the shapes once you have a rough idea of your pose.

The basic guidelines I use when drawing the female figure are the simplified rib cage, spine and hip bone. Use lines of movement to angle the torso, shoulders and hips accurately.

Foreshorten your subject if they are pointed toward or away from the viewer; using subtle distortion will create realism and show attention to detail. As your subject moves farther from the viewer, the lines and shapes get smaller, while anything coming closer to the viewer will elongate. Think of the body as made up of cylindrical shapes that distort as the body is angled in different ways.

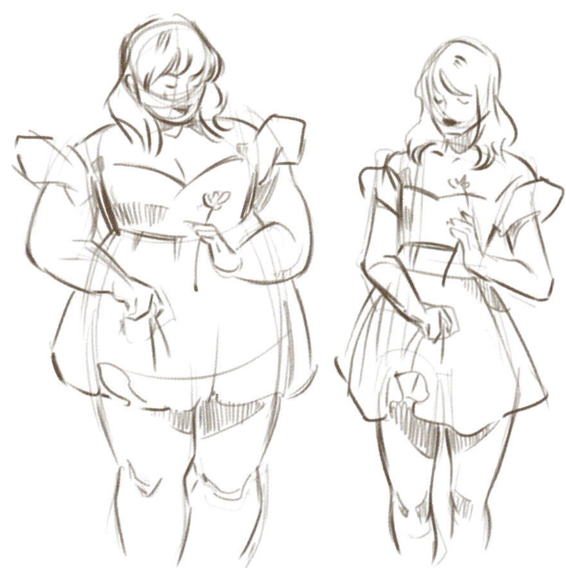

Add details to the basic guidelines, continuing to focus on drawing flowing lines in the hair and clothing.

Use angular lines for smaller or more petite subjects and more rounded lines for fuller figures and larger body types. You can stylize your subject and their body in a way that simplifies and flatters their figure, no matter what size or shape they are. Every individual has their own unique shape; find a way to best represent that shape in your own style.

PROJECT 1: PAINT A FULL-BODY SKETCH

Use a reference photo to create a full-body sketch, emphasizing the energy line (see Design Principles, page 91, for more on energy lines). What shapes are you utilizing to simplify your sketch? How are you adding details to those basic shapes? Refer back to Chapter 1 (page 11) if you need a refresher on setting up your canvas and downloading my favorite brushes.

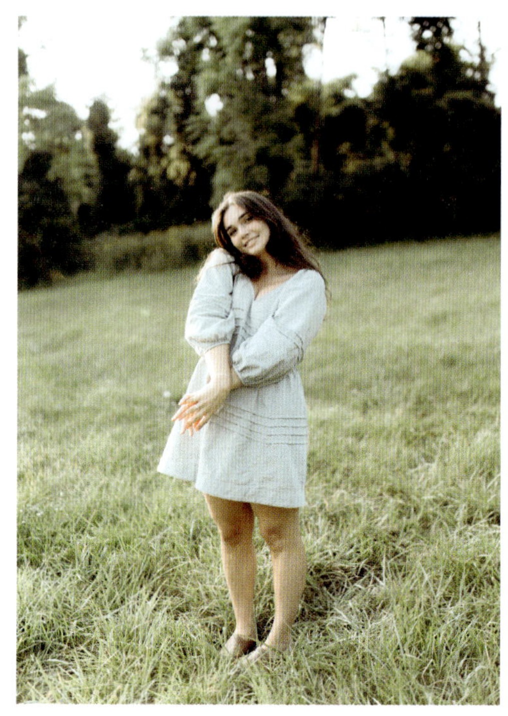

1. Draw the basic form of your subject. Utilizing an energy line that shows how the spine is angled, use any of the brushes (Airbrush, Oil brush or Pencil brush) to draw the basic shape of the head, rib cage, hips, shoulders, elbows, wrists and knees.

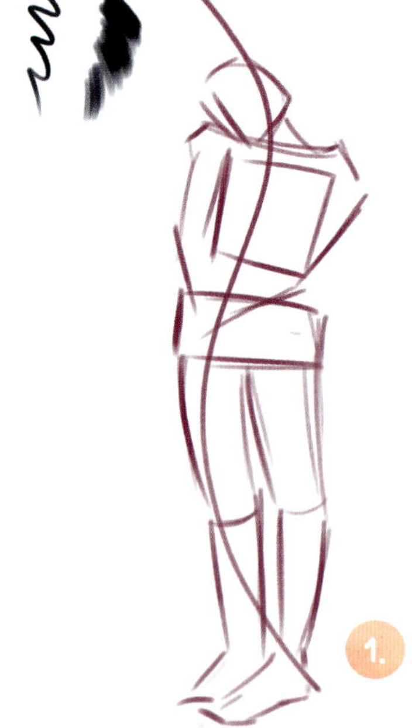

2. On a new layer, begin fleshing out your subject and adding soft, fluid lines that show the general shape of the body. You can set the opacity of your first rough sketch to 20% to 40% to trace over. The female body, in many cases, has more fat than the male body, so unless you're drawing someone specifically muscular, you can use softer shapes when drawing women. Use sweeping, fluid lines to draw the body instead of short, jagged lines.

3. Skip this step if you're not comfortable adding any extra elements yet. But, if you are comfortable with giving this a try, on a new layer, block in the basic shape of the hair (see page 64 for rendering hair), face (see page 35 for rendering facial features) or clothing (see page 134 for rendering fabric).

4. Analyze the reference photo and add blocks of shadows to continue rendering your subject. Use soft pressure with your brush to add shading and differentiate these lines from your sketch. Indicate where any highlights will sit on the subject in the same way you drew the shadows, but without adding shading to the blocky shape.

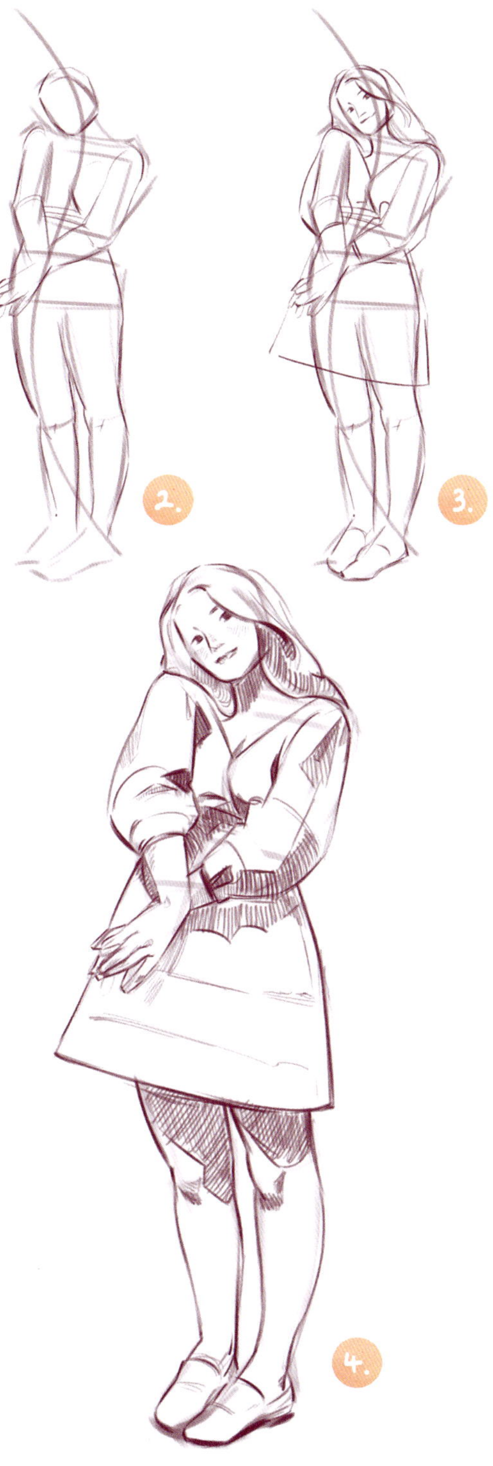

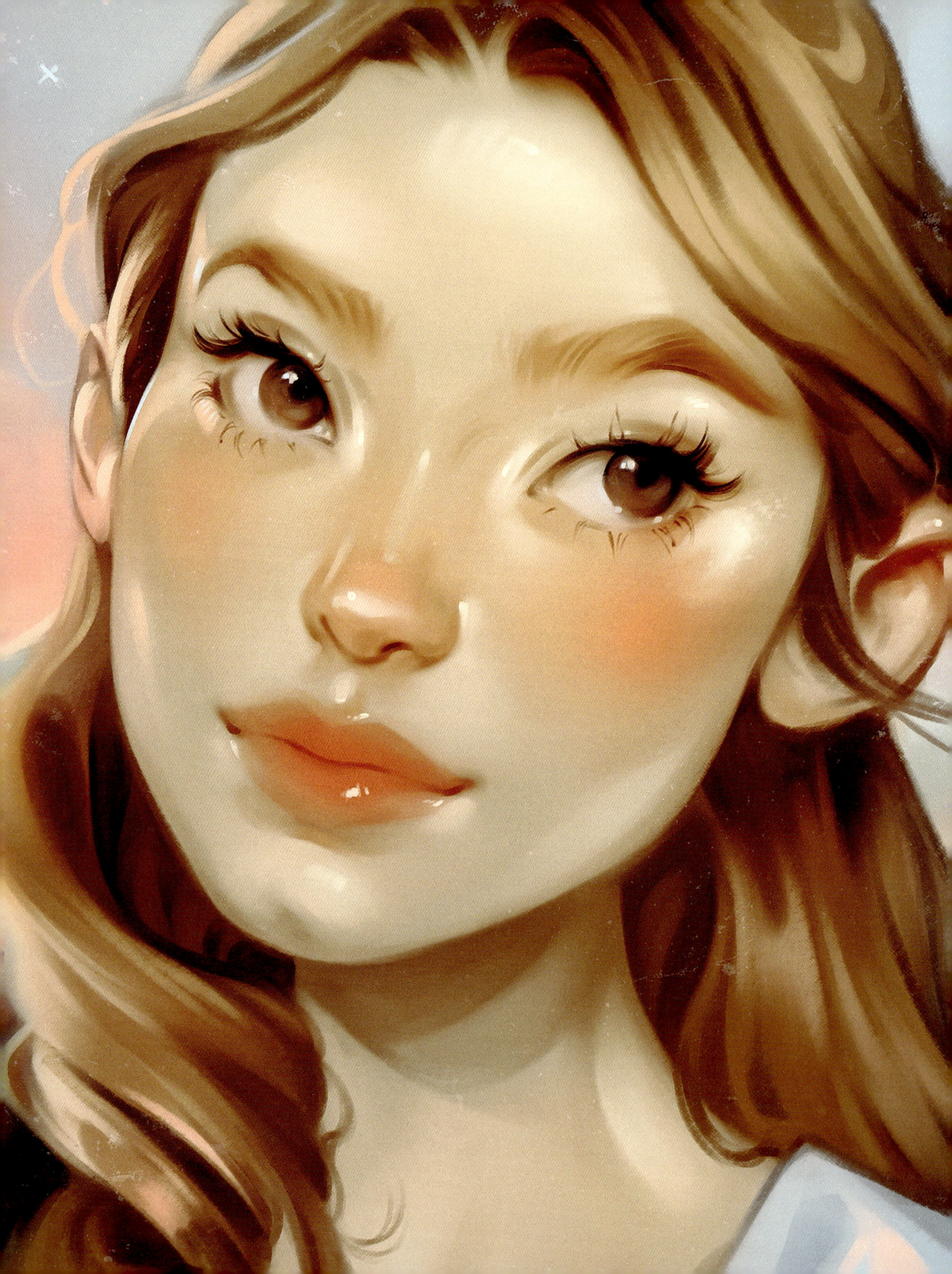

Eyes

Eyes are the most captivating feature of the face; I've always drawn big and bright eyes, and I think they are one of the defining features of my work. I have learned some tricks along the way to simplify the process and enjoy the time spent painting them.

First off, it's important to remember the spherical nature of the eyes; the eyelids will wrap around the eyeball, and depending on the lighting situation, the inner and outer corners of the eyes and eyelids will be more or less shadowed. Think of the eyeball as having an X and Y axis crossing over the center of it. Establishing that point on both eyeballs will help you draw them in the same direction, as well as at the same angle. Practice drawing the eyeball with the sphere and axis until you are comfortable drawing the eyes from different angles; you will eventually be able to draw the eyelids and iris without these guides, but they are very useful, especially for beginners.

When drawing both eyes, try to work on them both at the same time in order to achieve as much symmetry as possible. If you fully draw and paint one eye before moving to the next, it will be harder to match the other eye up to the original.

The eyelids have thickness, so the top lashes will cast a shadow on the whites of the eyes, or the *sclera*. If the top eyelid is casting a shadow in this manner, the top of the iris will be darker than the bottom of it. Because of the spherical nature of the eyeball, the undereye area will often be slightly shadowed as well. When drawing eyes closed, account for the curvature of the eyeball. The tear duct is not positioned on the eyeball, but rather on the very edge of it, so the eyelids covering the tear duct will not move drastically. Accentuate the crease of the eye socket and skeletal structure underneath.

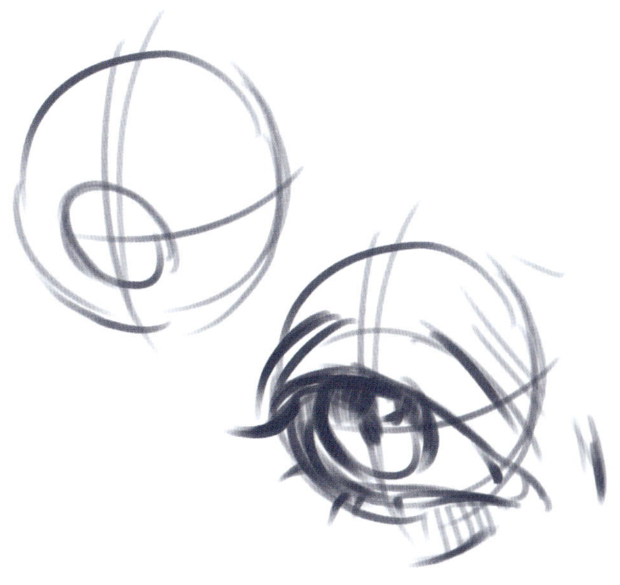

Start with a simple spherical shape as your guide and then add the details on top. This is a good exercise to practice drawing eyes.

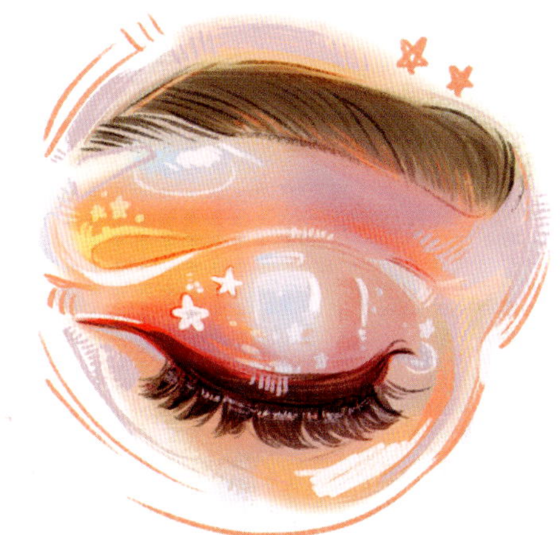

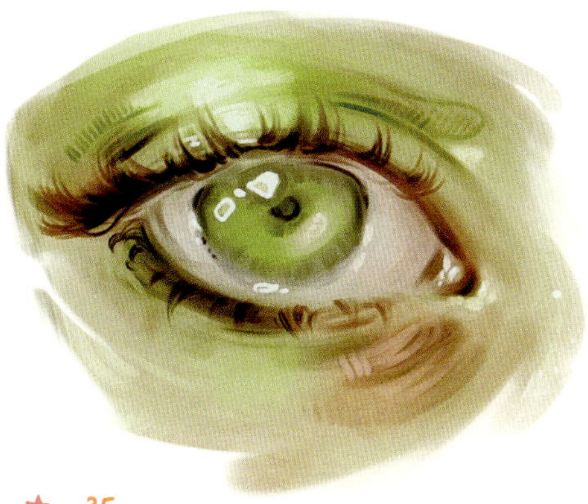

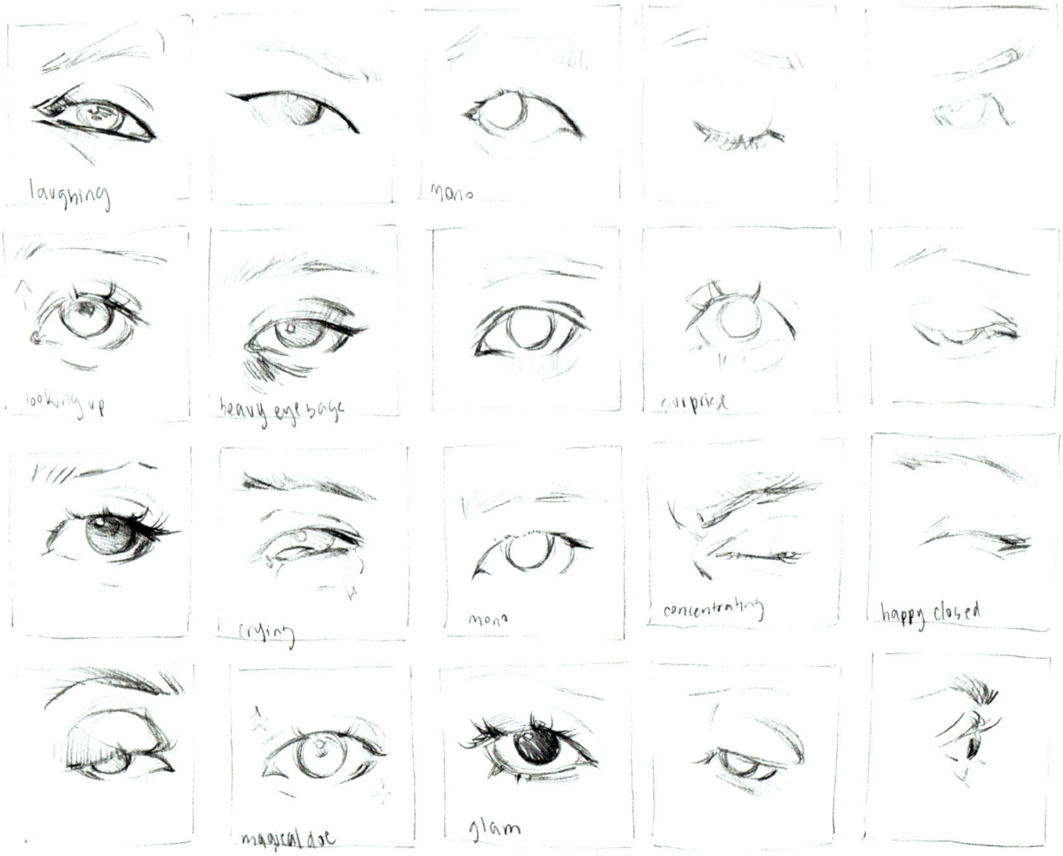

Practice drawing eyes with different expressions in a physical sketchbook or in your painting program.

When placing the eyes on the face, draw in the bridge of the nose as well as the shape of the eyebrows to give yourself a rough idea of the proportions of the face. The distance between the eyes is roughly the length of one eye.

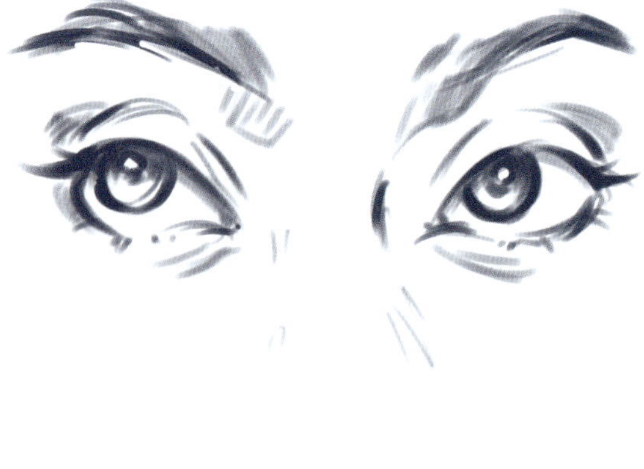

Eyelashes

When drawing the eyelashes, remember that you are drawing individual hairs coming from the edge of the waterline, and that they are coming out from a sphere. Eyelashes will not all go out in the same direction, but rather perpendicular to their surface; they also clump together, so when drawing eyelashes, draw some of them sticking to each other. You can foreshorten eyelashes pointing straight at the camera for a natural and realistic appearance. Add variation in the size, shape and length of each eyelash; drawing a thicker base with a tapered end will look realistic, but sometimes I like to paint the ends a little thicker to look like clumped-up mascara.

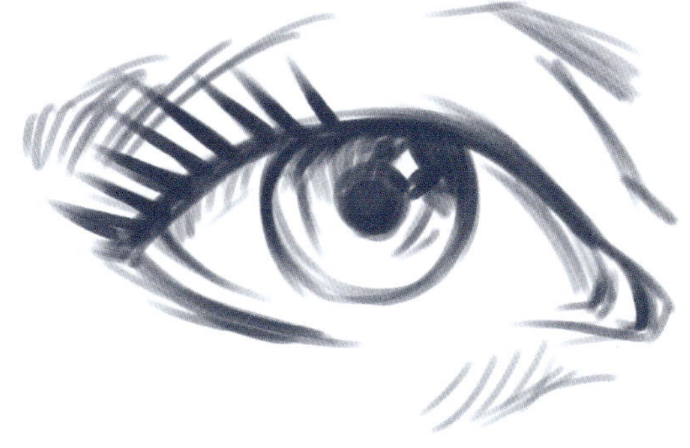

Wrong. The eyelashes are sticking straight out from the lash line, with no foreshortening or curl.

Eyebrows

When painting eyebrows, use light and feathered strokes to create the illusion of a soft, fluffy eyebrow, making sparser marks toward the front of the eyebrows. Blocking the eyebrows in with a darker tone will make them look harsh and unnatural, so build up the tones and shading in the brows for a balanced addition to the face.

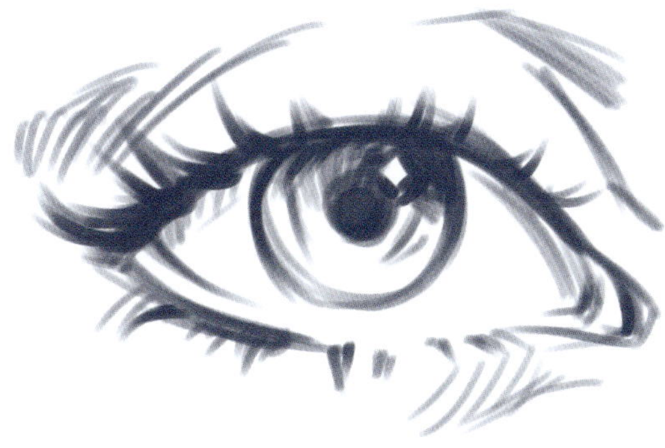

Right. The eyelashes bend naturally around the spherical eye, curling and tapering.

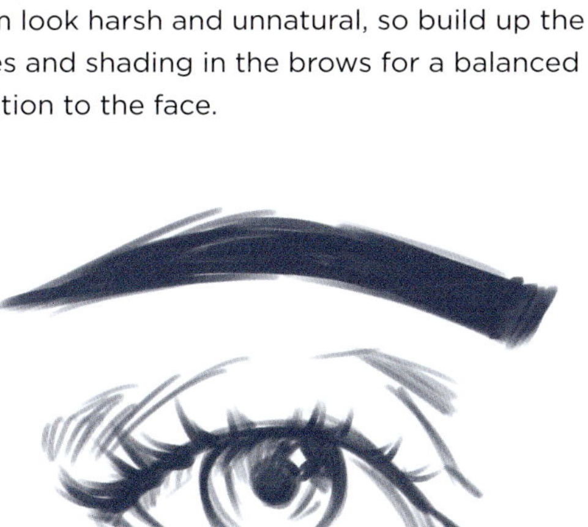

Wrong. This eyebrow shape looks like it has been drawn on with a marker. There are no natural gaps in the hair strokes.

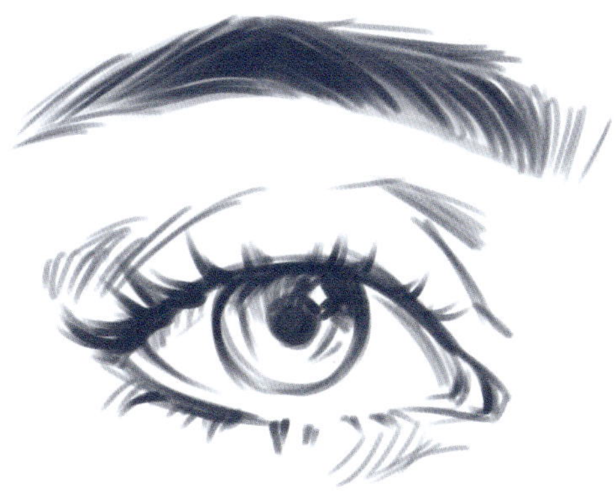

Right. The eyebrows follow a growth direction and pattern, with variations in the individual brow hairs.

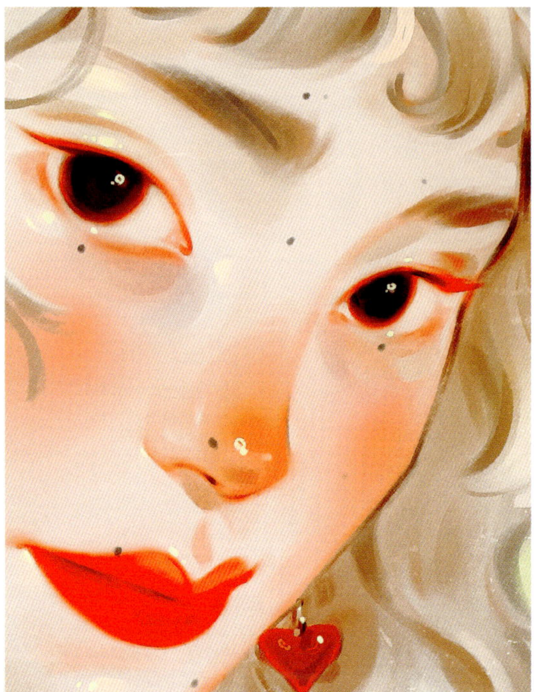

The whites of the eyes are not actually bright white, but rather a grayish color.

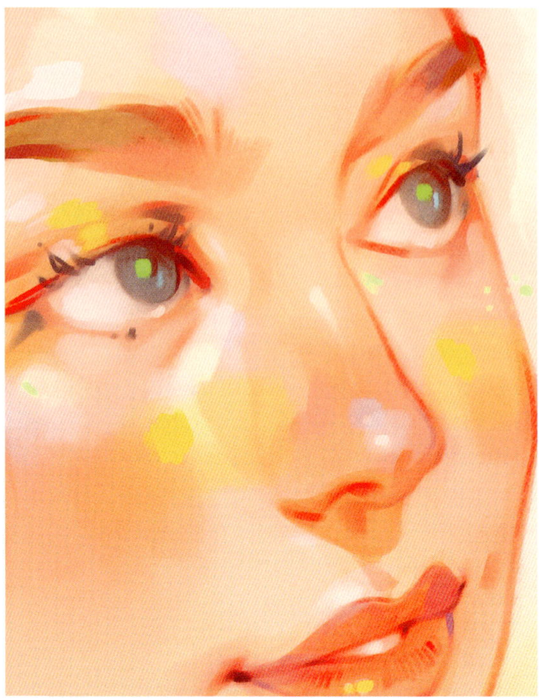

You can creatively highlight and shade the eyes using a variety of colors.

Coloring in the Eye

The color of the whites of the eye, or *sclera*, is not a true white, but rather closer to a grayish blue green. Sometimes, venations will add pink or red tones to the sclera, especially if the subject is tired or using substances. In addition, remember to paint the lacrimal caruncle, a.k.a. the *tear duct,* to add the same pink and red tones into the eye area. This can be a detail to add to your piece in order to explore more of the story behind a character. While you don't have to go into photorealistic detail in your paintings, making deliberate decisions to include small details like these will keep the viewer interested in the final piece. The color of the *iris* is going to have tonal shifts; often, there will be flecks of different colors and tones in the iris, so feel free to study references to get an understanding of what colors you might add to your pieces.

This is where you can take creative liberties with your color choices and realism. Since the eyes are so expressive, feel free to push color and value to create a more impactful piece. Another feature to notice is that the edge of the iris, or *limbal ring,* is softly diffused into the sclera rather than having an abrupt edge.

Add highlights to the inner corner of the eye, under the eye bags, in the middle of the eyelids (or whichever direction the iris is facing) and across the brow bone. Add tonal variations of blues, purples and greens to the undereye area. Due to the glossy surface of the eyeball, most lighting will create a sharp and defined highlight on the eye; you can add a softer, diffused highlight to the opposite end of the iris as light refracts through the pupil of the eye. You can also highlight the edge of the iris, waterline and tear duct to make the eyes pop.

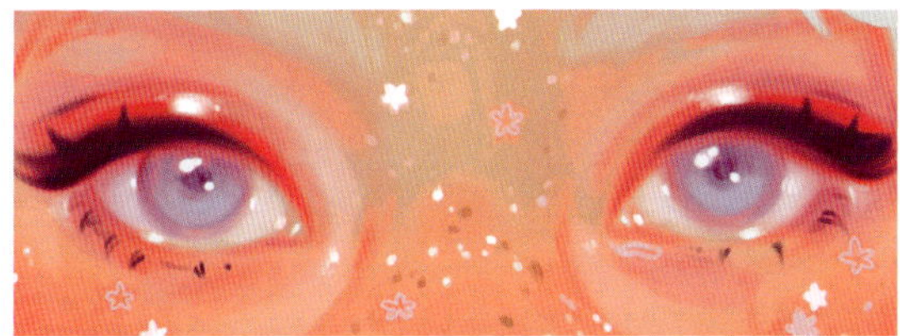

Round eyes

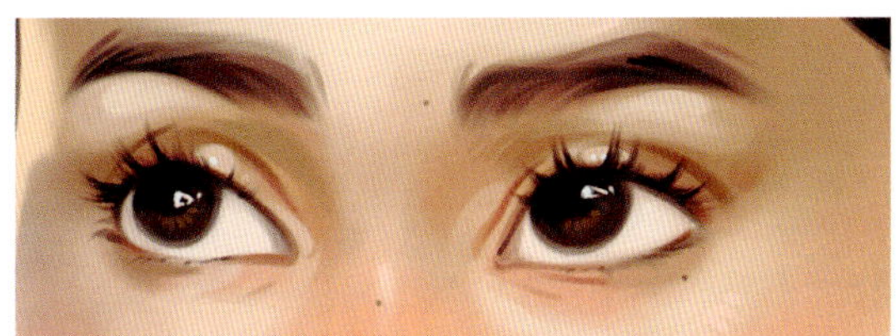

Deep-set eyes

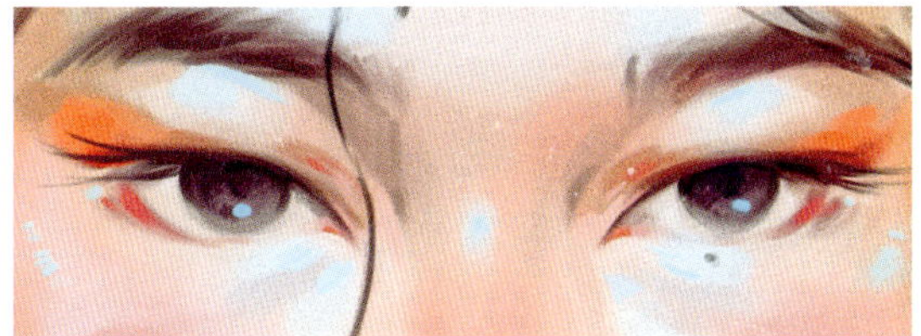

Monolid eyes

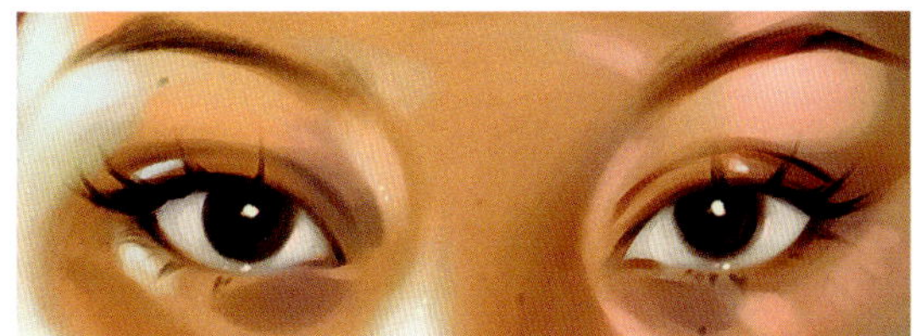

Upturned eyes

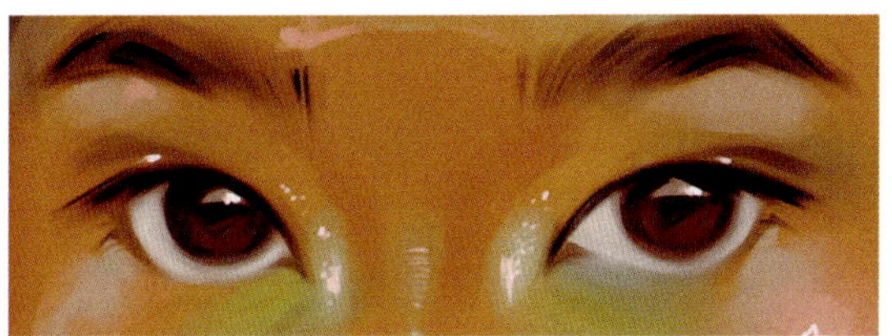

Hooded eyes

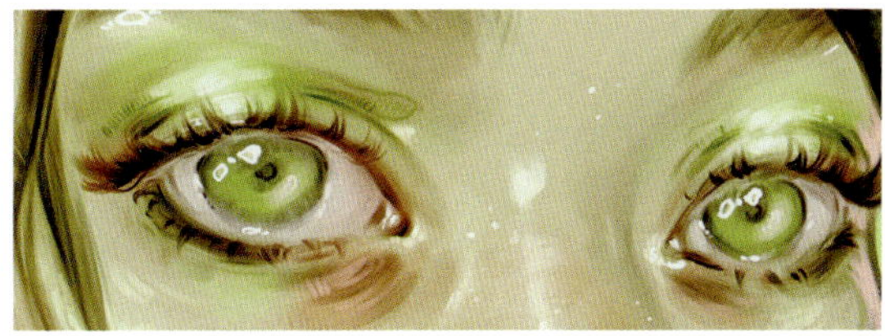

Protruding eyes

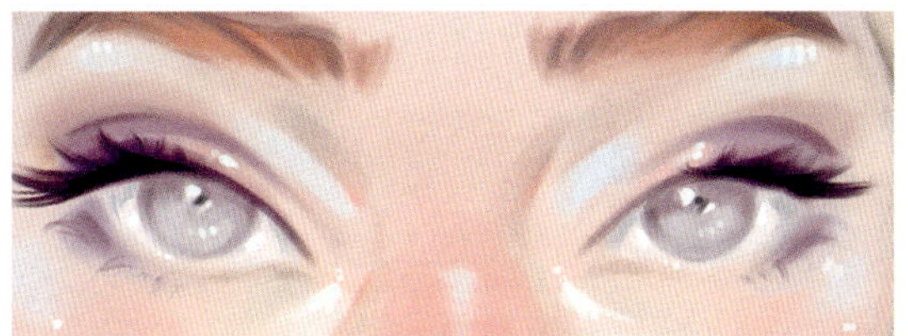

Almond-shaped eyes

Shapes of Eyes

There are six different eye shapes, which can all be various levels of inset or protruding: round, monolid, hooded, downturned, upturned and almond shaped.

Round eyes are especially round and wide without coming to a sharp point in the inner or outer corners.

Monolid eyes do not show the crease of the eye, while **hooded eyes** do show a slight crease.

Downturned eyes are lower at the outer corners than they are in the inner, and **upturned eyes** are higher in the outer corners than they are in the inner.

Almond-shaped eyes have a defined inner and outer corner and a significant crease.

Some people have wider-set, close-set, deep-set or protruding/bulging eyes. Study your reference to portray your subject in an accurate and flattering way.

PROJECT 2: PAINT A CLOSE-UP OF AN EYE

Practice painting an eye using one of the six different eye shapes listed on the previous page. Use soft marks to blend the shadows and highlights together and hard-edged strokes to emphasize the eyelashes, as well as crisp reflections in the eyes.

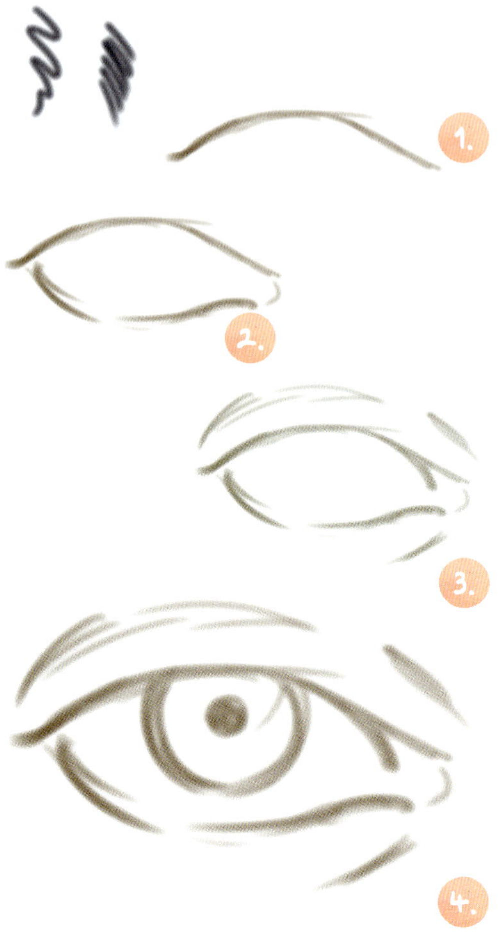

1. Create a square canvas of 4 x 4 inches (10 x 10 cm) at 300 dpi (see page 16 for canvas sizing). After setting the base layer to a background color of your choice, create a new Multiply layer for your sketch. Using the Soft Airbrush (see page 17 for brushes) with a medium-toned bronze (or a warm dark brown if you're painting a darker-skinned subject), begin by creating a hill shape with a steeper slope on one side than the other; this will be the top eyelid. The side with the steeper slope will be the outer corner. I am painting the right eye in this project.

2. Add the bottom eyelid to your sketch. Connect the inner corner of the eye with a round tear duct and follow the shape of an imaginary 3D eyeball with the bottom eyelid. You should have the widest point of the eye be wherever the iris will be looking. For me, this is going to be right in the middle.

3. Add rounded lines around the top and bottom eyelids; these are going to be the creases of the eyelid. Use round, fluffy curves for youthful eyes and thinner, longer lines for aging or sunken eyes. Connect the inner corner with a curved line to delineate the pink area of the tear duct from the rest of the sclera.

4. Add the iris and pupil to the eyeball; the more of the round iris you can see, the wider and more surprised the eye will look. Remember that the top eyelid will naturally rest on top of the iris if the eye is in a relaxed position, so place the pupil centered in the iris. If your eye looks like

mine, the pupil should be closer to the top eyelid than the bottom edge of the iris.

5. Let's add some shadows to the eye. Considering that the eyelid is sitting on top of the spherical eyeball, it will cast some shadows on the iris and sclera. Place a gradient shadow on top of the iris, leaving a small circle clear of shading to represent the reflection of a light source. I like to add some shadow around the top and sides of the iris, or limbal ring.

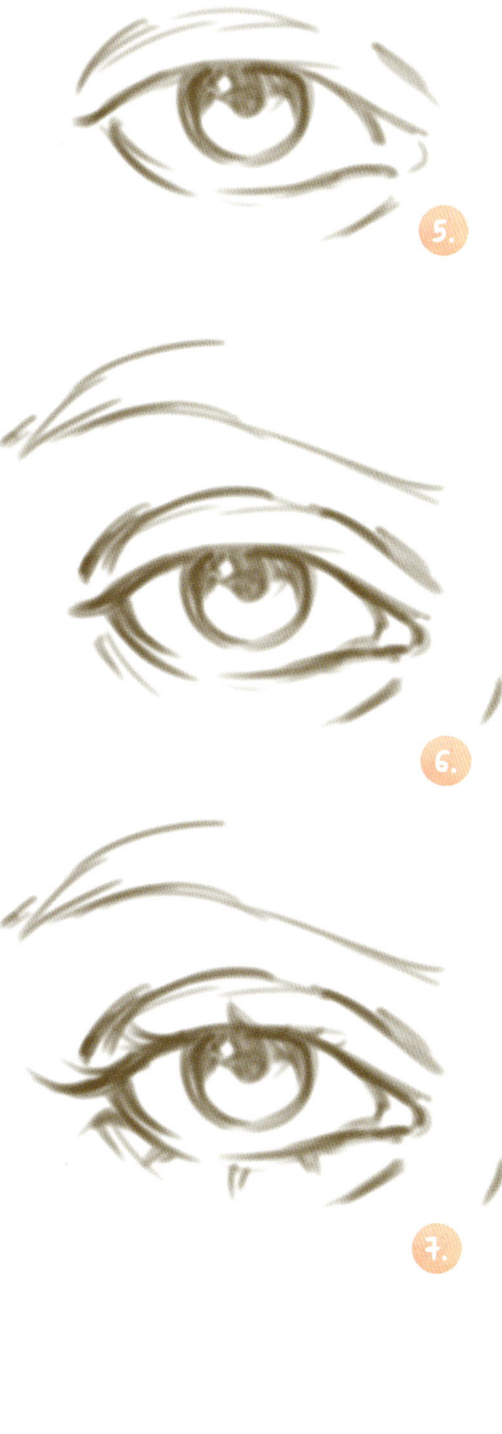

6. Define the edges of this rough sketch to add some more dimension to the drawing. Mark the thick edge of the bottom eyelid, as it is generally visible whenever you look directly at someone's eyes. Remember that this sketch will become a guide for shadows and highlights in the painting stage, so deepen parts of the sketch that will be defined with either shadow or contrast. For the surrounding area around the eye, map out the general shape of an eyebrow. The inner and outer corners of the eyebrow will sit slightly past the inner and outer corners of the eye. The shape of the brow can greatly impact the emotion of the subject (see page 45 for expressing emotions).

7. Add the eyelashes to the eyelids. To create curled, long lashes, use longer, vertical curved stokes. Draw short lines in the center of the eye to indicate that the eyelashes are pointed straight at the viewer and longer lines as they curve around to the corner of the lids. Use heavy pressure at the base of the eyelash and flick your pen upward to draw the wispy curved line of a lash. Set your sketch layer to Multiply (see page 18 for adjustment layers).

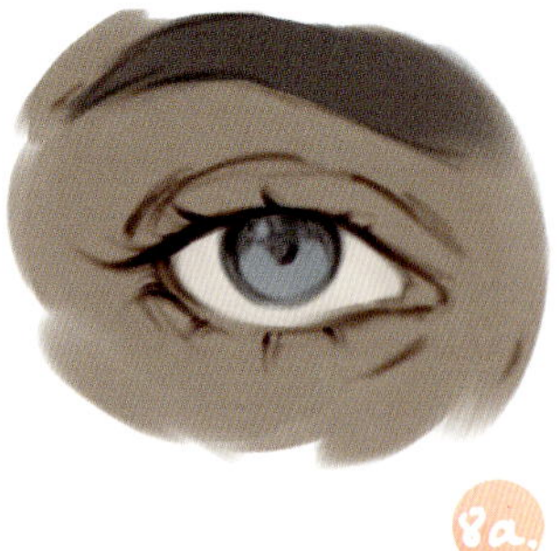
8a.

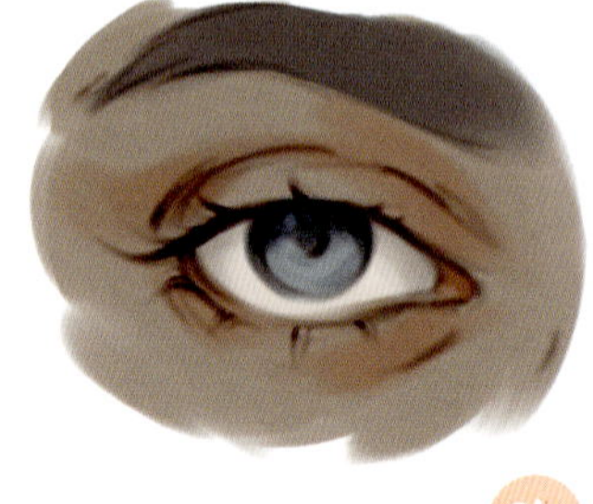
8b.

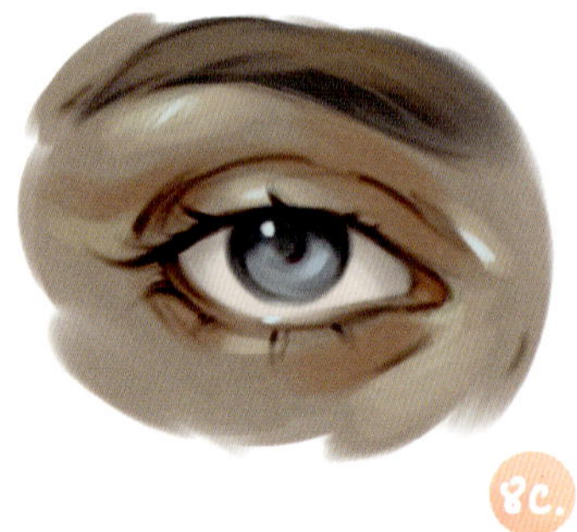
8c.

8a. On a new layer underneath the sketch, using the Soft Airbrush or Oil brush, add the base colors; I used the Oil brush to add some texture. Since I'm painting an isolated feature of the face, I want to add some interesting circular brushstrokes to the skin to frame the eye. Choose the skin tone, eyebrow color, grayish white of the sclera and desired eye color. Unless you are painting a fantastical subject, use desaturated blues, greens and browns for the base eye color.

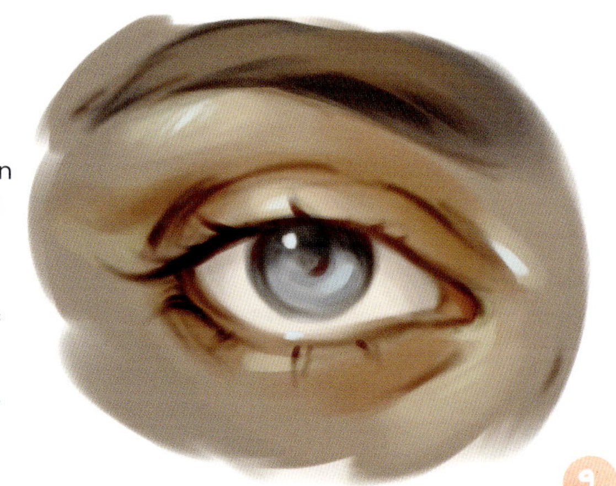
9.

b. To begin fleshing out the three-dimensional shape of the eye, add warm shadows underneath the bottom eyelid, around the corners of the eye, under the front of the eyebrow and across the crease of the top eyelid. Since the top eyelid casts a shadow, add a cool gray gradient across the top of the sclera and use a darker blue to deepen the shadows on the iris. Lastly, use a deeper, saturated tone for the tear duct.

c. Color pick your base skin tone and move the color wheel slightly over to the yellow to change the hue, choosing a lighter tone for the highlights. Add highlights to the brow bone, middle of the eyelids, corner of the eye and under the bottom eyelids. Then, with a pastel cool blue, purple or pink, add bright highlights to the iris, waterline, inner corner and brow bone. Keep these marks sharp instead of soft and diffused to indicate glossiness. Using a variety of colors for the highlights will create a shimmery, opalescent effect.

9. Add a new Soft Light layer (see page 18 for adjustment layers) above the other layers. Using the Soft Airbrush, gently paint over the base colors with brighter yellow, soft orange-pink and blue to unify the colors and add saturation. Feel free to use several adjustment layers and play with the layer opacity to achieve your desired effect.

10. It's time to begin rendering the painting; right-click on any layer and select "Merge visible into new layer" to flatten your image. Every time you would like to make a risky addition to the piece, you can right-click your working layer, select "Duplicate layer" and paint on that new layer to essentially save your process.

11. I like to begin working on either the focal point or the most challenging area of the painting first, to be sure that I nail it before continuing on to the rest of the piece. In this case, using the Oil brush, begin fleshing out the iris, color picking from the tones you have already placed down on the canvas. You should be able to have a wide variety of tones and values to choose from for this step, but you can also utilize the color wheel to add in any pops of color you feel are needed. Diffuse the edges of the limbal ring to melt the iris into the whites of the eyes. Define the edges of the sharp highlight, as well as the pupil and any variations in the color of the iris.

12. Refine the skin, color picking from the shadows and highlights you've placed down. Use gentle pressure and the Eyedropper often when creating a smooth gradient. However, you should still maintain some geometric shapes in the shadows and highlights. Press harder for a sharper edge to these shapes, referencing your Navigator window (see page 14 for program layouts) to check that the whole image looks good from a distance.

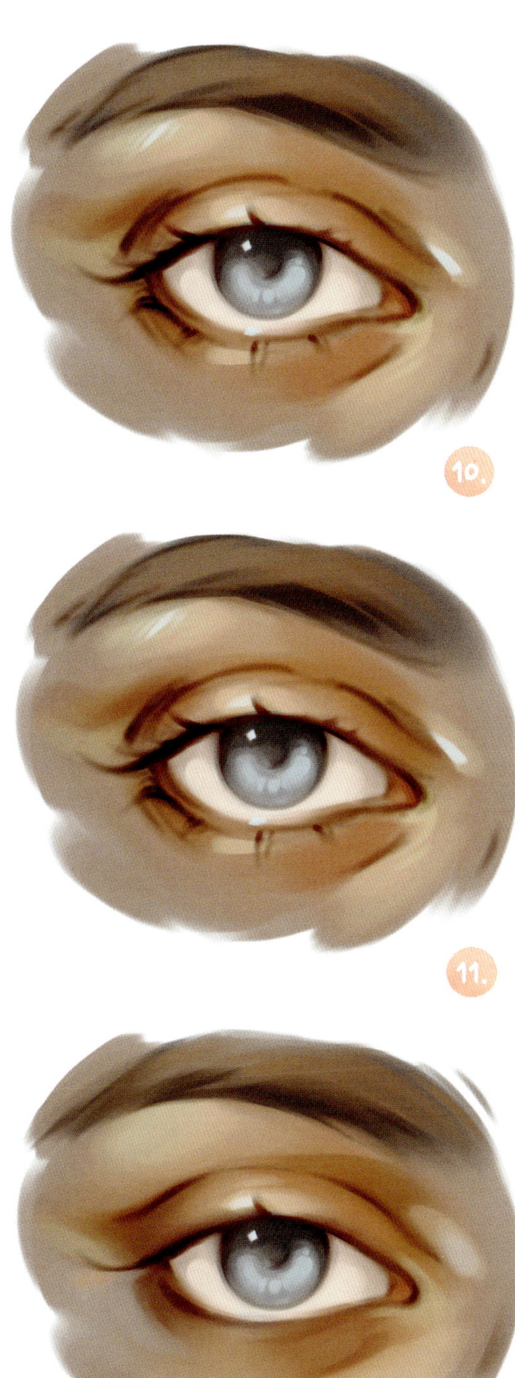

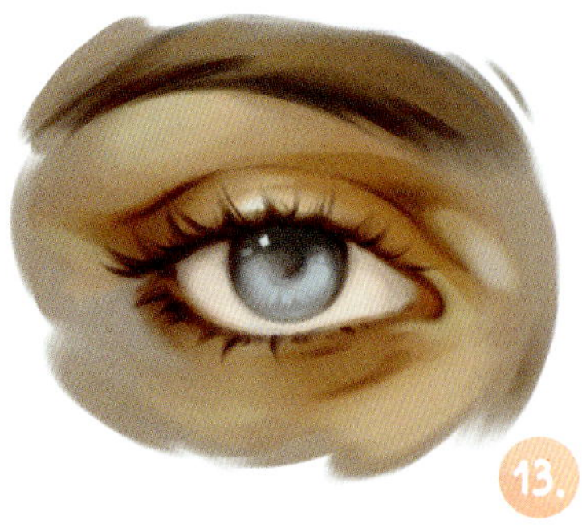

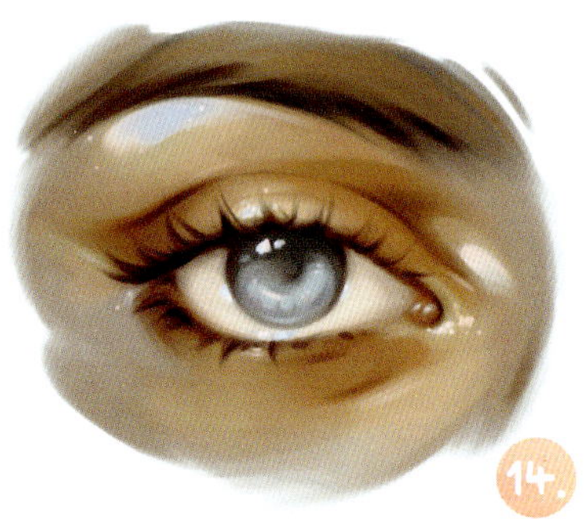

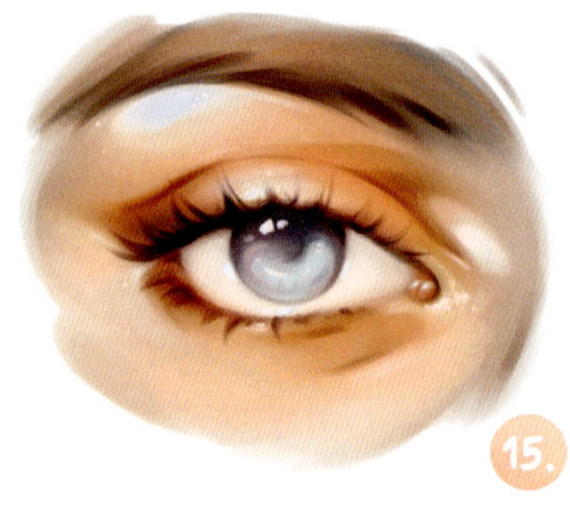

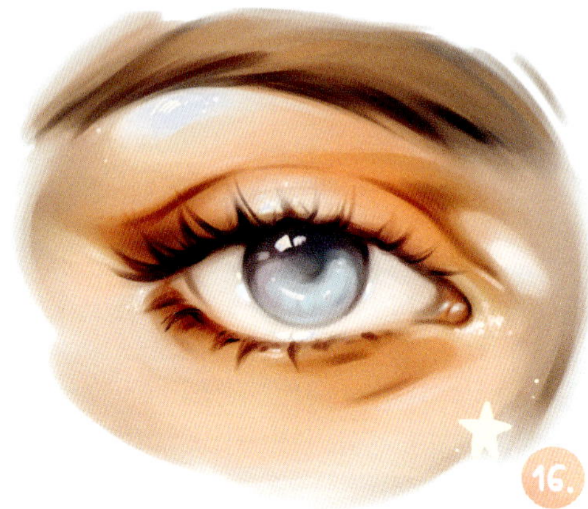

13. Finish the basic rendering of your painting. There should be no sketch lines visible after this step (unless that is a stylistic choice of yours). If any of the highlights you've placed down are hindering you from rendering the piece, paint over them for now; you'll have the chance to add them back in when adding your finishing details. Use soft marks to blend the edges of the eyelids to create dimension.

14. Add contrast through sharp details; paint the eyelashes using the same tips from Step 7 and add back the blue highlights on the brow bone, bottom lash line and inner corner of the eye. Minimize your brush size and paint in some shadows, almost in the same direction and shape as fine lines and wrinkles. Add small pink dots across the highlighted areas to add a magical glitter effect. Reference the Navigator window to assess whether the details are effective or overwhelming and erase them if they create visual clutter.

15. Play around with adjustment layers to color grade your painting. I used a Soft Light layer to add a unifying pink glow to the painting, darkness to the lash line and a smoky effect to the outer corner. I also add a Tone Curve layer to adjust the highlights, shadows and overall colors, shifting them to a pink hue.

16. Add Smart Sharpening to the painting and add any last details; I add my signature wonky star and marks, as well as some small finishing highlights. (See page 152 for details on finishing touches.)

Eye Expressions

Drawing expressive eyes is achieved through changing the movement in the eyebrows as well as how the eyelids interact with the actual eyeball. When drawing somebody with strong, urgent and intense emotions, you would usually point the front of the eyebrows inward; the eyes will either narrow or widen, depending on the emotion. When drawing someone with a more passive, open emotion, you can raise the front of the eyebrows and widen the eyes or squint the outer corners. You can achieve a wide range of emotions by slightly varying the shape of the eyebrows and eyelids. Make a collection of reference photos of faces expressing different emotions, and study the ways the eyes and eyebrows move and fold depending on the expression.

PROMPT: PAINT FIVE SETS OF EYES

Use reference images to paint sets of eyes using different shapes, angles, colors and expressions. Take note of how you improve your efficiency as you go from each set of eyes to the next. Write down any tricks you've learned or any pointers on anatomy and expressive emotions that you might want to reference later.

Do you have a set of steps you find yourself following when drawing each pair of eyes? Notice how different eye shapes inform how much of the iris and pupil you can see; monolid eyes cover more of the eyeball than wide almond-shaped eyes do.

Some eyes have pronounced tear ducts and waterlines, while some eyes have subtle shapes.

Are you adding wrinkles to the expressions you're drawing?

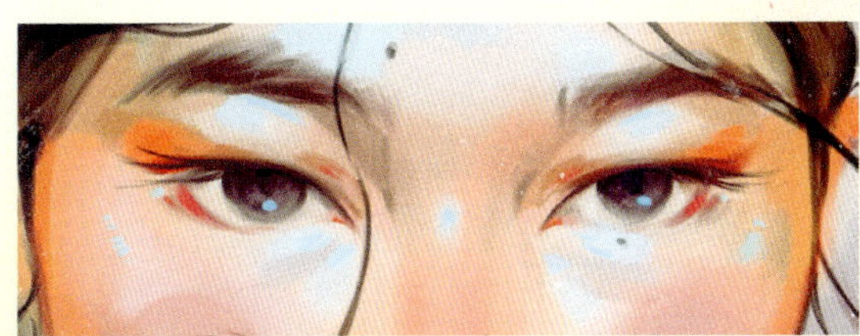

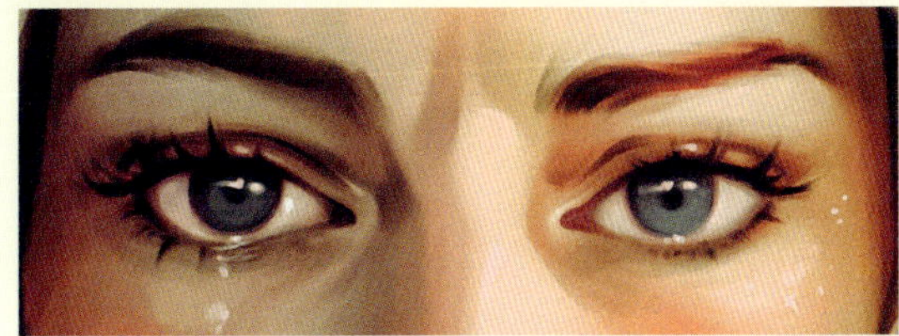

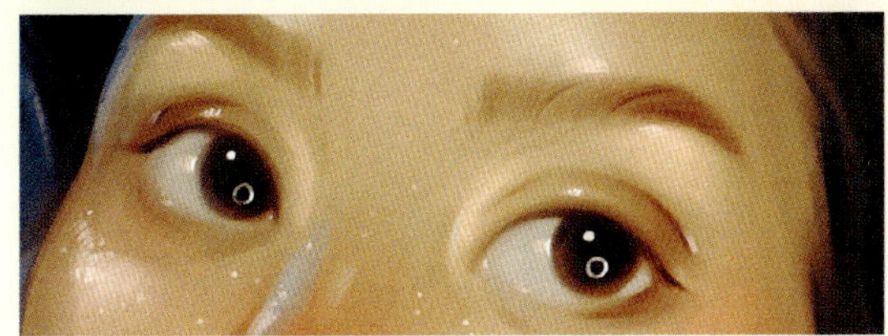

LIPS

When sketching the lips, use soft pressure to flesh out the curves of the lips. Don't use harsh lines around the edges of the lips unless you plan on painting a solid lipstick color with a defined edge; there is usually a slight gradient from the skin around the lips to the actual pigmented area, so avoid harsh lines or colors for a natural look.

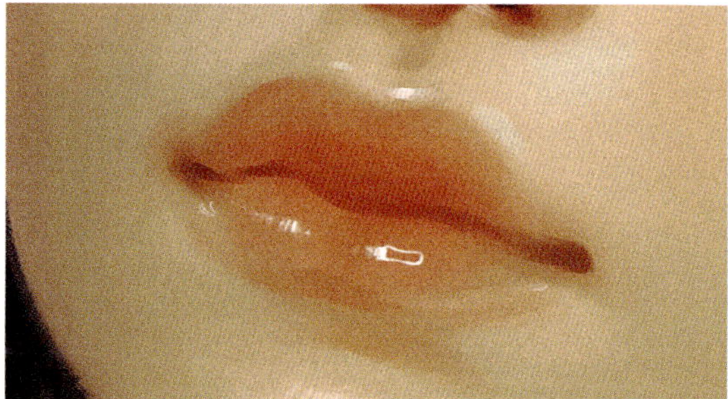

Blurred lip outline

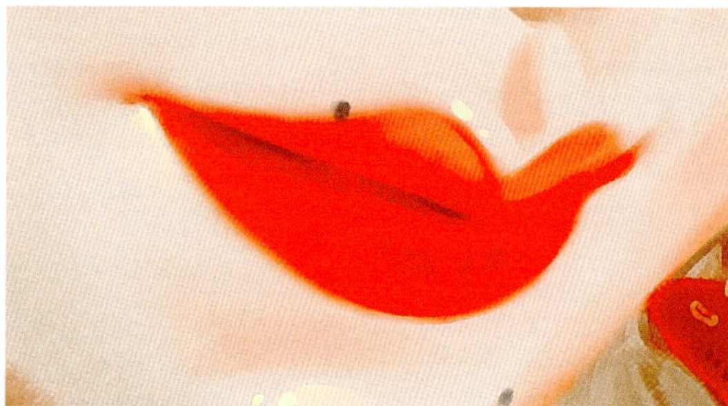

Sharp lip outline

Start with a small mark at the center of the lips and then draw the corners of the mouth. Connect the three points across the curvature of the teeth.

Lips curve inward into the mouth, so draw shadows meeting in the middle of the top and bottom lip; the corners of the mouth also curve in and are shadowed, so create a diffused shadow that becomes deeper as it closes in on the corners of the lips. Don't exaggerate this shadow too much since it will affect the expression.

Use your brushstrokes to indicate curvature and fullness, especially as you paint the shadows on the open lips.

The full mass of the lips isn't pigmented, and the edges are often raised and full without being pink. If they are full, you might also draw a slight shadow around their perimeter. There will also be a cast shadow under the bottom lip; how big that cast shadow is will create the illusion of a fuller or thinner lip.

Create the sketch using rounded marks to accentuate the three-dimensional fullness of the lips, and then use that sketch as a guide to add color, highlights and shadows.

When drawing lips at different angles, keep the concept of foreshortening in mind: If the face is extremely angled up or down, the lip farther from the viewer will appear thinner due to the condensed angle. Whatever is closer to the viewer will appear larger.

The lips fold and wrinkle in a cylindrical pattern around each of the top and bottom lips. Sometimes, there is a slight indent in the middle of the bottom lip, while there could be a slight extruded angle in the middle of the top lip.

There will be fewer folds if the lips are tightened; they will also be flatter as the skin stretches across the teeth. Painting small folds in relaxed lips is a good detail to add to your pieces to create more visual interest.

Consider the shape of the Cupid's bow and whether it is rounded or angular.

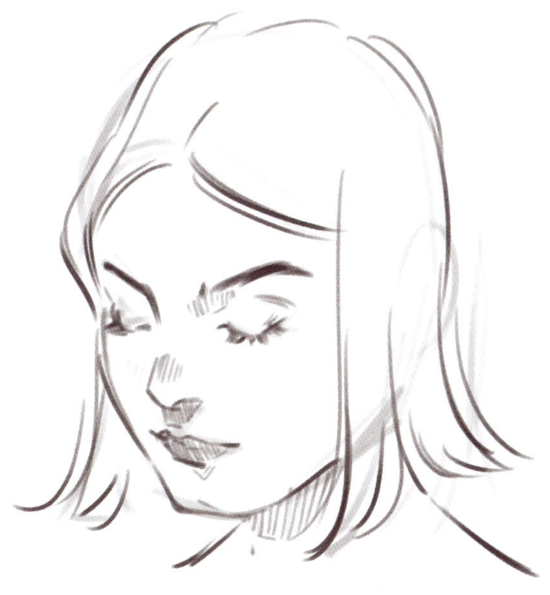

The downward angle of the face will foreshorten the fullness of the lips.

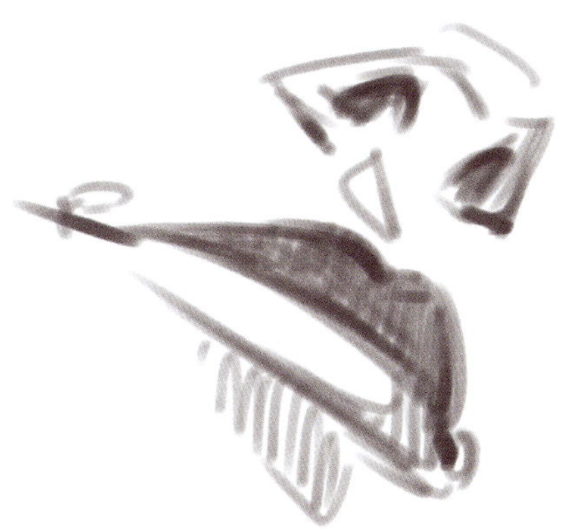

Practice different angles, remembering that lips follow the curvature of the teeth.

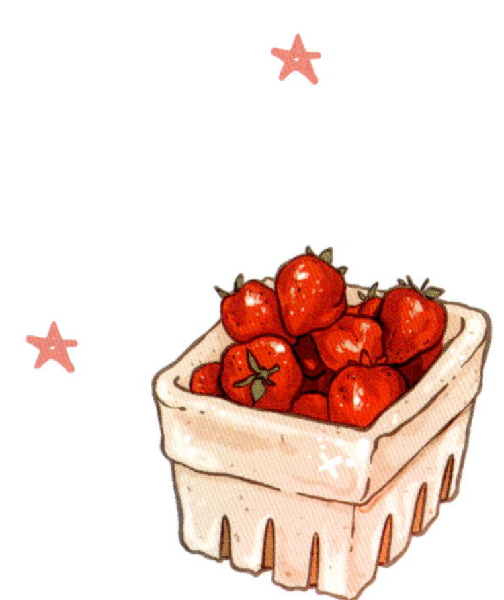

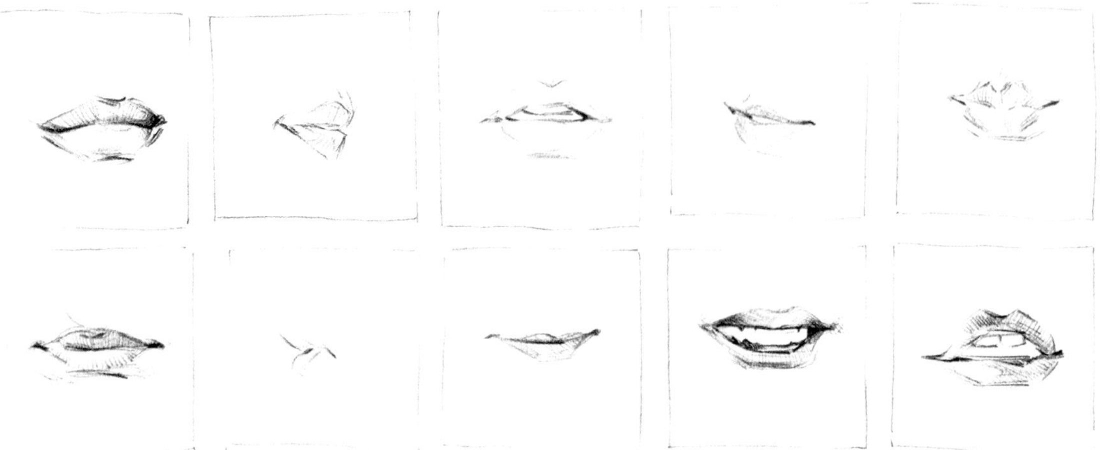

Draw a variety of expressions to familiarize yourself with the general shapes that make up the lips.

When adding highlights, add them to the Cupid's bow, *philtrum* (the vertical indentation in between the center of the nose and Cupid's bow) and corners of the mouth.

Consider the glossiness of the lips. If your subject is wearing lipstick, there might be a harsh defining line at the edge of the lips as opposed to a softer gradient. If they are matte, do not add any highlights; there will likely be low contrast. As the lips get glossier, you can paint brighter, larger and sharper highlights.

When drawing open mouths, remember their fullness and how the top and bottom lips interact with each other. Unless your subject has their mouth wide open, the top and bottom lips will still be touching close to the corners of the mouth instead of perfectly swiveling open from the corners.

When painting teeth, use the same principles as drawing the whites of the eyes. Teeth are not usually bright white, but rather a gray to yellow tone. Instead of defining each individual tooth, block in the general shape of all the teeth and add small details around the gums and bottom edges of the teeth to define them in a subtle way.

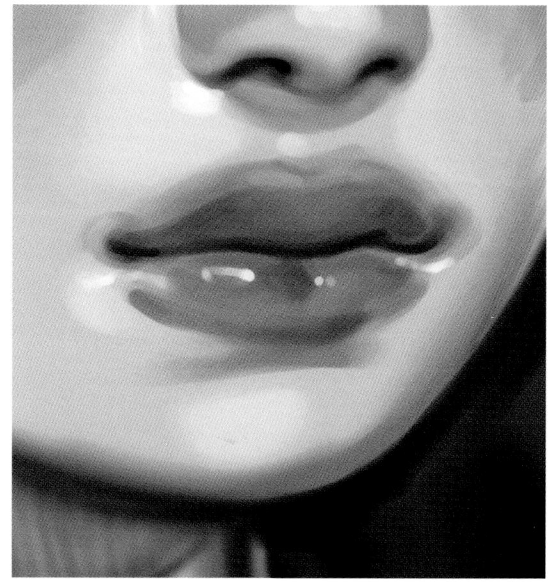

Add glossy highlights to the bottom lip and philtrum when the light source is shining from above the subject.

PROJECT 3: PAINT A CLOSE-UP OF A SET OF LIPS

Paint a set of lips from reference or imagination. Use a variety of marks to add softness and fullness to the lips, as well as shadows, creases and glossy highlights. Adapt these steps to paint thinner, fuller, glossy or matte lips.

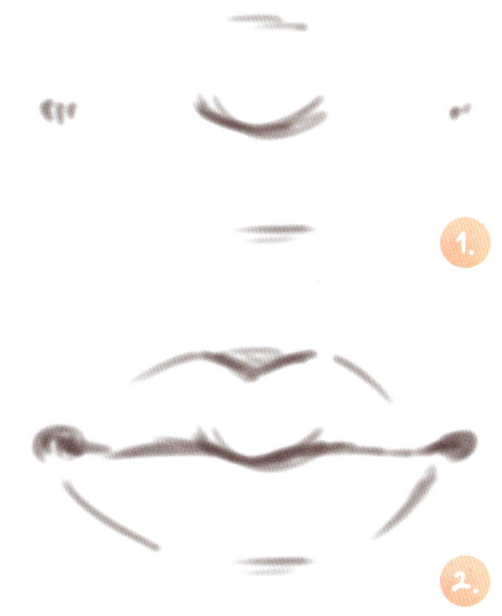

1. Create a square canvas of 4 x 4 inches (10 x 10 cm) at 300 dpi (see page 16 for canvas sizing). After setting the base layer to a background color of your choice, create a new Multiply layer for your sketch. Using the Soft Airbrush (see page 17 for brushes) with a dark burgundy (or a medium-toned bronze, if you're painting a lighter-skinned subject), begin by sketching out a small curve in the center of your canvas; this will be the center of the lips' parting. Create a small dash above and below that curve to indicate the top and bottom of the lips, and two dashes on either side of the curve to indicate the length of the mouth. The farther from the central curve these four dashes are, the more plump or thin the lips will look. Adjust these to your preferred size and effect.

2. Connect these dashes to create the outline of the lips; the Cupid's bow will make a rounded heart shape in the middle of the top lip. I like to use a soft spiral movement in the corners of the mouth to indicate the skin folding into itself and creating a shadow in the corner.

3. Sketch in the rough shapes of the shadows and highlights. I create two soft triangles, one above the top lip to indicate the philtrum's shadow, and one in the middle of the bottom lip to indicate the shadow of the indent. Draw in the double lip line; this can be omitted or more pronounced depending on the shape of the lips you want to paint. Set your sketch layer to Multiply (see page 18 for adjustment layers).

4. Using the Soft Airbrush or Oil brush on a new layer underneath your sketch, paint in the base skin tone. I am using a warm dark brown and the Oil brush to create some painterly strokes framing the drawing.

5. Using a darker, warmer-toned brown, softly paint in the shadows of the philtrum, the corners of the mouth and the bottom lip's shadow. Since I am painting full lips, I also added a soft shadow cast by the top lip.

6a. When coloring in the lips, you can really choose endless colors and finishes. For my painting, I wanted to paint a pink glossy lip with a brown lip line. To begin, diffuse a dusty rose color in the center of the lips; because the skin is darker, this dusty pink will look more like a bright pastel pink.

b. Selecting a wine burgundy color, gently shade in the outer lips, leaving the brighter pink in the center.

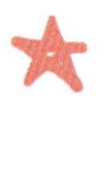

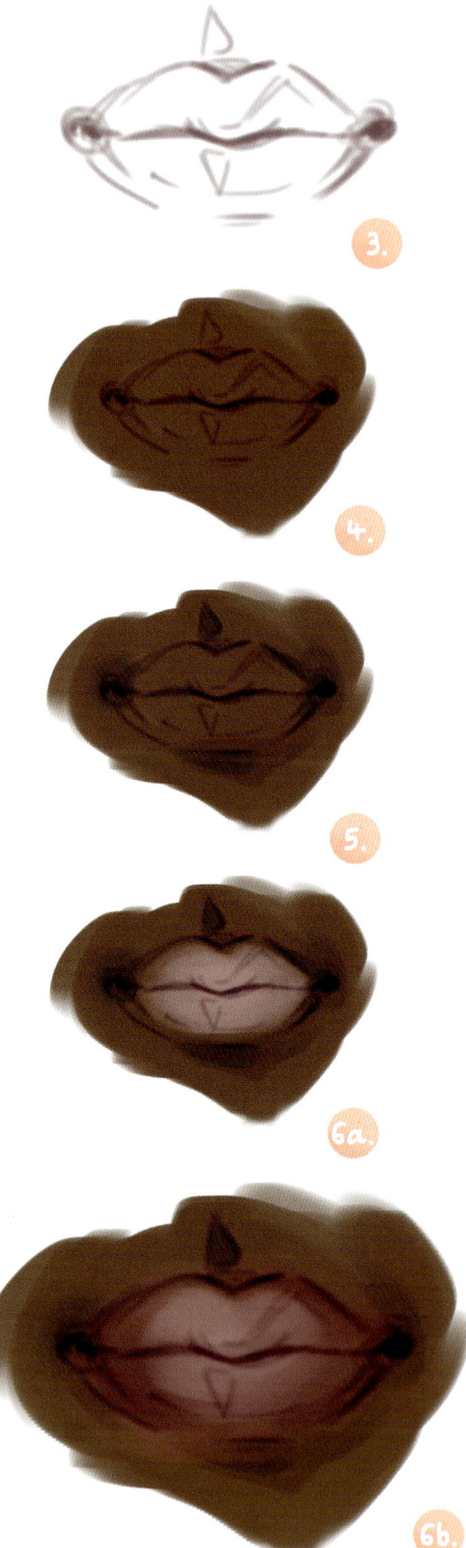

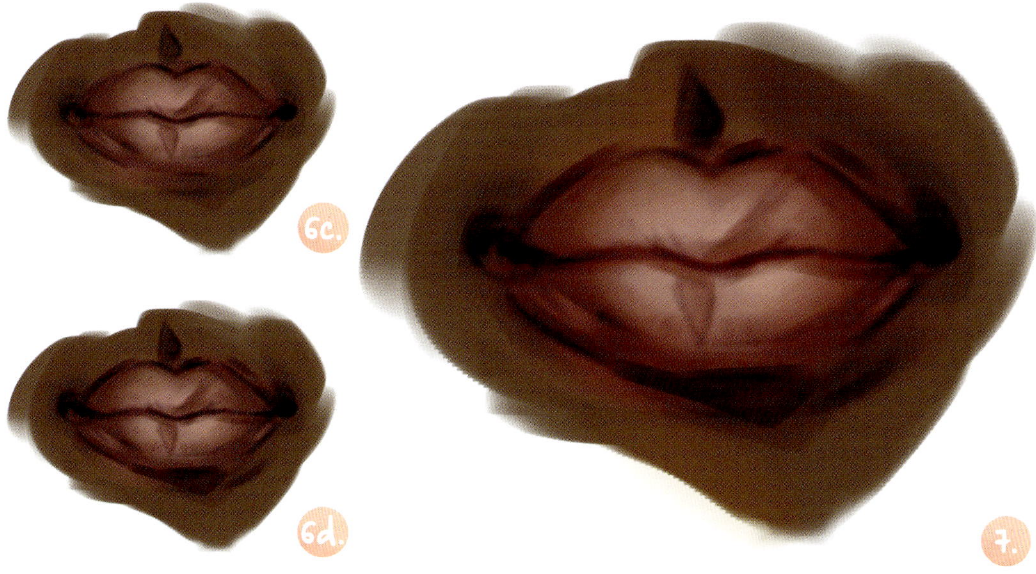

c. Using a lighter pink than the one in the center of the lips, begin adding highlights to the center of the lips. Since the lips are plump and fold inward at the center, leave a shadow in the middle of the lips and focus the round highlights in the middle of each lip.

d. Using a dark reddish brown, gently sweep it over the borders of the lips to deepen them. Use harder pressure with your brush and define the lip line, corners of the mouth and shadows under the top and bottom lips.

7. On a new Soft Light layer above the rest of the layers (see page 18 for adjustment layers), use the Soft Airbrush with a soft pastel coral to add a gentle gradient to the inside of the lips. Select a desaturated dark brown from the color wheel and paint around the edges of the lips to add more dimension and depth. Your colors should be unified and ready to be rendered.

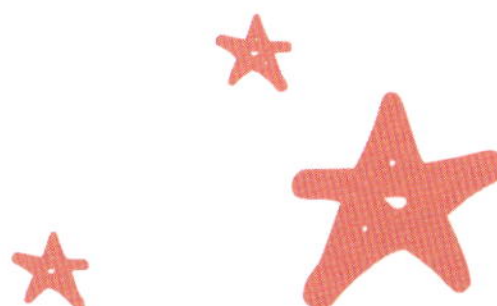

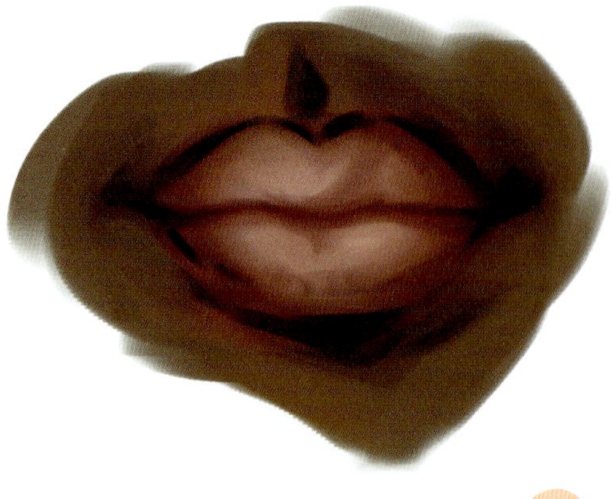

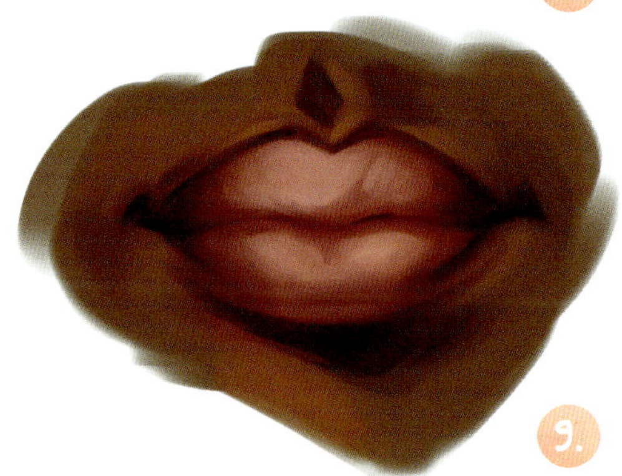

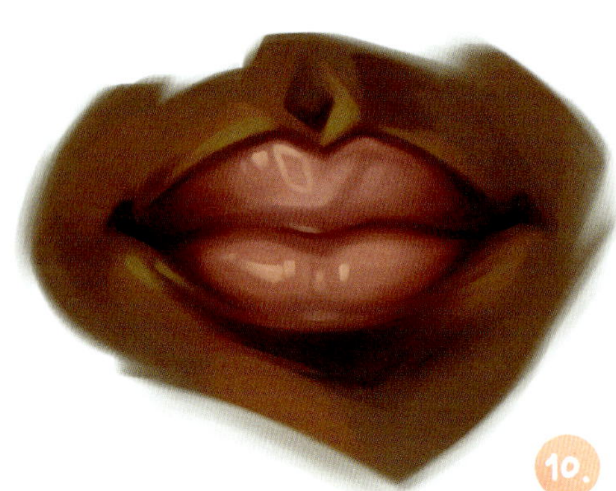

8. It's time to begin rendering the painting; right-click on any layer and select "Merge visible into new layer" to flatten your image. Every time you would like to make a risky addition to the piece, you can right-click your working layer, select "Duplicate layer" and paint on that new layer to essentially save your process. Color picking from your canvas, use the Oil brush and begin defining the edge of the lips, shading in the corners of the mouth and rendering the folds of the lips. Add natural texture to the lips by adding folds and lines in the lips; perfectly smooth lips with no fine lines will appear to have lip filler that has plumped and smoothed them.

9. Smooth over the skin around the lips to blend the highlights and shadows. Color pick over the brown lip line and define it and the philtrum according to your desired shape. Add some brightness to the skin right under the corners of the mouth to create dimension, as well as above the lip line to define the lips. Softly blend the bottom lip lines into the rest of the skin and add some darkness to the inner corners of the mouth. The darker these marks are, the plumper the lips will appear.

10. Select a yellow-toned highlight from the color wheel to add some extra dimension to the highlighted areas of the skin. Color pick the pink tone of the lips and shift the hue of that color to a brighter pastel coral tone on the color wheel to begin painting in some glossiness on the lips. If you are struggling with how much definition and realism to add to the painting, view your Navigator window (see page 14 for program layouts) and analyze if the painting could be sharpened up with some more graphic shapes in the highlights and shadows.

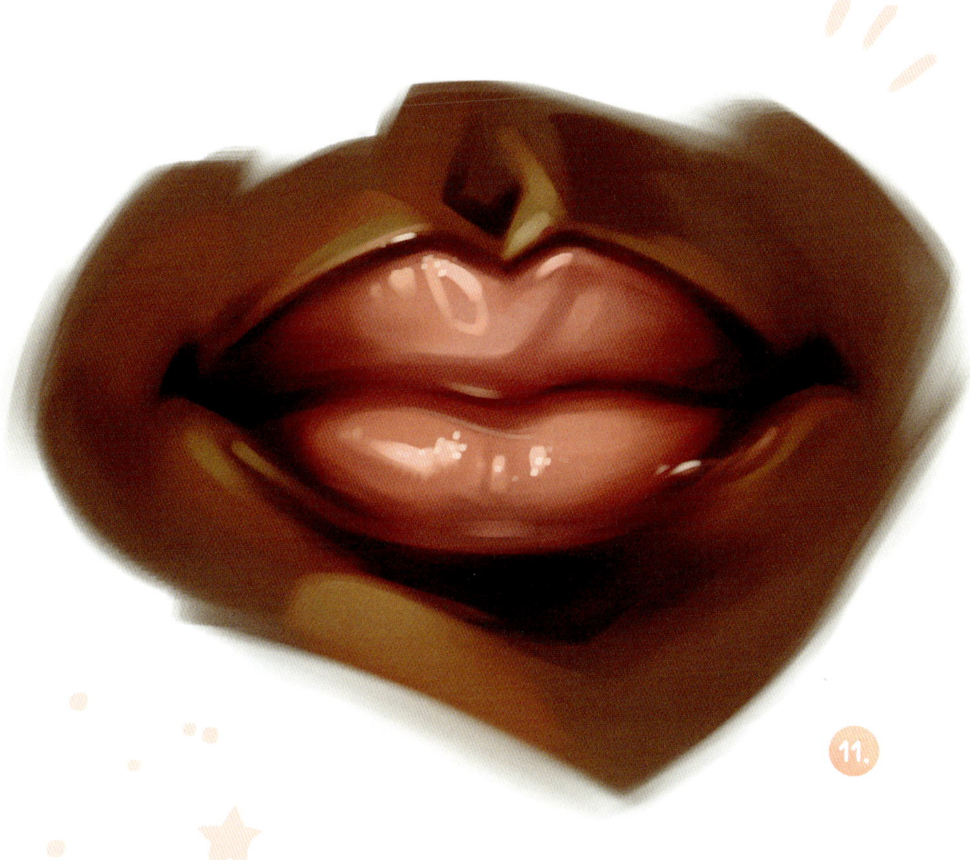

11. Use a Soft Light layer or Tone Curve layer above the rest of the painting to add any unifying colors to the piece; I applied the Soft Airbrush on a Soft Light layer to enhance the shadows with a cooler purple tone and lift the highlights to a pastel yellow. Using a bright pastel pink on a small size of the Oil brush, add sharp, glossy highlights to the painting. Think of where a lip gloss would be applied and add reflections and glitters to those areas. Finish the piece with any glows or signature details, like my wonky star and exclamation marks, and add Smart Sharpening to the finished painting. (See page 152 for details on finishing touches.)

PROMPT: PAINT FIVE SETS OF LIPS

Use reference photos to sketch different lip shapes, angles, colors and expressions. Take note of how you improve your efficiency, and write down tricks you've learned or pointers on anatomy and expressive emotions that you might want to reference later.

Are there any basic shapes that you find yourself using to build the structure of the lips? Some lips have a larger top or bottom lip, and most people don't have perfectly symmetrical faces. Experiment with glossiness, texture, gradient and contrast in each exercise.

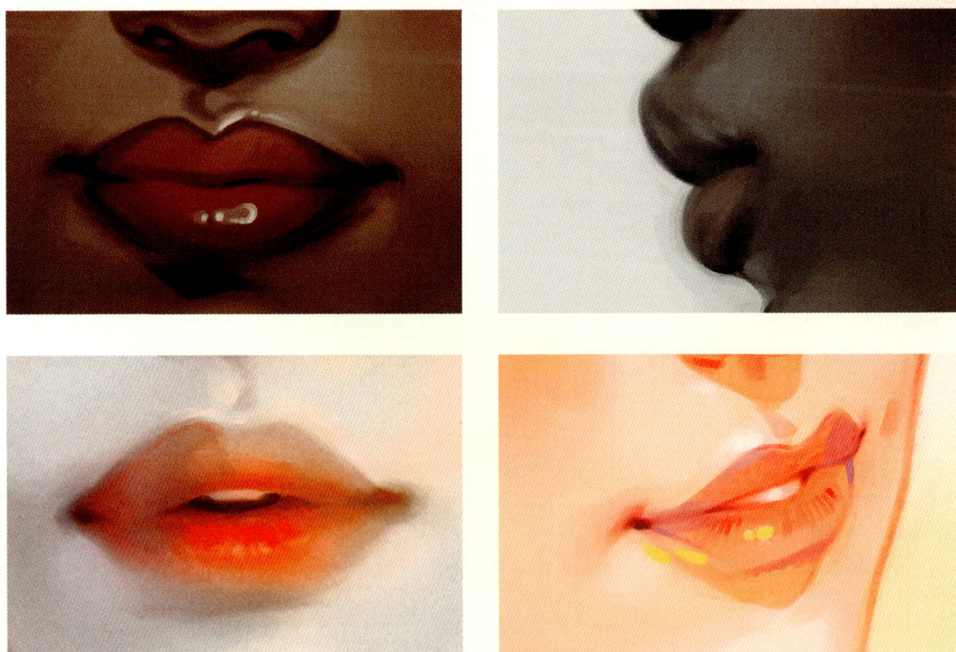

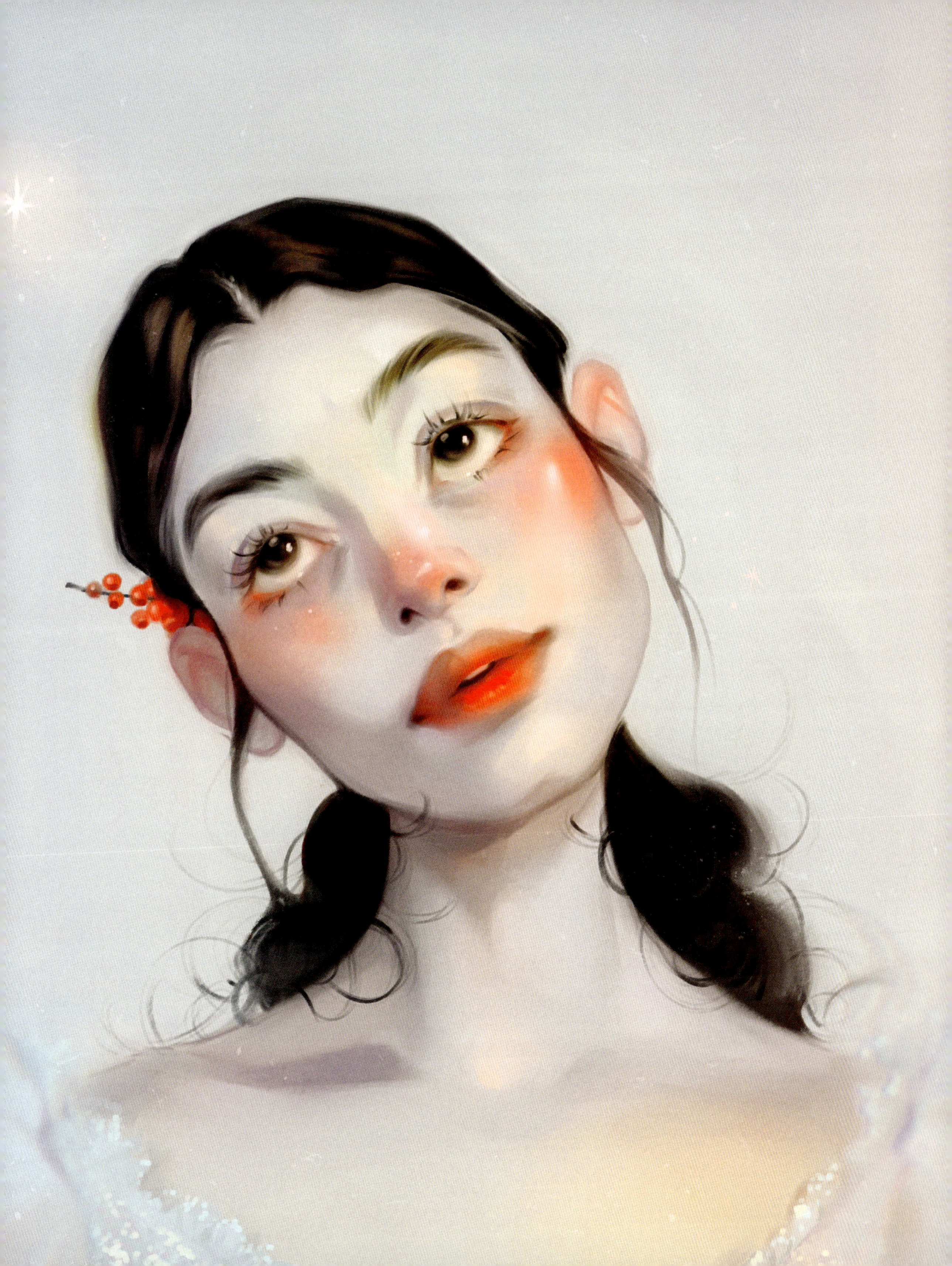

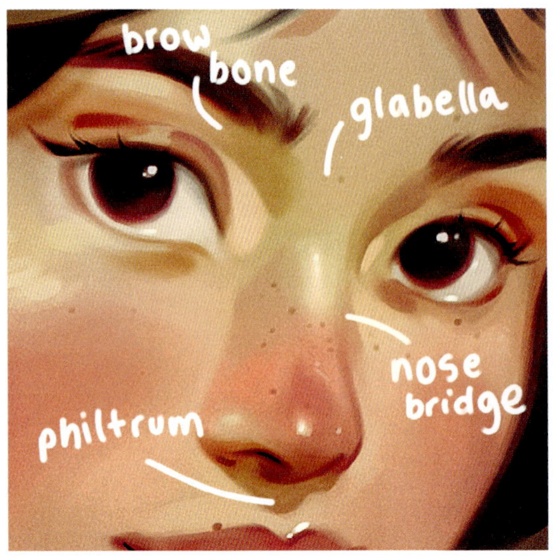

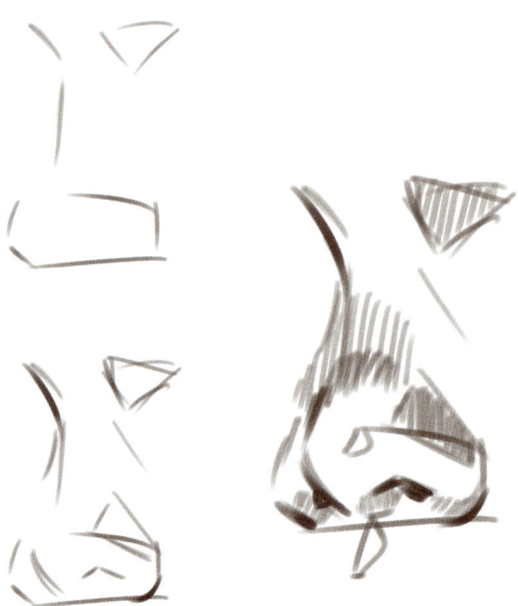

Work with small marks to map out the curves and edges of the nose. Once you have blocked in where the shadows and highlights will go, shade them in.

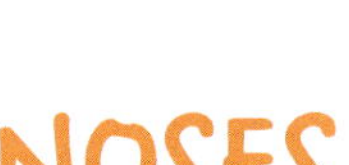

NOSES

When learning how to draw and paint noses, you must first step back and break down the nose into a couple of simple shapes. The bottom of the nose will either look like a diamond or a triangle with one of the tips cut off; the tip of the nose will cut that basic shape into something similar to a heart or arrow. This shape can be angular or softened depending on how pointed or fleshy, wide and flat or narrow and long the nose, which is determined by your reference and the ethnicity of your subject. Connect that base with the bridge of the nose as it connects to the eyebrows and the inner brow bone. The inner brow bone and *glabella* (the flat part between the eyebrows) will be lightly shadowed as they are slightly inset in the face. Use delicate shading to indicate this shadow; using harsh shading can give your subject a stern or harsh look.

Work from simple shapes to details. Study the basic shapes that make up the nose in your reference and replicate them in your drawing. Once you have these rough shapes drawn, start adding details like the nostrils and sides of the nose. When adding values, study your reference and block in the values and colors before going in with details. Every nose will be shaped differently, so there isn't a clear-cut way to describe this process other than emphasizing simplification of forms. Pay attention to your reference: Does your subject have a prominent or flatter nose? Use contrasting tones when painting a larger, stronger nose and more subtle tones when painting a nose with a subtle bridge.

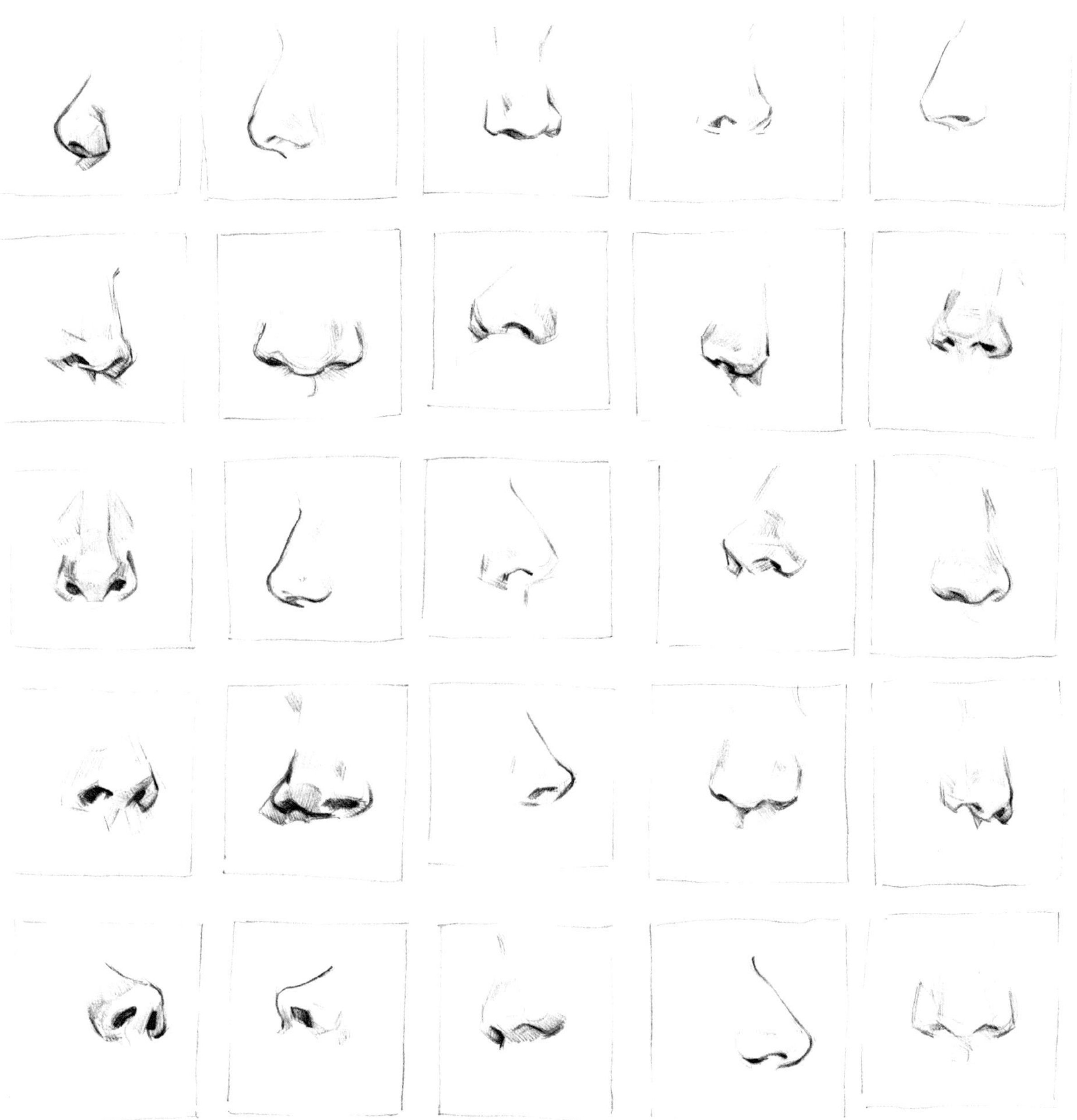

Practice drawing different shapes, sizes and angles of the nose from references to get used to them from your imagination.

Colors

Use subtle tones to show the variations in shadows and hues in your painting. Since the nose is so delicate, using highly contrasting colors will bring more attention to the nose. The tip of the nose is fleshier than the rest of it, so there will oftentimes be more warm and pink tones found in the tip of the nose rather than the bridge. Because of the fleshy nature of the nose, the nostrils will often not only be shadowed with a dark and muted color, but also, since all skin has transparency, refract some light and include bright pink and red midtones.

Add highlights to the edge of the nostrils, tip of the nose, along the nose bridge and in the creases of the nostrils. Build up these highlights gradually, and make sure to gradate the shadow under the nose seamlessly into the philtrum and Cupid's bow.

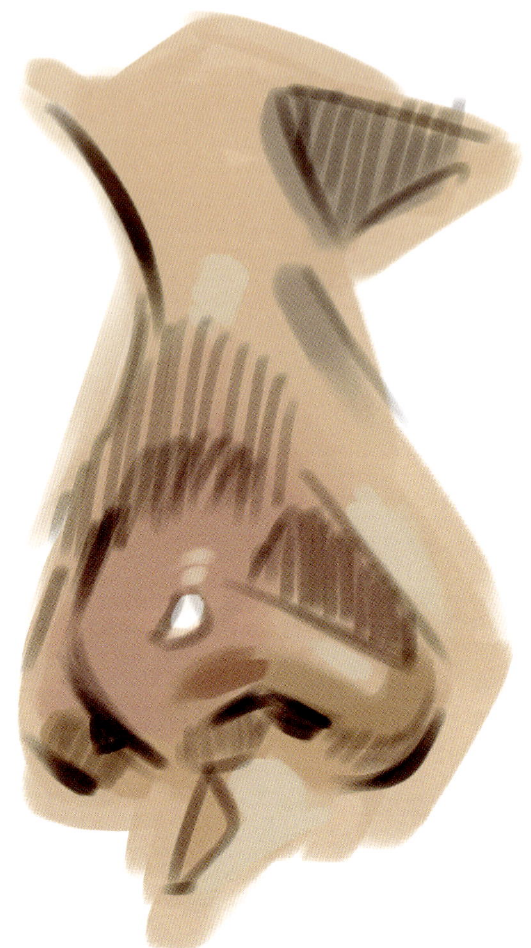

Color in the nose according to your personal preferences. I like to add a pink hue to the tip and nostrils.

Angles

When viewing the nose at different angles, break the bottom of the nose, the sides of the nose and the nose bridge into their own respective simple shapes. The profile of the nose is, at its base, a triangle. You can add crooks or different angles to this triangle to draw different nose bridges and shapes, but you can often use this basic shape as a guideline when sketching. There is no easy hack to drawing and painting noses other than diligent study of references and application. Once you become comfortable replicating a reference, you will be able to draw noses realistically from your own memory.

PROJECT 4: PAINT A CLOSE-UP OF A NOSE

Mastering painting the nose is difficult; I still struggle with different angles! Use reference photos for different shapes, sizes or angles that you want to paint. Write down challenges, tricks or improvements you learned from your process.

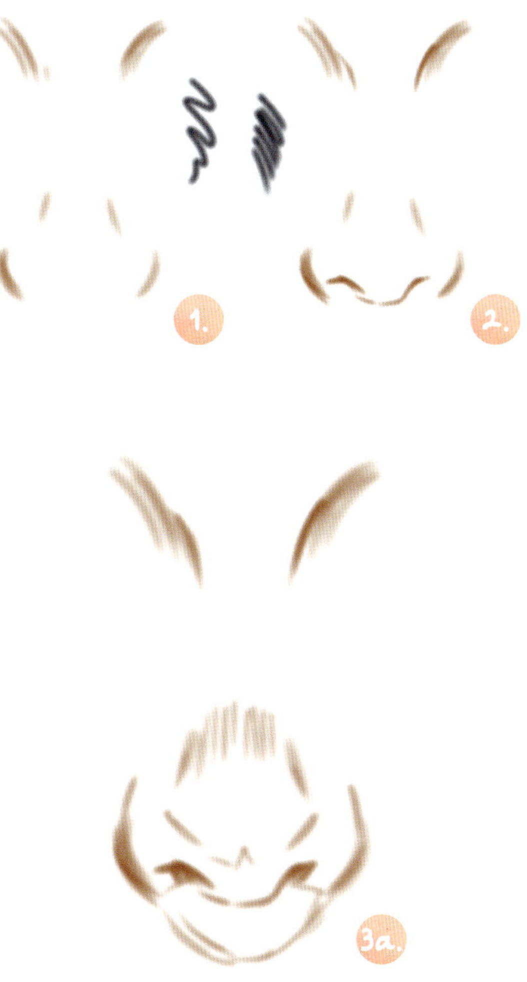

1. Create a square canvas of 4 x 4 inches (10 x 10 cm) at 300 dpi (see page 16 for canvas sizing). After setting the base layer to a background color of your choice, create a new Multiply layer for your sketch. Using the Soft Airbrush (see page 17 for brushes) with a medium-toned bronze (or a warm dark brown if you're painting a darker-skinned subject), begin by sketching out the rough shape of the nose bridge and nostrils. These marks will be relatively symmetrical, as we are looking straight on at the nose. The top curves represent the nose bridge fading into the eyebrows, the middle lines are the tip of the nose and the bottom curves are the shape of the nostrils.

2. Next, draw in the nostrils; use angular lines to create sharper features, and softer curves to draw a fleshier or rounder tip of the nose. Keep the marks of the nostrils dark since these will be contrasted in the painting stage.

3a. Roughly shape the contours of the nose; add vertical shading to the nose bridge, then softly outline the tip of the nose, with or without the small indent at the bottom of the tip (I like to draw this in most of my paintings). Fill in the nostrils with shading and indicate where the tip creates a shadow over the rest of the philtrum and lips.

b. Draw two triangles on both sides of the nose bridge. These are going to be the slopes that connect the nose to the rest of the face; imagine these are at a downward angle, almost like a mountain. These triangles will be receding in shadow compared to the top of the nose bridge. The little circular marks above the triangles indicate the shadows cast by the brow bone. Lastly, the soft triangle under the nose indicates the shadow of the philtrum. All the marks you've made in Steps 1–3 can be elongated or widened depending on the shape and size of the nose you are drawing. Set your sketch layer to Multiply (see page 18 for adjustment layers).

4. Using the Soft Airbrush or Oil brush on a new layer underneath your sketch, paint in the base skin tone. I am using an olive-toned tan and using the Oil brush to create some painterly strokes framing the drawing.

5. With a warmer golden color, paint in the highlights. The bridge and tip of the nose will be illuminated, as well as the face surrounding the sides of the nose and nostrils. Avoid the shaded area of the nose bridge since the slope will indicate a button shape to the nose.

6. With a cooler red tone, paint in the shadows of the nose. With a more saturated red color, add a fleshy tone to the shaded nose bridge and nostrils. Use a cool, desaturated brown to add shading to the sides of the nose, brow bone and the shadow under the tip of the nose. This variety in hues and tones will be sufficient for color picking in the painting stage.

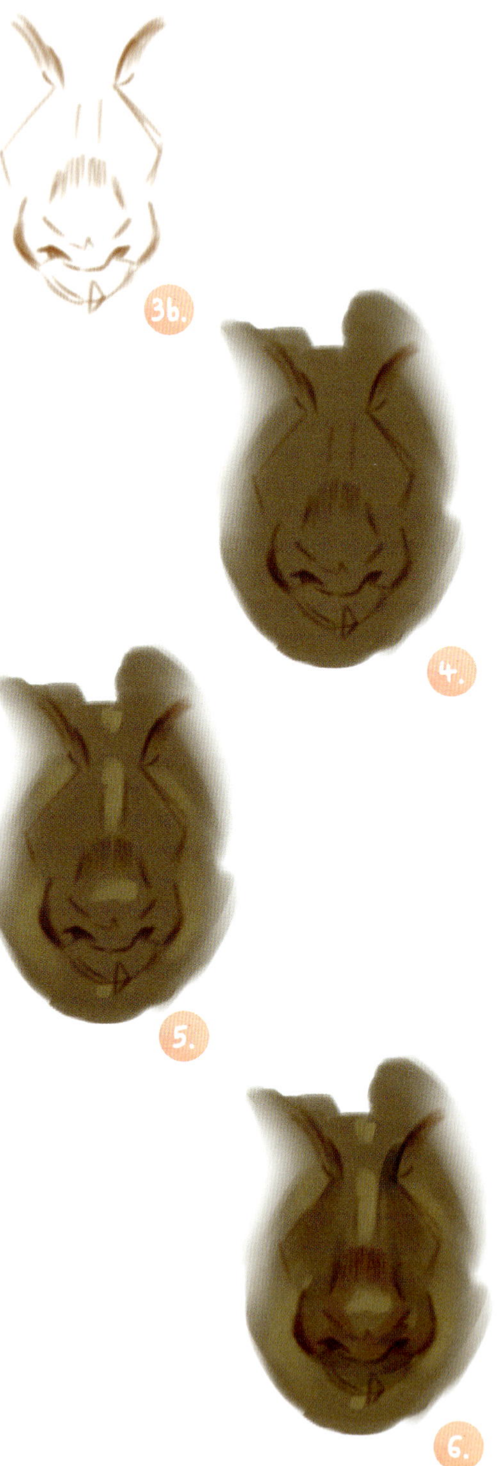

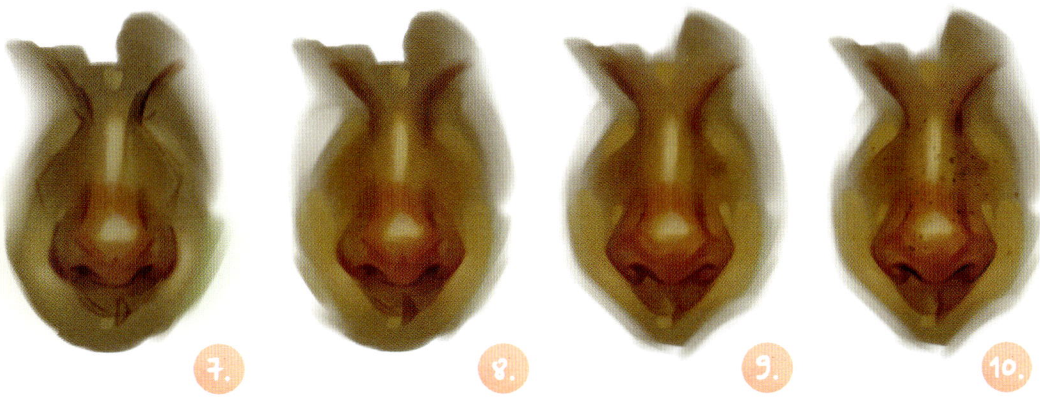

7. Add a new Soft Light adjustment layer (see page 18 for adjustment layers) above the rest of your layers and use the Soft Airbrush to gently paint in some warm highlights. I like to add some more warmth to the tip of the nose, since I like the sunburnt or blushing look; you can omit this if you don't enjoy it stylistically. Use this step to finesse your colors and bring a cohesive tone to your painting.

8. Right-click on any layer and select "Merge visible into new layer" to flatten your image. Every time you would like to make a risky addition to the piece, you can right-click your working layer, select "Duplicate layer" and paint on that new layer to essentially save your process. With the Oil brush, begin rendering the nostrils and tip of the nose. Use hard pressure to add a sharp, defined edge to the side of the nostril, and then blend softly in circular motions to diffuse that mark into the rest of the skin. The basic sketch and color of the nose are already on the canvas, so work on blending the sketch into the rest of the painting.

9. Continue rendering the painting, focusing on defining the darkness of the shadowed nostrils, tip and sides of the nose. Paint with a mixture of soft blended marks to soften the colors into one another, and with assured strokes to add painterly texture to the angled areas of the face.

10. Let's add some freckles! If you are nervous about this step, create a new layer on top of your painting, and play around with the opacity of the layer if you feel that the freckles look too strong or dark. Using a dark, desaturated brown, make soft oval marks over the nose bridge and tip. Consider the direction the skin is lying/moving and paint the freckles following that direction. You can minimize your brush size to add smaller clusters of faint freckles, and maximize the brush to add larger, darker beauty marks. Make sure to soften the edges of each freckle; I paint them each in a quick spiral pattern, pressing hard to begin with and easing my pressure as I move across the spiral to diffuse the edges. Make sure to place these marks irregularly. Placing freckles equidistantly will create a Raggedy Ann® doll effect rather than a natural, sun-kissed one.

11. This next step is optional, but looking at the sketch, I found it awkward to have a floating nose on a canvas without any context. I added some subtle sketchy lines around the nose bridge to indicate where the eyebrows and eyes would begin if I was to continue rendering the piece into a full portrait.

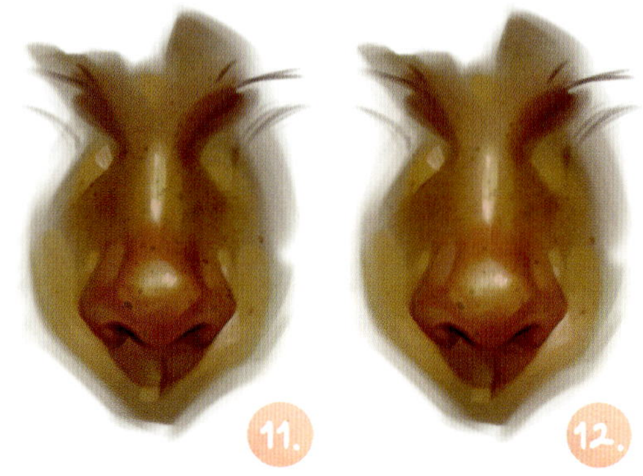

12. On a Soft Light layer above all the other layers, use the Soft Airbrush to add any highlights or shadows to the piece to unify the tones. I used a soft pastel pink to lighten the nose bridge and slightly shift the colors from yellow to pink. If you are unhappy with the colors, use a Tone Curve layer to adjust the brightness and contrast of the piece, or to shift the hues and unify the painting.

13. Lastly, add any final details to the painting. Use a pastel pink to add a glossy shine to the nose tip and bridge, and gently brush over the freckles with the base skin color to soften their appearance. Lastly, add Smart Sharpening to the image. (See page 152 for details on finishing touches.)

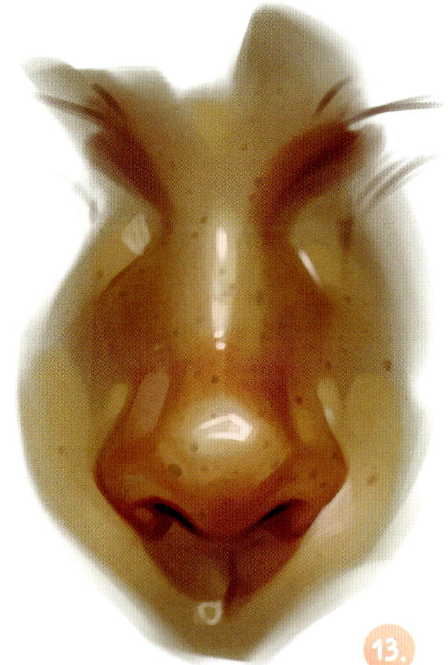

PROMPT: PAINT FIVE NOSES

As with the eyes and lips, use reference photos to paint nose sketches with different shapes and at different angles. Try to simplify the reference into the simplest shapes possible and write down any tips that work for you.

Try to use loose, quick strokes to lay your sketch down so that you don't get caught up in details too quickly. Experiment with the length and width of each nose. Some might have wide bridges, while some may have wide nostrils.

Which angles are difficult to draw? Dedicate more practice to improving your workflow with that angle. How do you prefer to use shading: simplifying and stylizing the shape or adding realistic dimension?

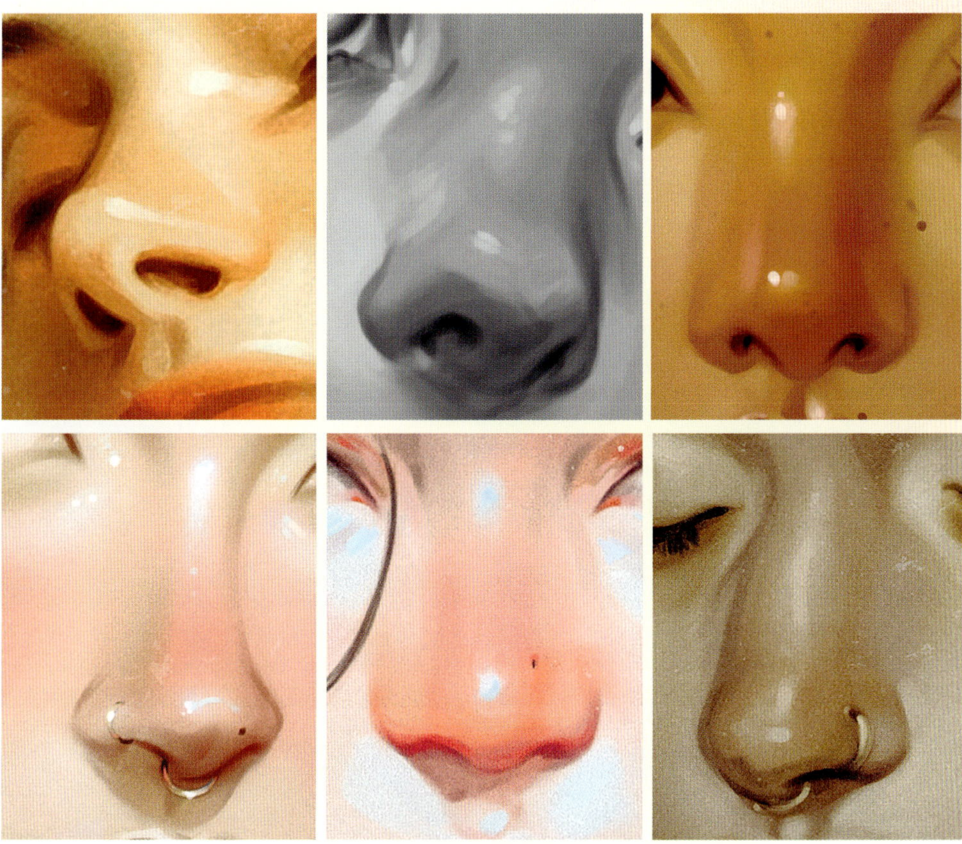

HAIR

Hair gives your paintings and characters personality, energy and dynamism. Understanding basic rules for how hair moves and flows will help you create beautiful portraits quickly, without hiccups in the painting process. There are endless possibilities when it comes to rendering texture, tones and hairstyles, making it one of the most creatively liberating parts of painting portraiture.

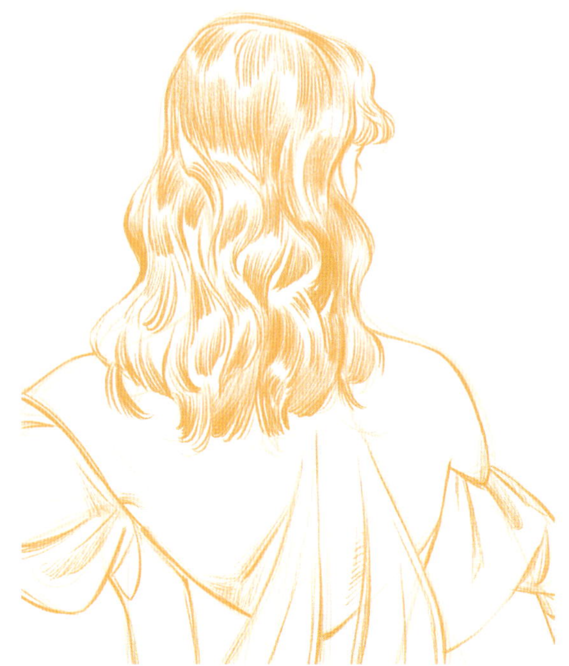

Sections

Think of hair as made up of larger sections. Painting every individual hair will be a time-consuming process that can only work well when painting a photorealistic subject. When stylizing hair, think of it in large, flowing chunks. Break the sections up, and add highlights and shadows to each of those sections as they move instead of focusing on drawing every strand of hair. If you're unsure how to break hair up in different chunks, look at reference photos of hairstyles you'd like to paint and trace out the individual segments of hair. Being able to simplify hair into blocky shapes will help you understand how to break hair up in those chunks when you sketch and paint; it can even be helpful to squint and see which shapes blend together and which stand out. You will be able to stylize or render the hair as much as you would like when you begin working on the details (see page 152).

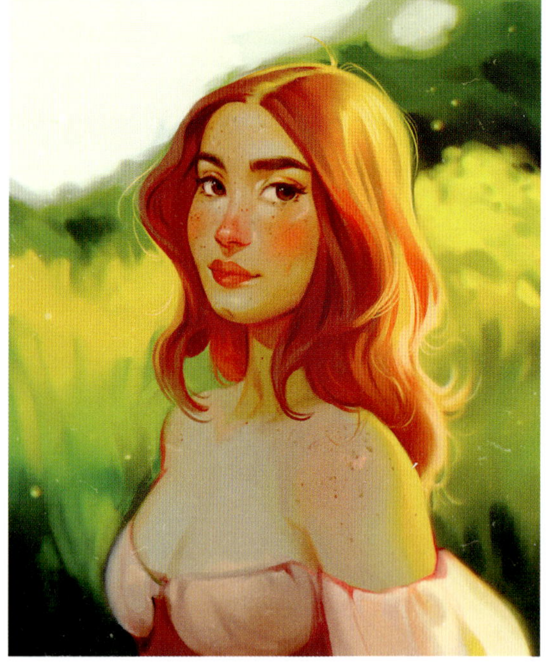

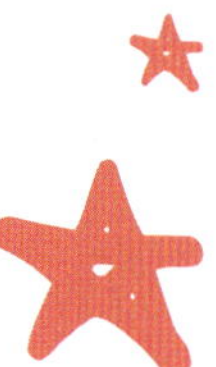

Contours

Thinking about hair in sections will help you properly develop the contours and curves of the hair. When shading, make sure that you're deliberate in the curve and placement of each stroke. Use each line as a tool for suggesting hair strands, highlights and shadows. The goal isn't to fill in the shape of the hair in one flat wash, but to create an illusion of depth, movement and curl. In the same way that you broke down the mass of the hair into chunks, break the shadows and highlights down into blocks with shading or color. This is going to guide you in your color placement as you paint in the details. I like to softly shade in my shadowed blocks to differentiate them from the blocks of highlights.

When you begin breaking the hair up in solid chunks, you can create definition within straight hair, waves or curls. Aim for using long, smooth strokes instead of short, jagged lines. Even straight hair will have one or two large waves in each section of hair based on the movement of the character, drape and wind. Using short, jagged lines also makes it difficult to add silky shadows, highlights and details to the hair. While shading it in quickly may seem like the simplest solution in the moment, investing some extra time into working with the contours of the hair to create flowing lines will look better and come naturally with practice. As you shade in the mass of the hair, use strokes that move with the length and curvature of the hair. Even though you're not drawing in each individual strand of hair, these contours will begin to add depth and dimension to the blocks of hair.

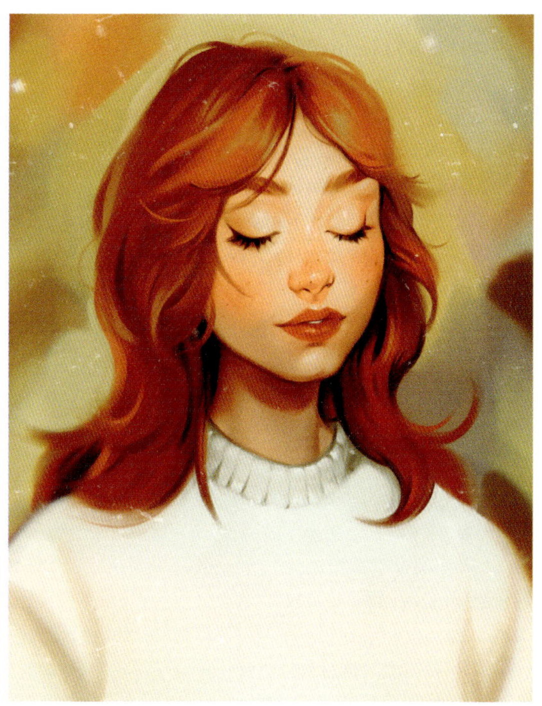

Paint wispy highlights to add details to the large sections of hair. It's not necessary to draw every hair strand in order to create depth.

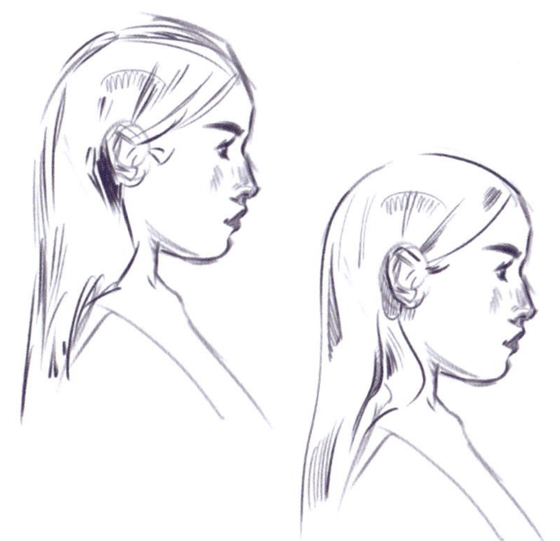

When sketching the hair, instead of using your wrist to draw short, choppy lines, use your elbow to create longer, smooth strokes. This will give the hair more movement and a polished look.

Hairstyles

When drawing different hairstyles, consider the weight of the hair and what is holding it up. Are you trying to draw a tight ponytail or a loose one? Depending on how tightly the hairstyle is held in place, there will be room for flyaway hairs and looser strands of hair. If you are struggling with drawing a braid or bun, simplify that hairstyle into simple geometric shapes; breaking a braid down into a combination of rectangular boxes can help you understand the general shape and direction of the hair. Add baby hairs for a natural, unkempt appearance and sleek down the hair for a more polished look. Remember to study any traditional or culturally important hairstyles and to portray them in a respectful way, especially since many women have been discriminated against or ridiculed for wearing their hair in a traditional style.

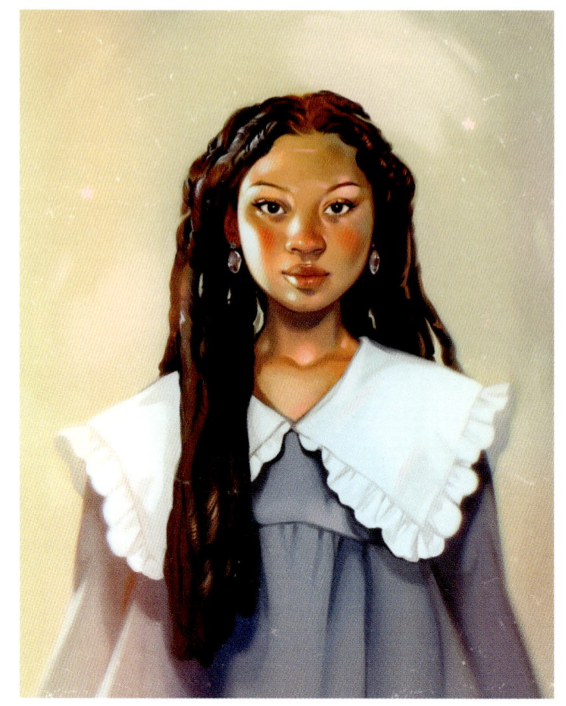

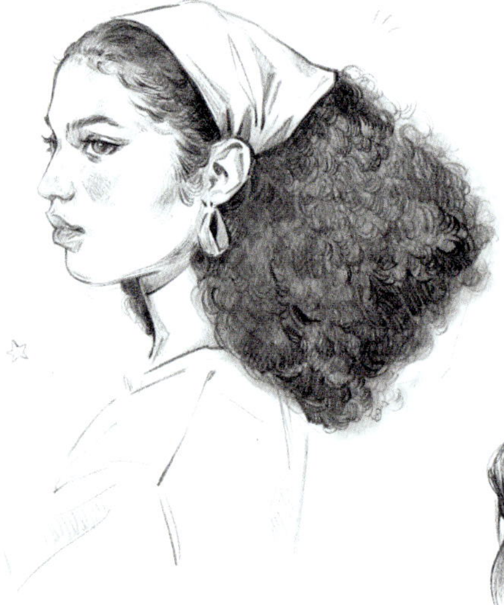

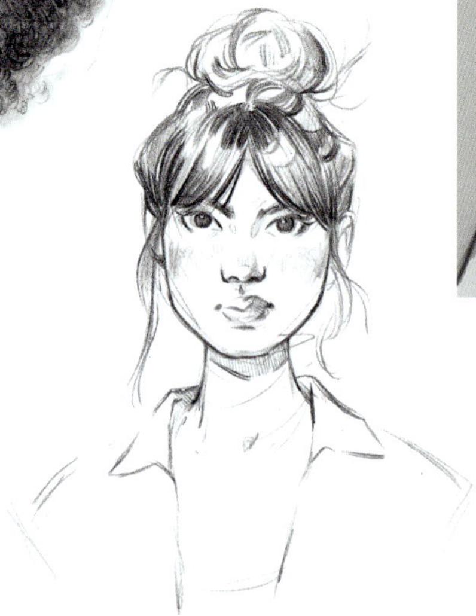

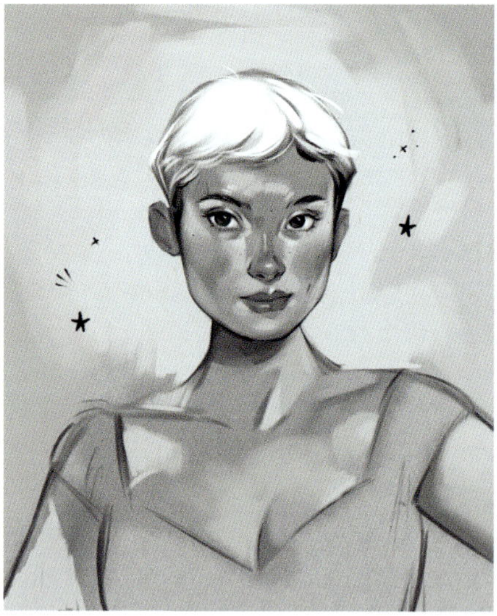

PROJECT 5: PAINT A CHARACTER WITH A HISTORICAL OR CULTURAL HAIRSTYLE

Make sure to choose something complex that you will have to break down into simple shapes and add detail to. Write down areas that you would like to improve on and things to keep in mind for your next painting. Writing about what you are proud of and what you can improve will help you keep those in the forefront of your mind when you are starting a new piece.

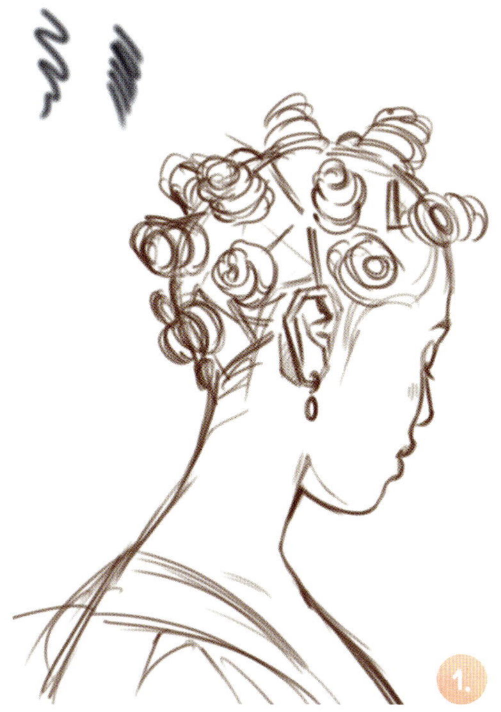

1. Create a canvas of 4 x 5 inches (10 x 13 cm) at 300 dpi (see page 16 for canvas sizing). After setting the base layer to a background color of your choice (I used a tan shade), create a new Multiply layer for your sketch. Using the Soft Airbrush (see page 17 for brushes) with a warm dark brown (or a medium-toned bronze if you're painting a lighter-skinned subject), begin by placing the rough shapes of the hairstyle you chose. I chose Bantu knots since there are many textures and shapes to highlight. Keep the part of the hair in mind and how messy or neat it needs to be for the hairstyle. Use flowy, free lines for hair that is loose, and smoother, streamlined linework for hair that is taut. The Bantu knots are tightly wrapped, so I use smooth lines to emphasize the shape of her skull, as well as the thick, wrapped knots.

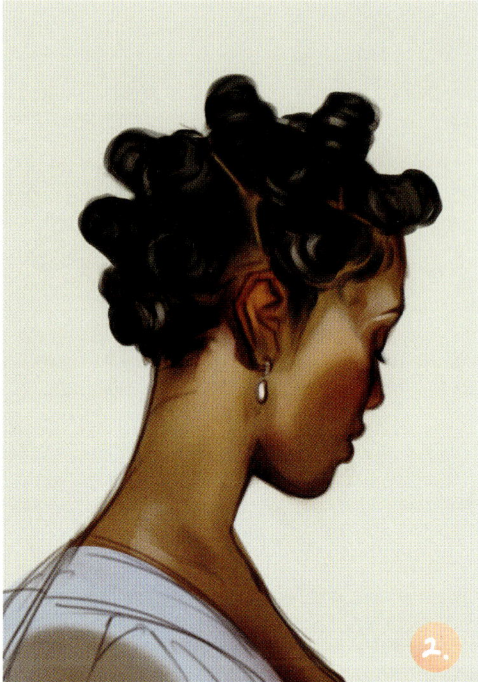

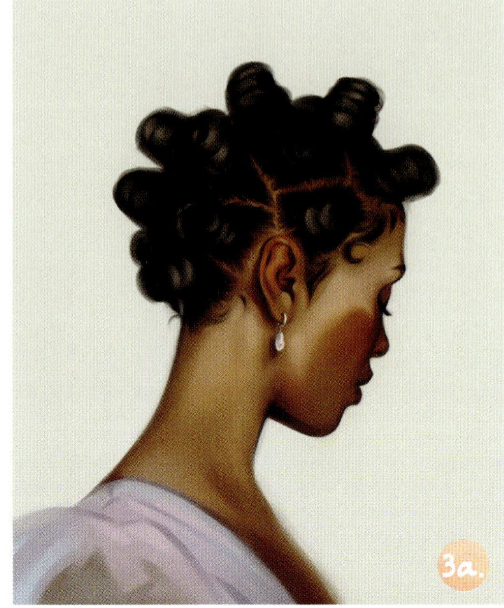

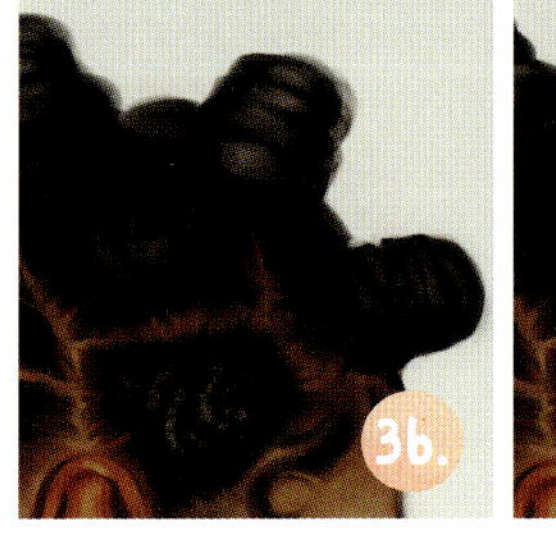

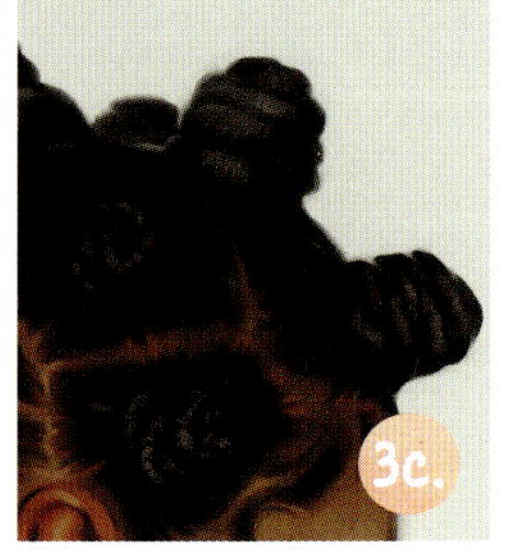

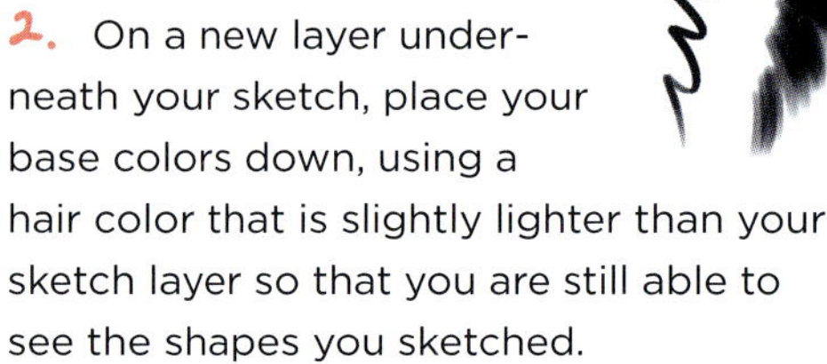

2. On a new layer underneath your sketch, place your base colors down, using a hair color that is slightly lighter than your sketch layer so that you are still able to see the shapes you sketched.

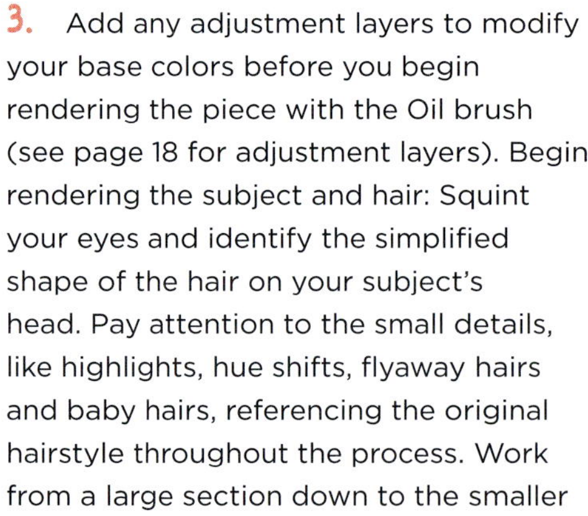

3. Add any adjustment layers to modify your base colors before you begin rendering the piece with the Oil brush (see page 18 for adjustment layers). Begin rendering the subject and hair: Squint your eyes and identify the simplified shape of the hair on your subject's head. Pay attention to the small details, like highlights, hue shifts, flyaway hairs and baby hairs, referencing the original hairstyle throughout the process. Work from a large section down to the smaller details instead of being bogged down by the individual strands to begin with. While it might make sense to draw every individual hair strand to add volume and dimension to the hair, it's better to work with large, blocky shapes that are blended into one another. At the end of the painting process, you will only need some choice, thin lines to create that dimensional detail in the hair. Focus on smooth transitions between the values and hues.

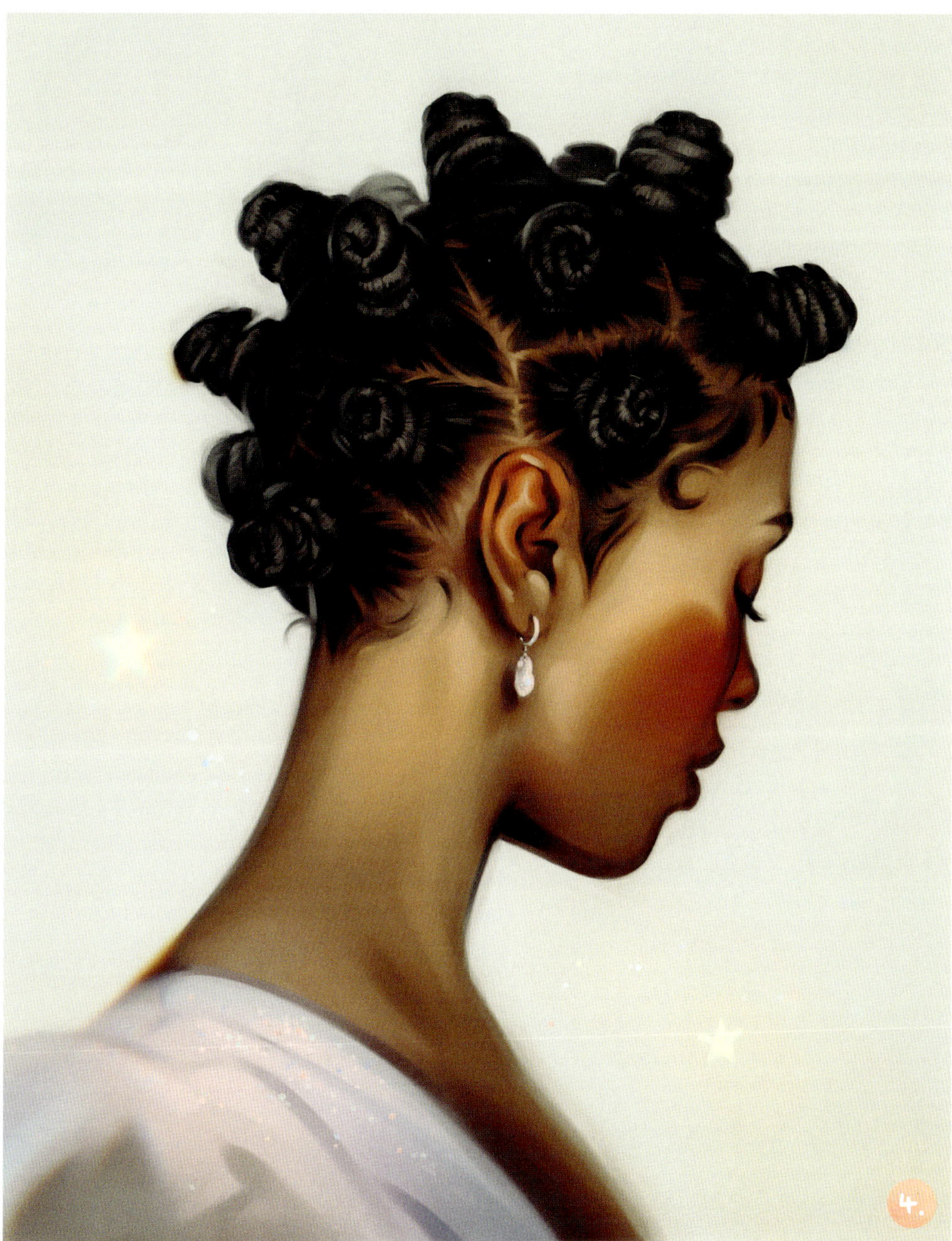

4. Finish up the details, like flyaway hairs and baby hairs, adding these on a separate layer in case you wish to remove them easily in the future. Add any adjustment layers and color grading to the piece to create a cohesive final image.

Movement

The movement of your subject's hair will vary depending on the fullness of the hair and the thickness of each strand. A thick head of hair will be heavier and weighed down by gravity more than a fine, thin head of hair. Heavier hair will move less as it's being blown by the wind, while fine hair will have more movement. You can add more volume to the scalp if the hair is thicker or add wispy strands to the head if the hair is thinner. Straighter hair will show more movement as your subject is turning their head, the hair is blown by the wind, etc., while wavy and curly hair will maintain the integrity of that hair texture when in motion: The tighter the curl, the more static it will remain.

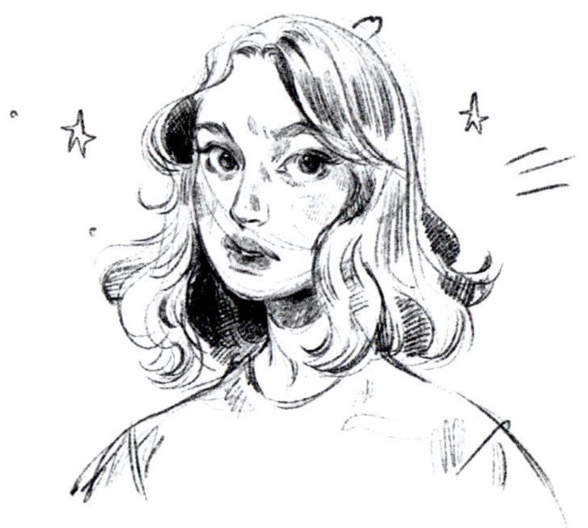

Using bouncy lines for the hair will create a whimsical and magical appearance.

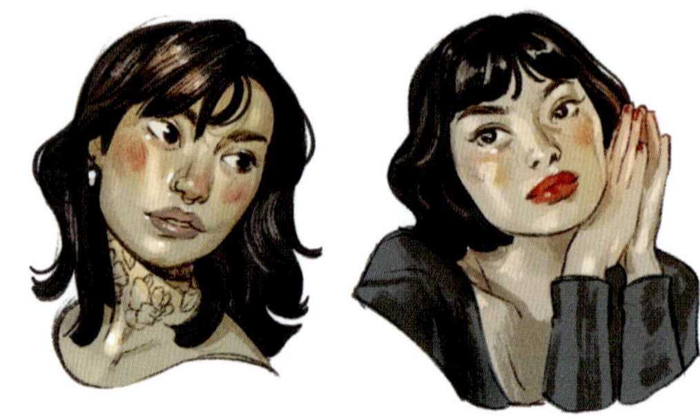

Tones

When painting hair, change up the hue and tones for the shadows and highlights. Adding variations to the colors you choose will create depth and interest, while staying in the same hues and tones when adding details and shading creates a flatter, less dynamic portrait. If you use a warmer tone for the highlights, consider using a cooler tone for the shadows.

Details

You can detail the chunks of hair by adding a couple of individual stray hairs; this adds an organic touch to your portrait. Imperfections are a good way of adding character and realism to your art, and flyaway and stray hairs will take your painting to the next level. Rim and backlighting can also add a special touch to your portrait. Creating a halo of light around the hair shows off the contours and can add further punch to the small details you've added.

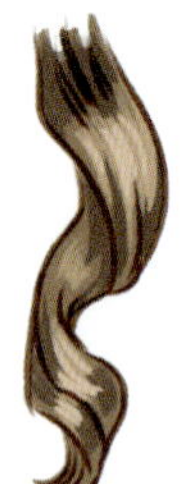
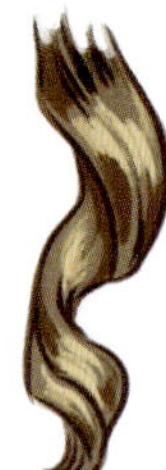
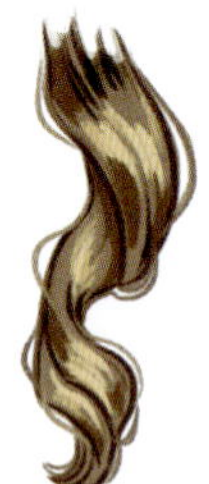

To create depth in the hair, use a variety of hues in the shadows and highlights. Add small strands of hair for dimension.

PROMPT: PAINT FIVE HEADS OF HAIR WITH DIFFERENT TEXTURES

Paint different lengths and textures of hair. You can paint a subject's hair blowing in the wind, a subject swinging their head, hair that defies gravity, etc.

Become familiar with the movement and bounce you can incorporate into hair. Write down anything you learned that could be useful for future reference. Do you have trouble painting movement? How do you portray weight in different hair textures and styles?

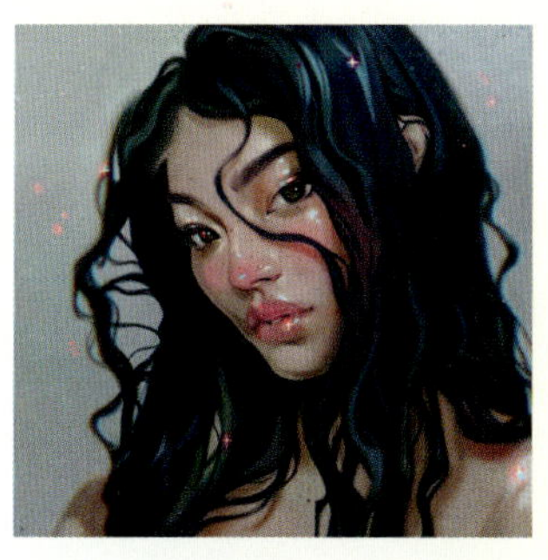
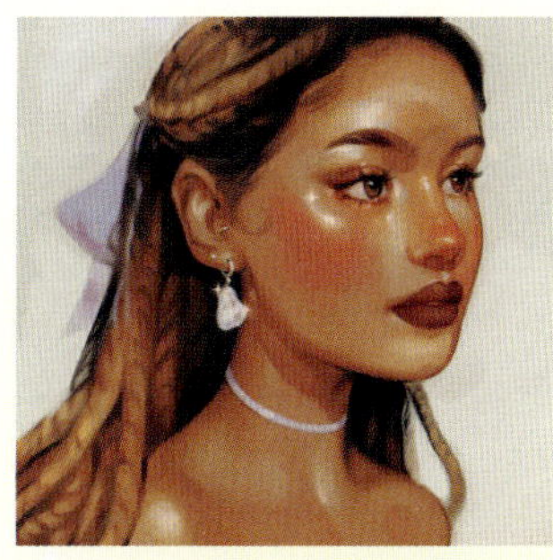
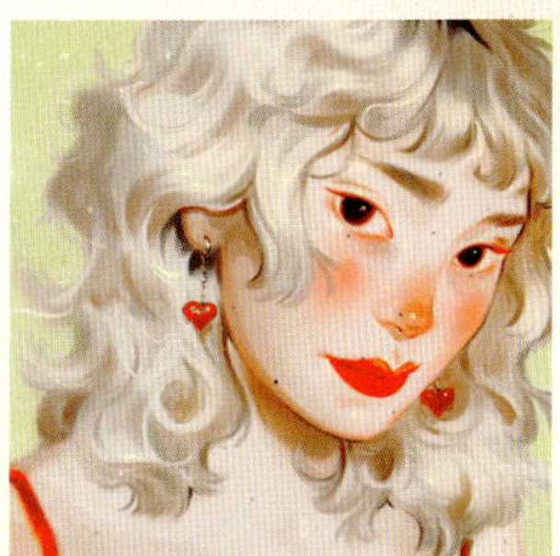
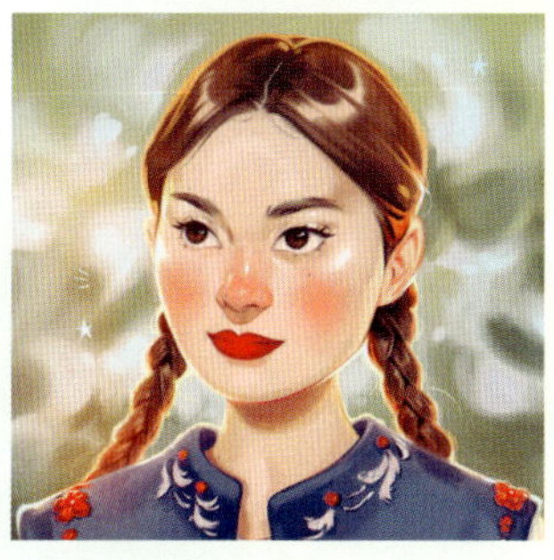
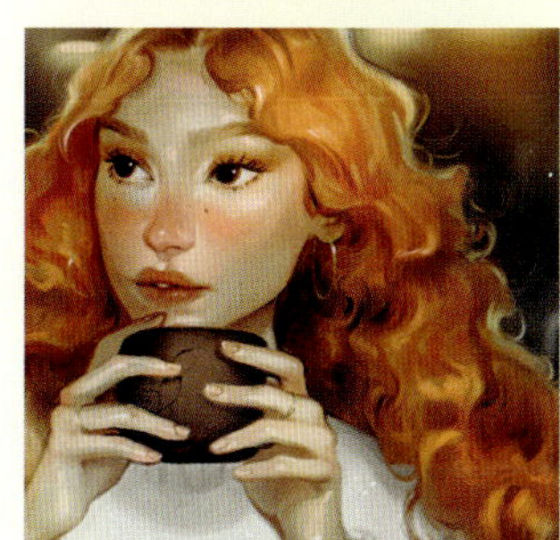
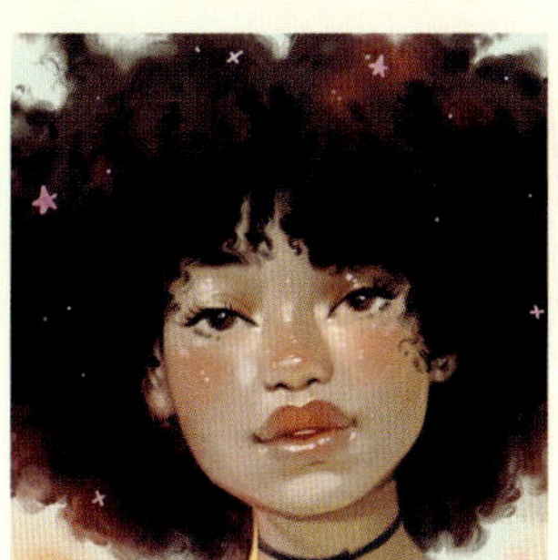

HANDS

Probably the most daunting feature for beginners to draw is the hands. While learning proper shading and drawing fingernails can be a learning curve, drawing the basic form of hands is relatively easy once you break everything down into simple shapes.

You can think of the palm as a rectangle with four cylinders coming from the top of it and one coming from the side. When adding detail to these simple shapes, round the palm off toward the wrist and make sure to add two joints in each finger to create three sections in each cylinder. The easiest way to fool people into thinking you've mastered drawing hands is to draw the hand as a mitt. Once you have the general mitten shape, draw out the individual fingers and connect them to the palm. Drawing the middle and ring fingers touching can be the easiest way to draw the hand; since you don't have to worry about each individual finger's angle, you can draw a relaxed hand that looks skillfully executed.

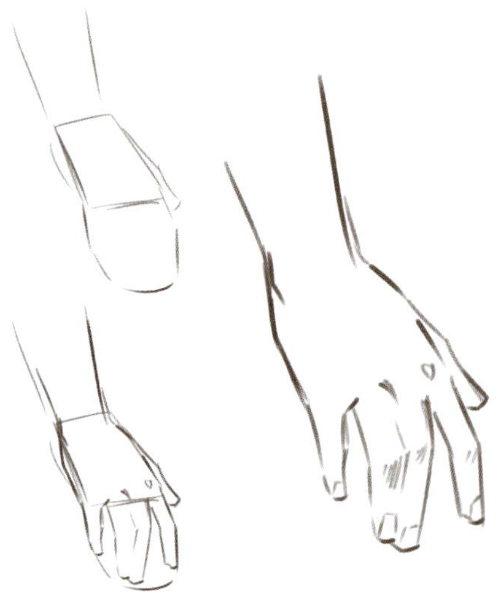

Draw a mitten shape before rendering the individual fingers and adding small details like the fingernails.

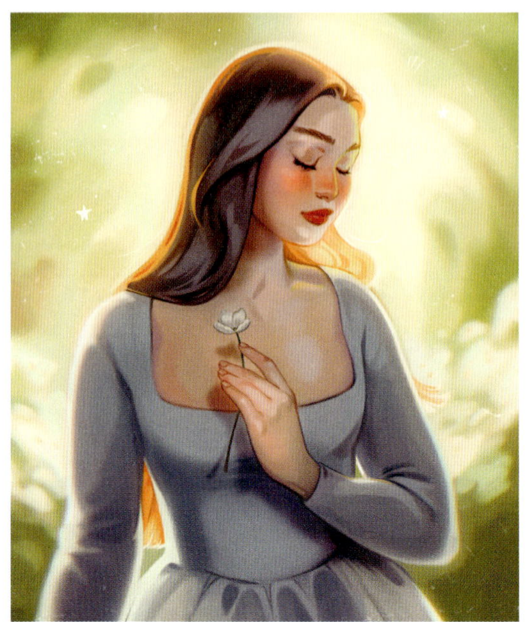

I photograph my own hands to use as references. Try posing your own and taking a quick picture to better understand the shapes and forms.

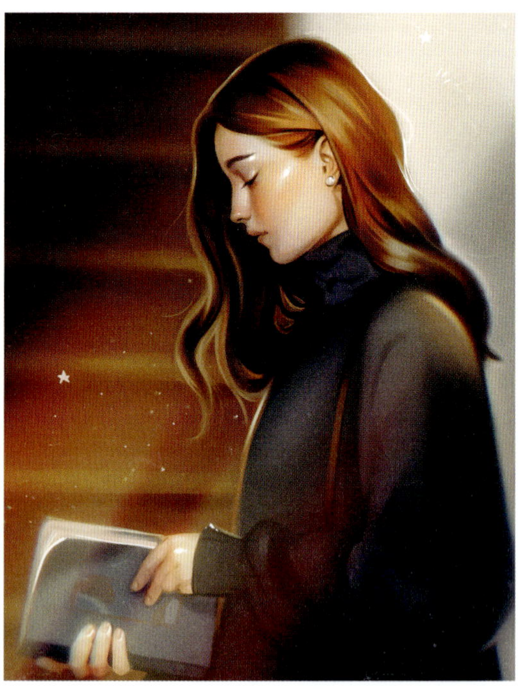

You don't need to sharply define the details in the hands to create impact in a painting.

You can either draw fingers tapered or squared off at the end; tapered fingers look classic and feminine, while squared-off fingers can look more cartoony and masculine. You can also draw hands with rounder, softer features, like undefined knuckles, or more angular knuckles and wrists. I recommend taking quick reference photos of your own hands to see what they look like in a very specific pose. Remember to utilize your mark-making to indicate the curvature of the palms and cylindrical nature of the fingers.

Arms

When drawing your subject, it might be hard to draw the arms and hands naturally posed. I used to start with the shoulder and work my way down to the wrist and hands when I wanted to draw a specific pose. This never worked out for me because I was subconsciously not taking angles and foreshortening into consideration. I would recommend placing the hand first and then connecting the arm to the hand. This makes it much easier and more natural to pose your subject.

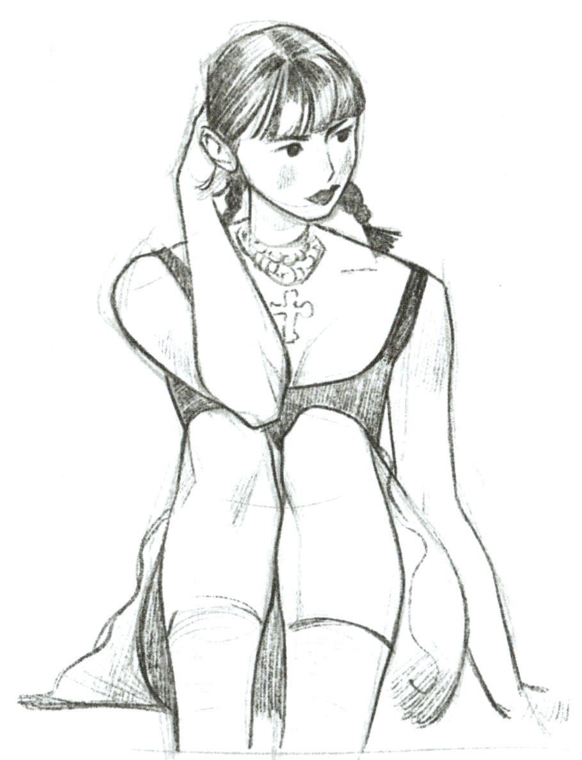

Foreshorten the arms to create the illusion of them extending toward the viewer. Begin by drawing the hands, then add the rest of the arms.

PROJECT 6: PAINT A HAND HOLDING A FLOWER

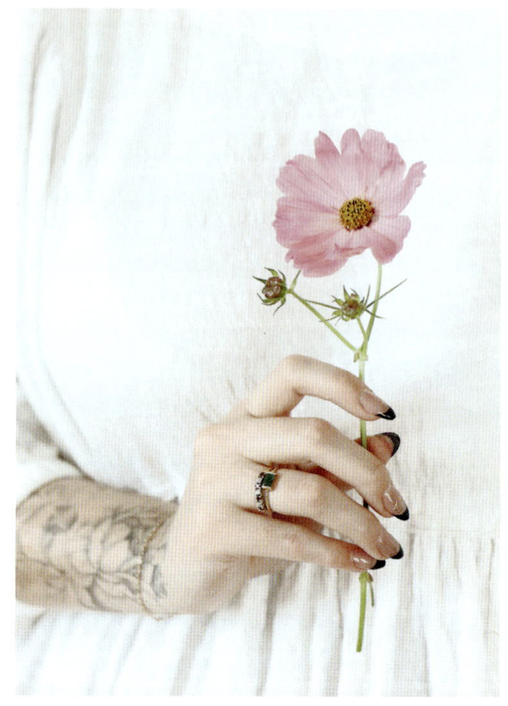

Even though I can paint well from my imagination, I often need a reference photo when rendering hands. As with the rest of my process, I recommend starting from large, blocked-in colors and shapes, and working down to small details like wrinkles and folds.

1. Take a photo of your hand holding a flower or follow along with my reference photo. Create a square canvas of 4 x 4 inches (10 x 10 cm) at 300 dpi (see page 16 for canvas sizing). After setting the base layer to a background color of your choice, create a new Multiply layer for your sketch. Using the Soft Airbrush (see page 17 for brushes) with a medium-toned bronze (warm dark brown if you're painting a darker-skinned subject), begin by sketching out the rough shape of the hand. Begin by drawing the silhouette of the hand, and then begin rendering the details inside the silhouette. Draw the rough shape of the flower and set this layer's opacity between 20% to 40%.

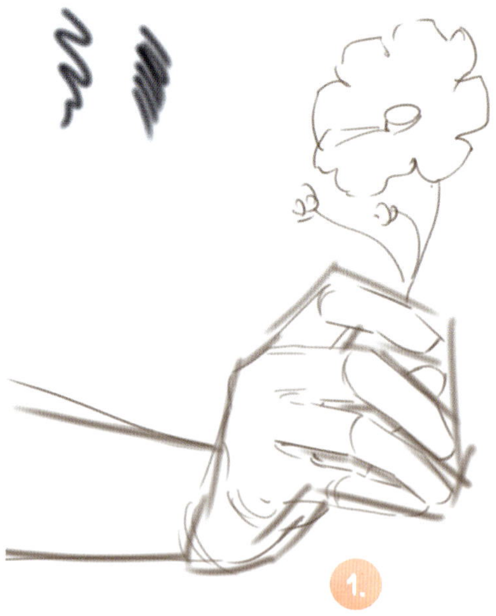

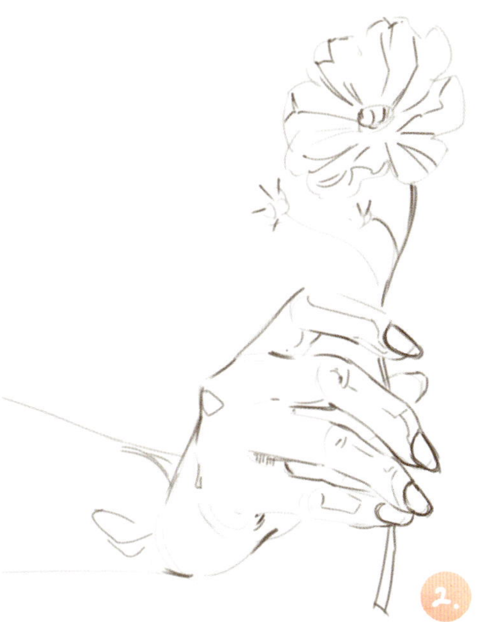

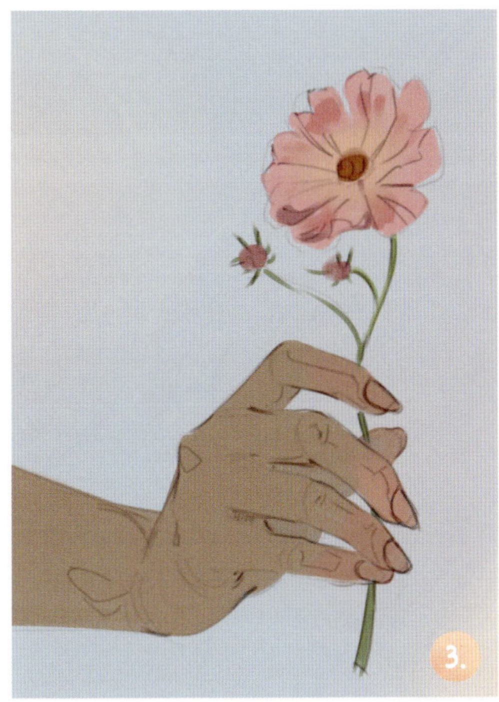

2. On a new Multiply layer above the previous, trace over the rough sketch with the same brush and add smaller details, like the knuckles, fingernails, wrinkles and folds. Render the details of the flower (see page 145 for drawing props).

3. Using the Soft Airbrush or Oil brush on a new layer underneath your sketch, paint in the base skin tone, as well as the flower petals and stem. Use a lavender tone to paint in the background, adding soft pink blurs toward the edges of the painting to create a pretty gradient.

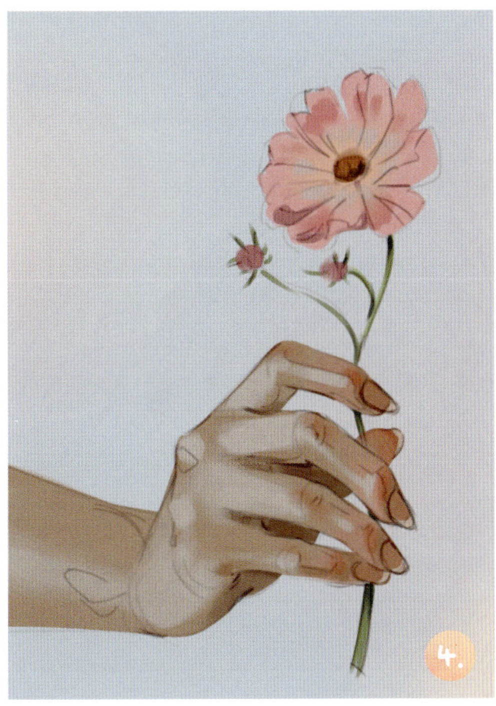

4. With a lighter cool tone, paint in the highlights. The tops of the knuckles and fingers will be illuminated more since they are closer to the light source. With a warmer shadow tone, paint in the shadows around the palm, fingertips, knuckles and fingernails to add dimension to the hand. Use similar toned highlights and shadows on the flower to keep the lighting and tones consistent throughout the piece.

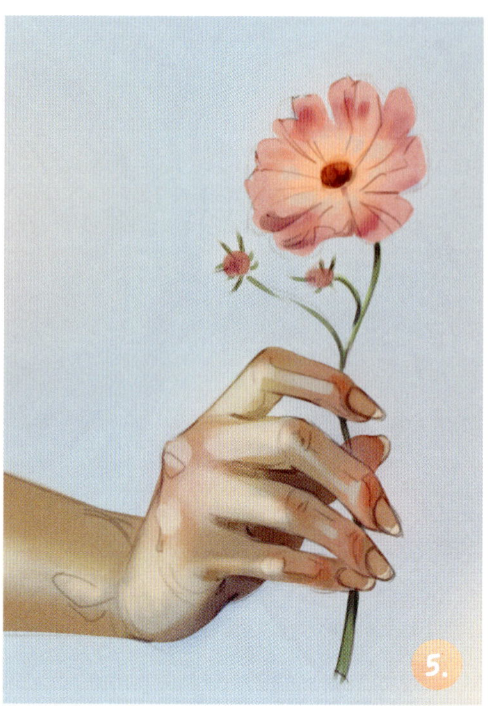

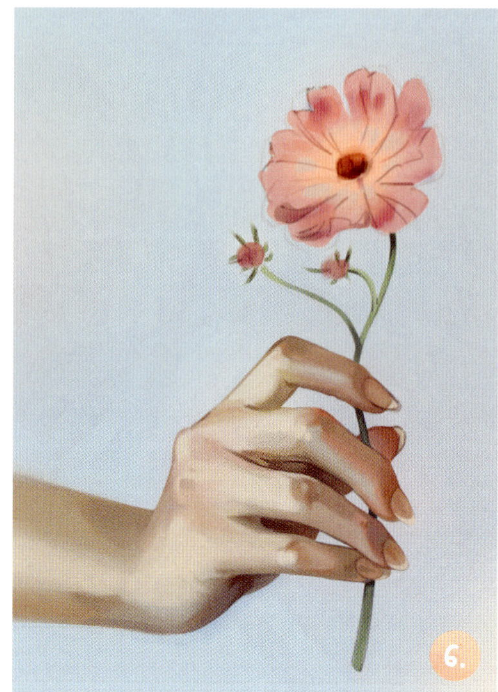

5. Add a new Soft Light adjustment layer (see page 18 for adjustment layers) above the rest of your layers and use the Soft Airbrush to gently paint in some warm highlights, as well as blushing around the tips of the fingers, fingernails, knuckles and flower petals. Tweak the colors using adjustment layers until you are pleased with the overall tones and values.

6. Right-click on any layer and select "Merge visible into new layer" to flatten your image. Every time you would like to make a risky addition to the piece, you can right-click your working layer, select "Duplicate layer" and paint on that new layer to essentially save your process. With the Oil brush, begin rendering the hands. I like to start with the fingers, working my way around the silhouette of the hand, then focusing on the fingernails and knuckles. Color pick from the background color to gently diffuse the edges of the fingers as they curve away from the viewer.

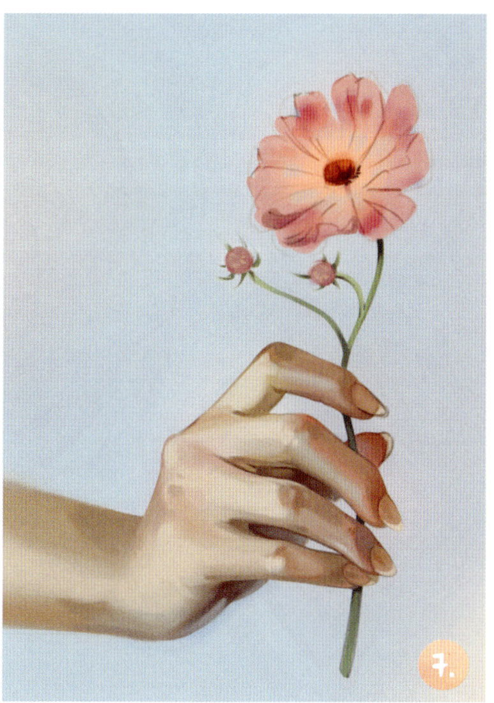

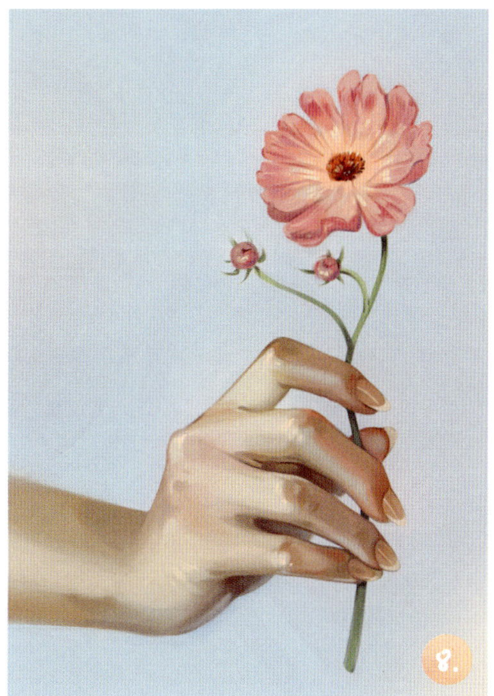

7. Continue rendering the painting, adding slight bounce lighting to the shadowed parts of the hand. While you are painting, position your own hand in the same angle to observe the shadows and wrinkles that you could add to your painting.

8. Finish rendering the flower, stem and any leaves you've added. Add deeper shadows around the skin that makes direct contact with the flower stem to show the stem pressing into the palm and fingers. For the nails, paint the white crescent, or *lunula*, softly with a slightly brighter tone than the base shade of the fingers. You can paint short or long nails, adding a creamy white length to the tips of the nails as they get longer.

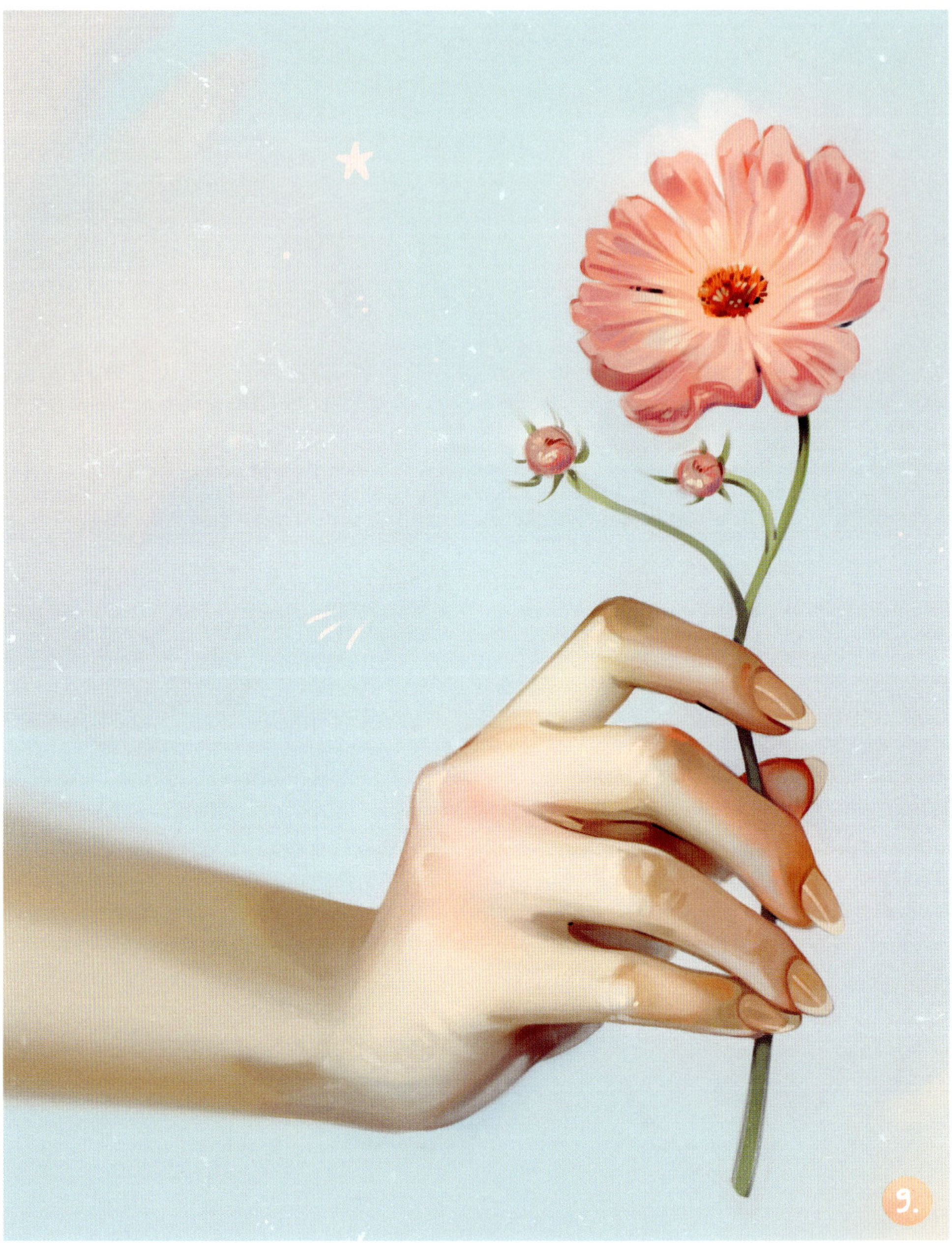

9. On a Soft Light layer above all the other layers, use the Soft Airbrush to add any highlights or shadows to the piece to unify the tones. Use a Tone Curve layer to adjust the brightness and contrast of the piece, or to shift the hues and unify the painting. Lastly, add any final details to the painting, including shine to the fingernails, high points of the knuckles and flower petals. (See page 152 for details on finishing touches.)

PROMPT: PAINT FIVE HANDS

Take five reference photos of your hands and simplify them into basic shapes. Practice drawing the palms and fingers in different angles; try to understand how the shape of the hand changes as the angles also change.

Are you able to streamline your process as you progress in your paintings? Write down any challenges you're facing when drawing or painting hands. Keep these in mind for later practice.

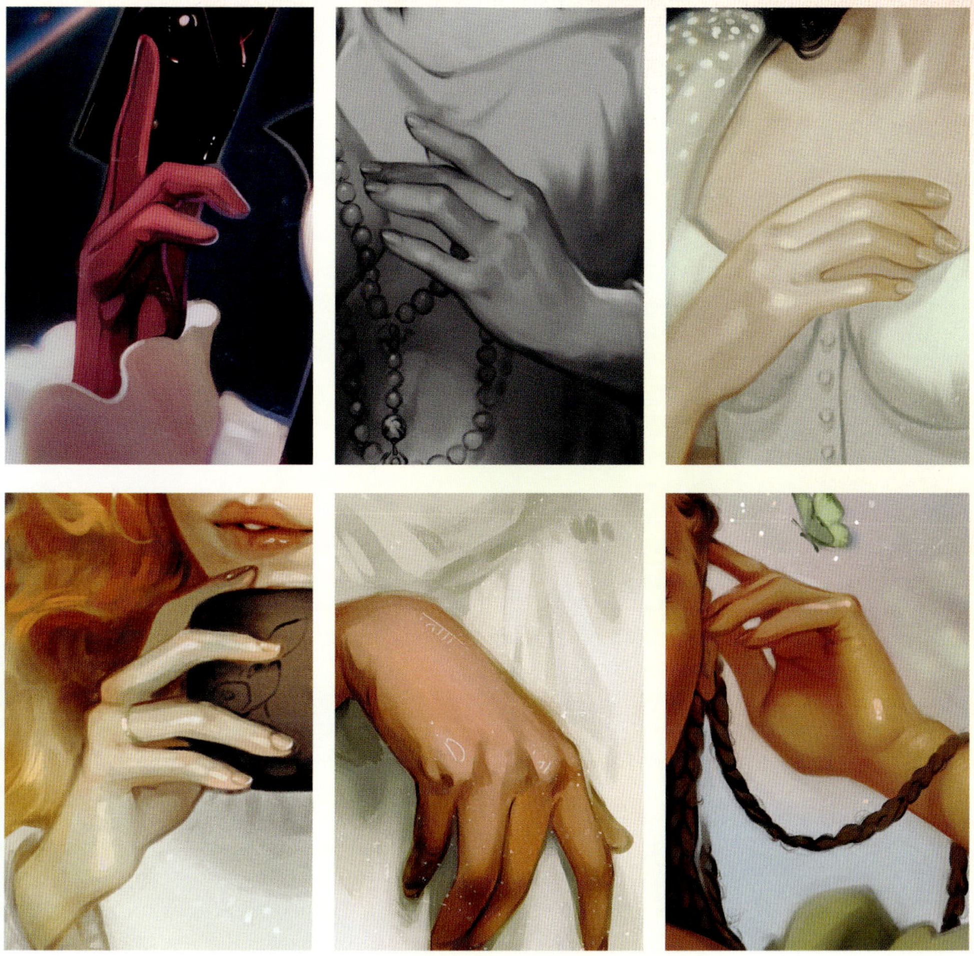

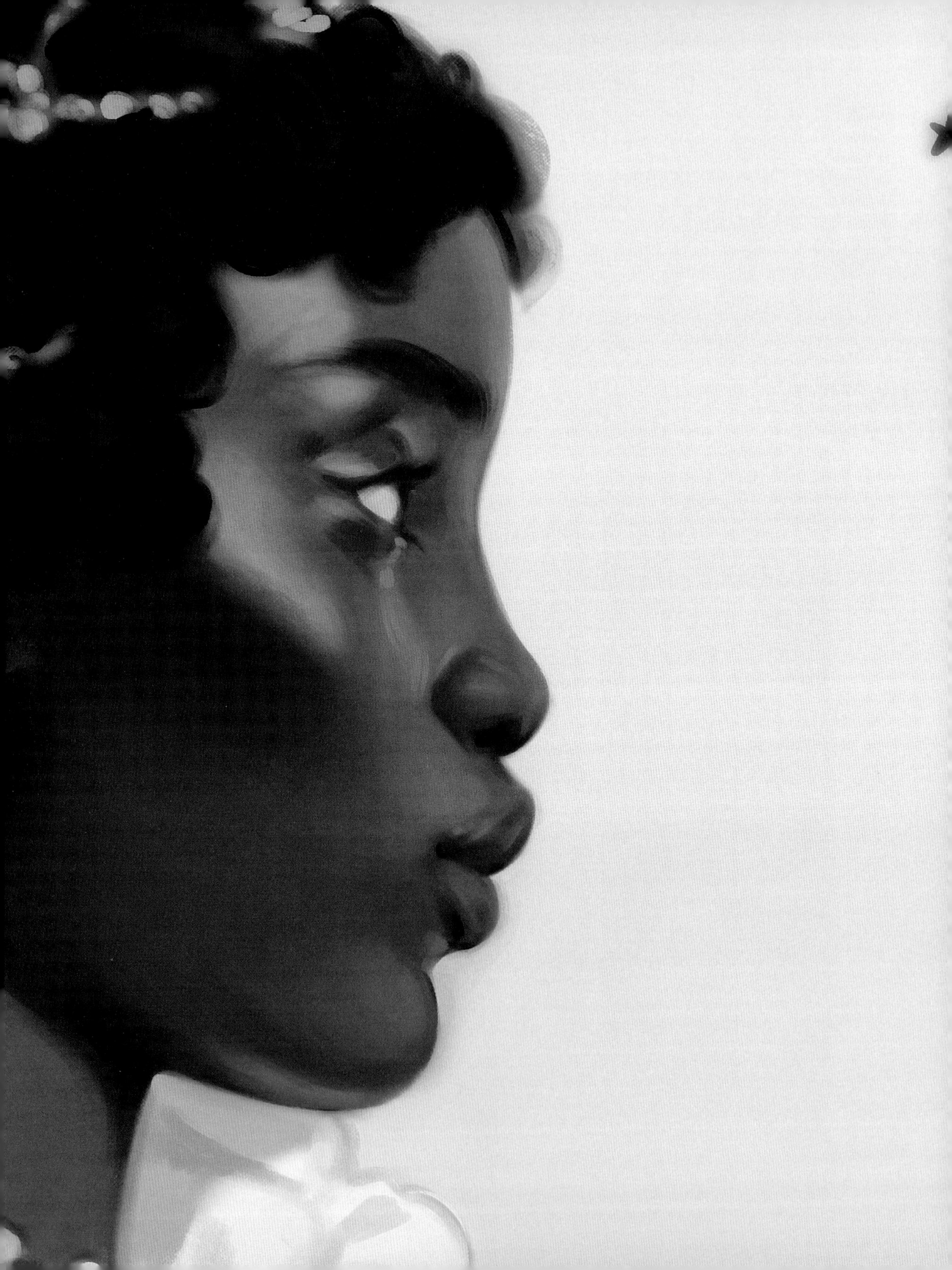

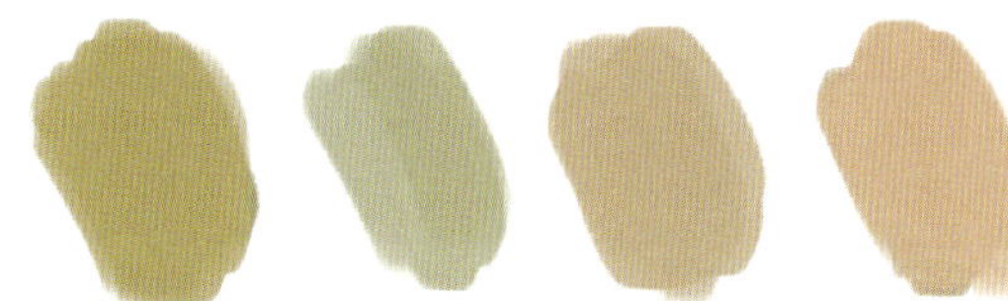

Warm, olive, neutral and cool

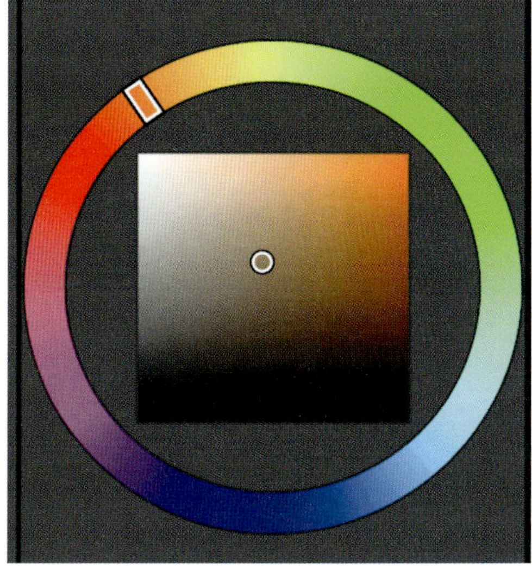

Keep the skin tone in the middle of the color wheel rather than close to the top or bottom. Using a midtone will allow you to add details without blown-out highlights or crushed shadows.

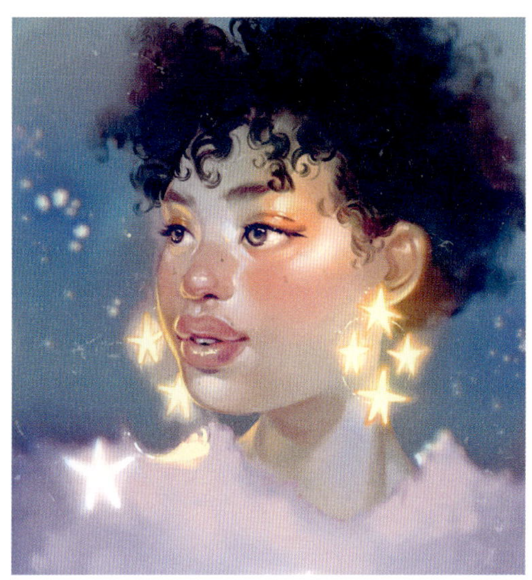

SKIN TONES

When choosing skin tones, start off with a midtone (whether drawing a model with a fair or deeper skin tone). Don't feel like you have to use an extremely bright tone or an extremely deep tone, depending on your subject. Remember how lighting affects your values; you can always lighten up or deepen tones with adjustment layers, but it is easier to come up with balanced details when working with midtones.

Each deepness of skin tone will have four undertones: warm, neutral, cool and olive. Warm undertones have a yellow or golden base, neutral undertones have an equally balanced mix of warm and cool tones, cool undertones have a pink or bluish base and olive undertones have a desaturated green base. Study the skin tone of your model and mix in shades of blue, pink, green and purple into the skin to make the skin more realistic. The bony areas of the face are cooler toned, while the fleshier areas are warmer. The forehead and jaw will have shades of blue and green in them, while the apples of the cheeks and tip of the nose will be pinker. When choosing colors for the face, make sure to vary the hues you're placing onto the face; only using values in the same hue will create a flat portrait.
If you have a hard time finding the perfect hues to add to your painting, color pick a blue, purple or green and use extremely light pressure to lay down a light layer of that color; use the Eyedropper to pick up the new shade and use it in your piece. Adding subtle layers of vibrant color will create depth in your piece.

When painting the face, unify the blush and contour shades in the eyes, face, nose and lips. Color picking from an existing shade you placed in the face and carrying it into another area can create harmony in your piece.

PROJECT 7: PAINT A SKIN TONE YOU'RE NOT USED TO

Use one of the color palettes I've created to follow this project. You can download these palettes for free at sarucatepes.com/resources. These palettes are not all encompassing in the variety of skin tones that exist, but they're moreso useful for demonstrating the relationship between midtones, highlights and shadows on the color wheel. Write down anything you learn about these color relationships, and think about how you can apply these concepts to all your portraiture.

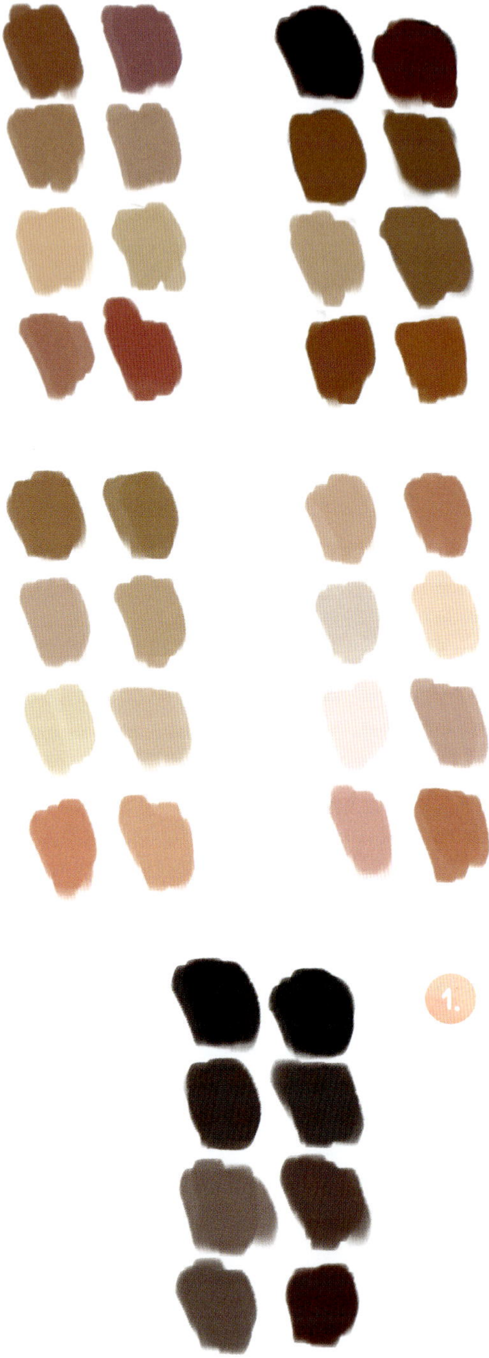

1. Select one of the color palettes I've created to practice mixing skin tones, challenging yourself to paint an unfamiliar skin tone. I am going to use the darkest color palette shown for this project. Look at the color wheel and notice where the shadows, midtones, highlights, blush and contour tones sit.

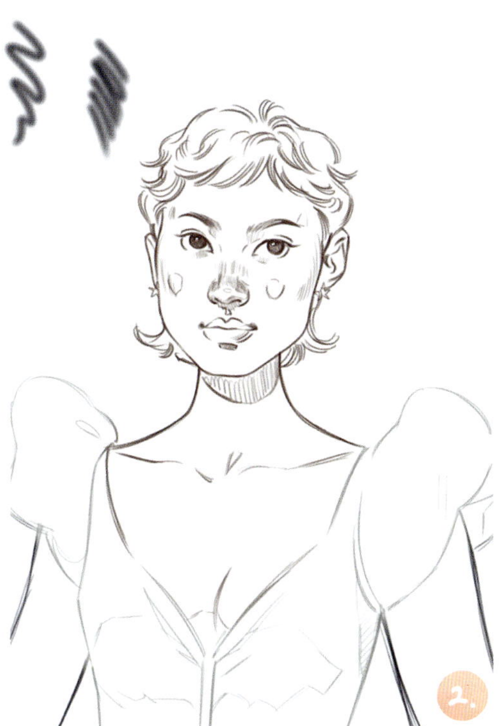

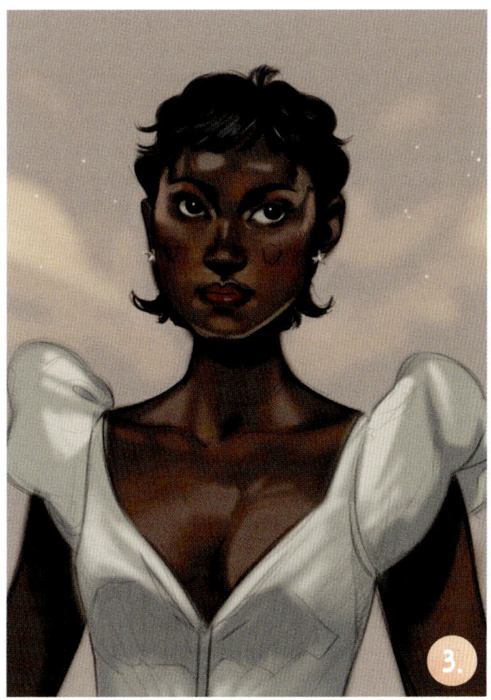

2. Create a new canvas set to whatever aspect ratio you want. On a fresh layer, use the Soft Airbrush (see page 17 for brushes) with the sketch shade from your chosen palette and sketch out your subject. You can paint a close-up portrait from imagination or a reference photo, keeping in mind that the focal point of this piece is painting the skin tones well. Set this sketch layer to Multiply (see page 18 for adjustment layers).

3. On a new layer underneath your sketch, begin color blocking your base tones. Fill in the background with a dusty rose color and pastel orange sweeping lines that indicate distant clouds. Place the midtones, shadows, highlights and blush on the face. Color pick between these colors to soften any edges for seamless color transitions where needed.

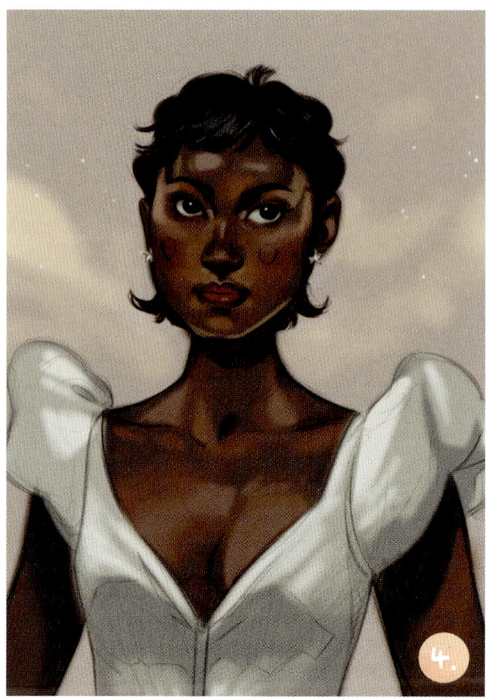

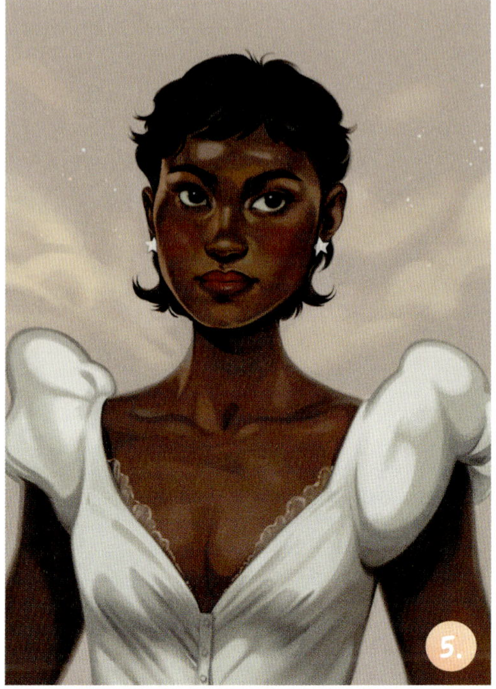

4. Add any adjustment layers (see page 18) that you need to make your base pop, like adding colorful flares or rim lighting on your subject. This will ensure that you are maintaining a cohesive palette, as well as emulating the dreamy look that photographs can achieve. Use curves to play with the contrast and overall hue of the piece.

5. Begin painting in the details on top of your base: in the lips, nose, eyelashes, hair, bodice and rim lighting. If you feel that you're color-picking too dull of a color, adjust the saturation and brightness to add boldness back into your piece. Vary the hues that you are painting with to add dimension to the skin. Step away from the painting process if you begin to feel unsure of your marks. Often, overworking a piece without breaks can lead to muddy tones and funky proportions.

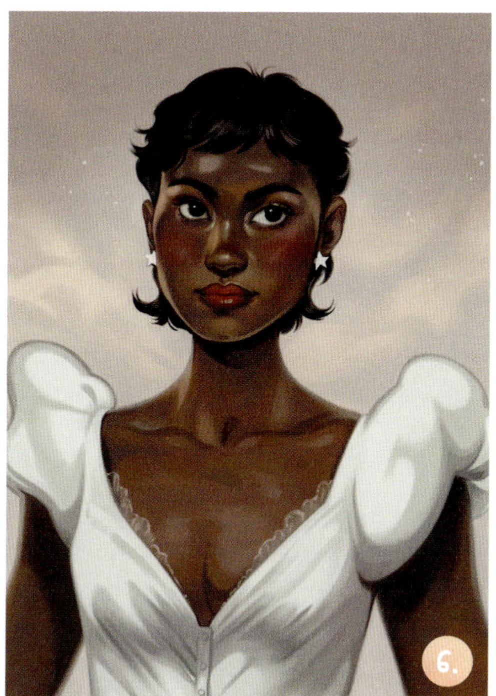

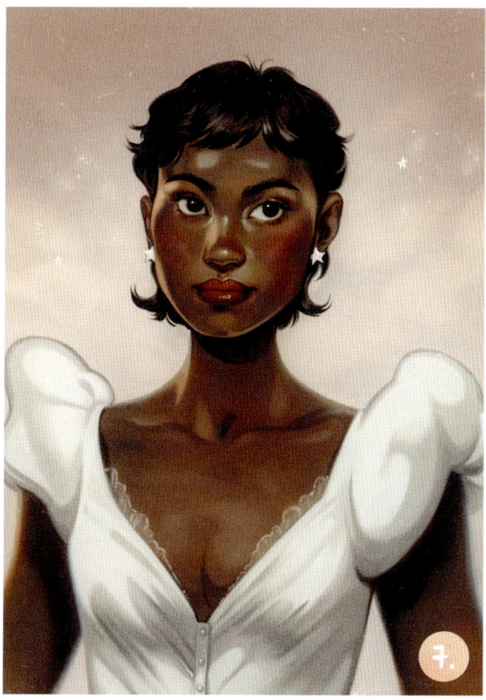

6. On a new layer, add colorful highlights, rim lighting or sharp details to your painting. Choose one bright pop of color to subtly add to highlights, rim lighting and even shadows to create more life in your painting.

7. Use adjustment layers to unify and brighten the final colors of your piece. Once you're finished with the painting, use the Eyedropper tool to inspect the final colors you added to your piece. Think about how you can incorporate bold colors in your next pieces.

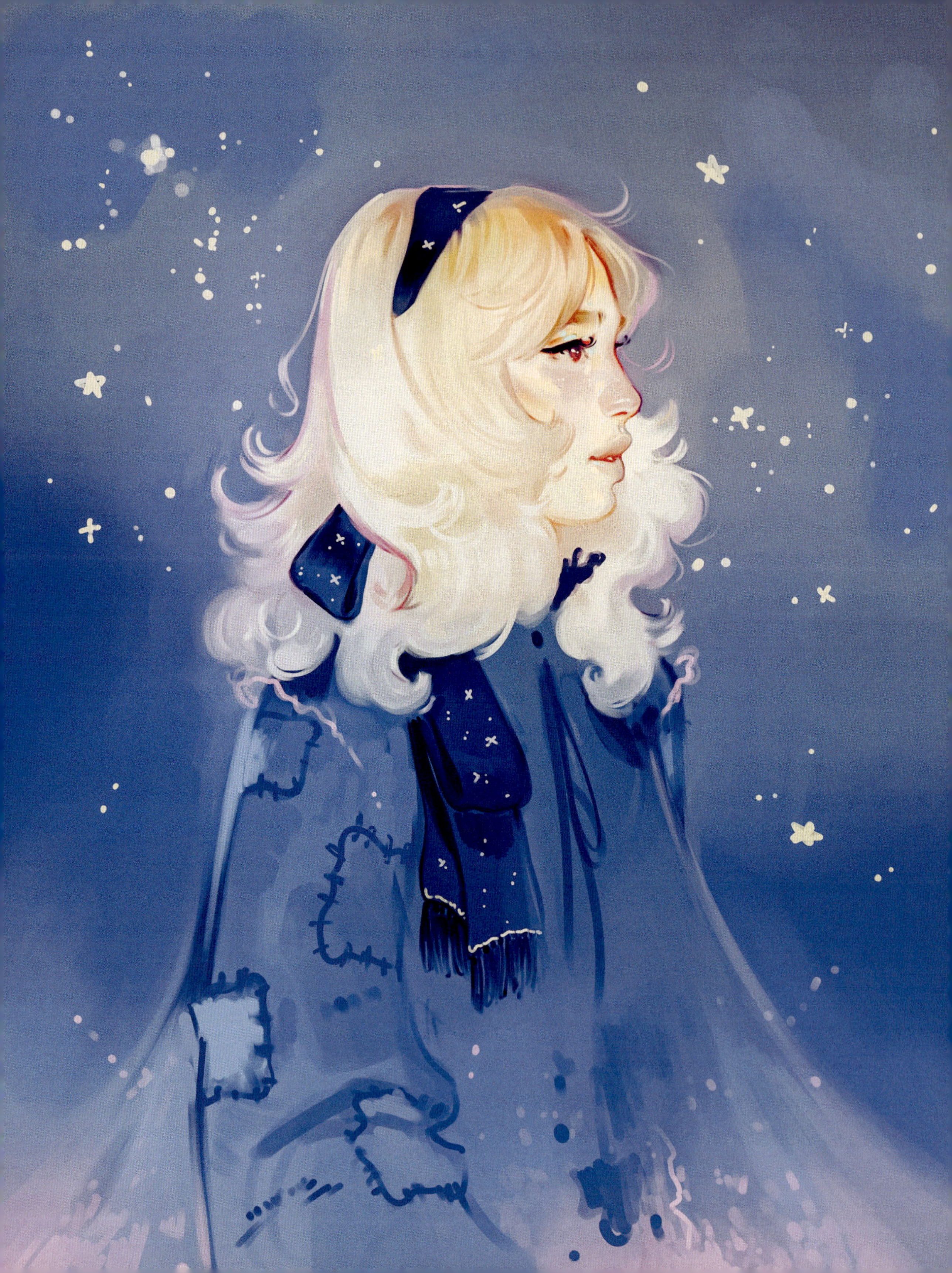

Chapter 3

CREATING COMPLETE PAINTINGS

In this section, we are going to slowly build upon the concept of composition. Once you learn about the compositions available to you, you will get some practice brainstorming your concept and sketching out thumbnails. We will build on that skeleton with colors, values and lighting.

COMPOSITION

Composition is a universal concept that applies to any visual art, including photography, design and cinema. Good composition will draw the eye in a fluid motion across the piece, often compelling the viewer to continue observation and study. Bad composition will be confusing to look at; the painting will look off without the viewer being able to recognize exactly what is wrong. Composition is made up of multiple design elements, including lines, shapes, colors, values, depth and texture. These elements are applied to design principles, such as balance, harmony, contrast, movement, emphasis and pattern. Lastly, many of these principles make up some of the most popular composition types: symmetry, rule of thirds, figure-ground relationship, golden ratio/Fibonacci sequence and Gestalt principles.

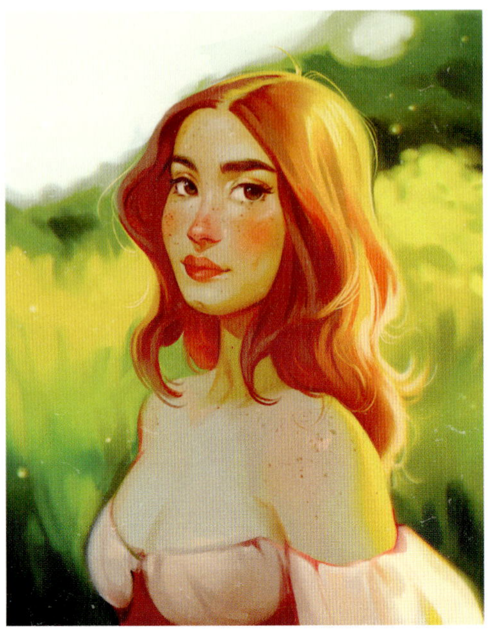

The leading lines of the bushes behind the subject lead to the subject's eyes.

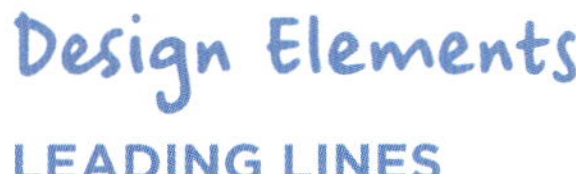

LEADING LINES

Starting with lines, you can use leading lines, whether actual or implied, to draw the viewer's attention across the piece. You can do this by being intentional and graphic with the shapes in your piece, or by making your subject look at another part of the painting. As a viewer, you will want to look at what the subject of the piece is observing—this is an implied line. You can be more literal with lines by framing a piece using solid objects like walls, doorframes and windows strategically placed. Usually these lines will be man-made, like fences in a field or trails in the woods. Even the human body can act as a leading line.

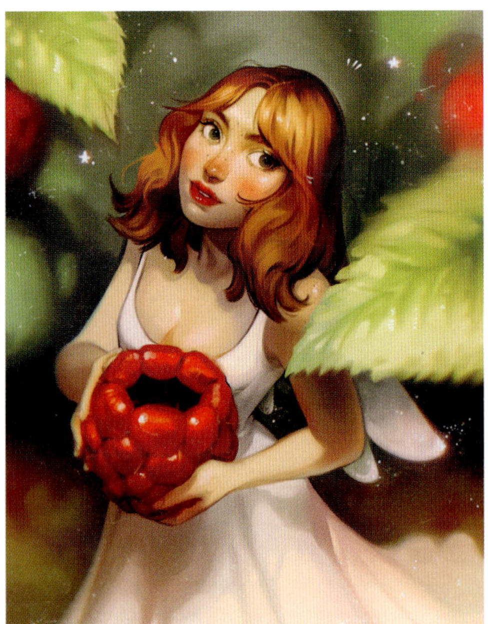

The leading lines guide the viewer's gaze, starting at the subject's eyes, moving down to the raspberry, following the train of the dress, then over to the leaf on the right side of the painting and finally circling back to the eyes.

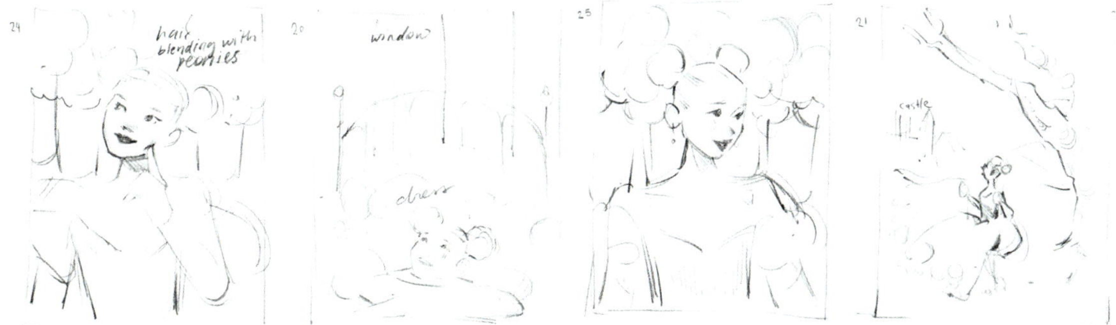

Keep this chapter's guidelines on composition in mind when crafting thumbnails.

MAPPING OUT ROUGH SHAPES

You can also utilize shapes to draw the eye across your composition. Simplifying the elements in an environment can show you the dominant shapes. Bodies of water, trees and mountains can all have striking silhouettes that draw the eye across the painting. The shape of your subject, their hair or an object they are holding can all be utilized to direct the viewer's gaze across a piece. If you are unsure about how to simplify shapes, look at the silhouette of something you want to include in the composition. If it is large on your canvas, much of the viewer's attention will go toward it.

COLORS FOR CONTRAST

Think about the colors of your piece; color can be used to bring something to attention or help it recede into the background. Any bright and saturated color will immediately draw the viewer's attention. Dark, muted tones will sink away. Choose your colors consciously to support your composition. The values of your colors are just as important as the saturation. A dark maroon red will fade into the background compared to a bright tomato red. Use shadows and highlights to draw the viewer's eye across a piece. While knowing correct color theory and lighting is important, as the artist, breaking away from the realism of your reference to tell a story is part of the creative process. Colors and values also tie into the way you portray depth and texture in your pieces. Use dark and muted tones with softened texture to depict depth, and use brightness, saturation and texture to bring elements of the composition closer to the viewer.

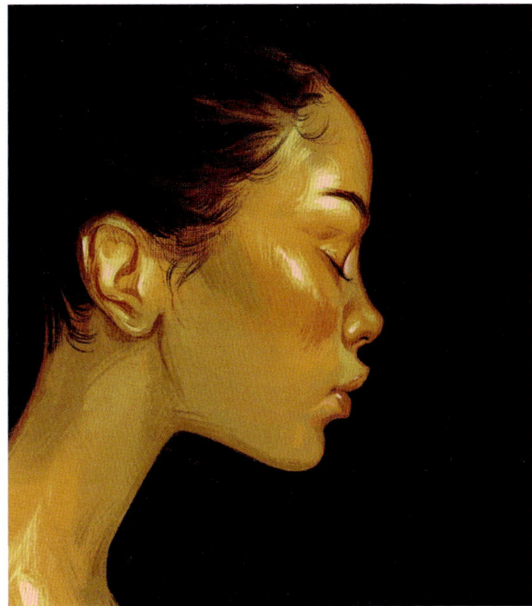

The subject's profile pops against the dark background.

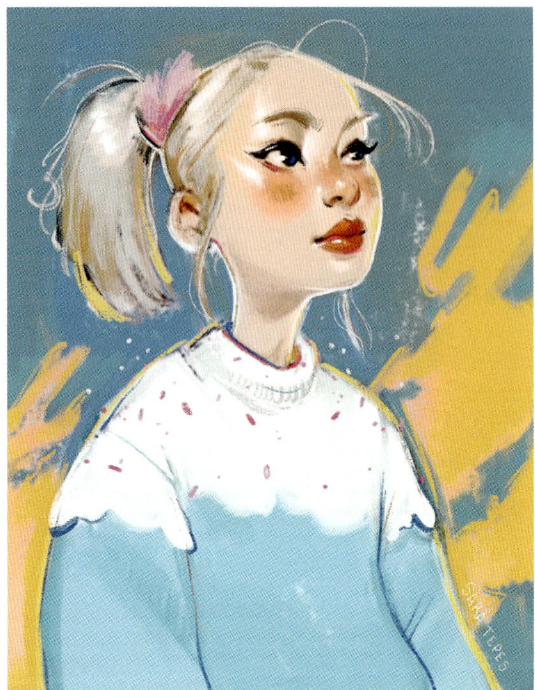

The teal background is darker than the subject's sea green sweater, and her bright, wispy hair contrasts with the midtone background.

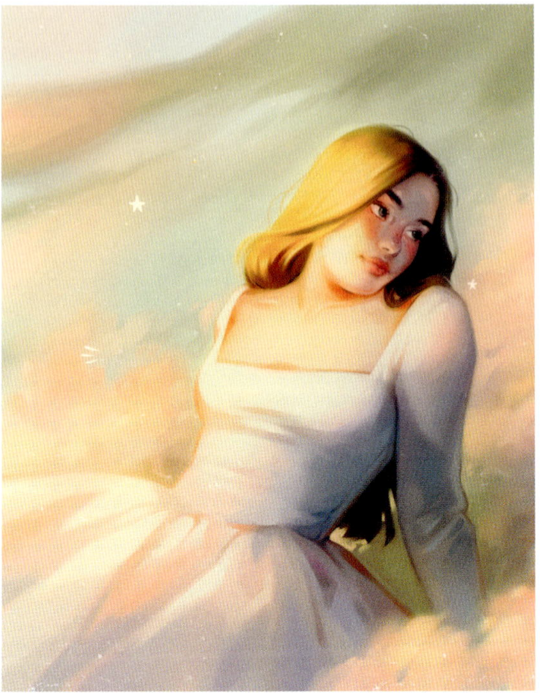

The contrast between the golden hour light and lavender shadows creates a dreamy quality to the painting.

Design Principles

Now that you know what design elements you can utilize in your composition, it's time to apply them to design principles.

PATTERN

One of the simplest design principles is pattern. Just as you can introduce pattern using shapes and colors on fabric, you can also create visual harmony by repeating light and dark values throughout a piece, ensuring continuity and balance. Once again, light tones come out toward the viewer, while dark tones recede into the background.

CONTRAST AND HARMONY

You can also add contrast by making these tones more extreme; however, be mindful of how your subject matter interacts with the lighting and contrast in your piece. If you use harsh colors and values to depict a serene subject, the composition will clash. In that situation, use harmony and balance instead. Choose shades and tones that are calm and similar in value. This diffused color palette and shade range will add a hazy, dreamy look rather than an intense one.

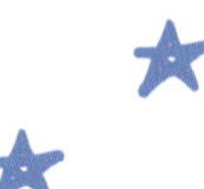

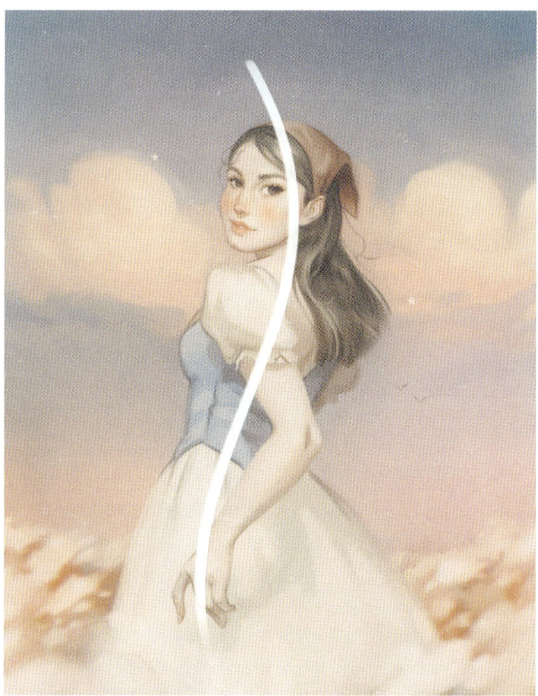

MOVEMENT

Lastly, use movement to draw the eye across your canvas. As stated before, the human body can be a leading line in your piece. Another approach to using leading lines is by incorporating them as energy lines—fluid lines that travel from the subject's head, along their spine and down to their feet. The energy line of your subject's body in motion can be used to draw the eye toward another part of the image. In addition, combining the concepts of pattern and movement can help you use rain, leaves, flower petals or grains of pollen in the environment to point toward the subject of your piece. The possibilities for combinations are endless.

Types of Composition

Now that you know how to mix and match design elements into design principles, you can combine all this knowledge into the most popular compositions. Almost every well-composed piece will keep one or multiple of these in mind; composition isn't limited to painting. Design and photography use these rules as well, so feel free to keep all of these concepts in mind next time you're flipping through a magazine or scrolling through a photography Instagram.

SYMMETRY

Symmetry is the most basic type of composition: Two halves of your image, whether vertically or horizontally, will be mirrored images of each other. You can take this concept as literally as you want. You can literally mirror one side of your image to the other or compose your subject symmetrically across the middle X or Y axis of your canvas. You don't need to copy the same elements across both halves of the piece, but rather, maintain the same weight, value and balance across the halves.

RULE OF THIRDS

The rule of thirds evenly breaks up an image into thirds, both vertical and horizontally. Placing your focal point on these lines or intersections of these lines will create a pleasing composition to the viewer. In my opinion, the rule of thirds is the most simple and effective rule of composition. Most any photo can be cropped to place your subject on a third instead of being centered in the photo, creating interest to the image.

FIGURE-GROUND RELATIONSHIP

Figure-ground relationship refers to a composition where you can see your subject's silhouette against the background; this relationship plays off the contrast between positive and negative space. This powerful composition creates depth and utilizes texture as a defining contrast between the foreground and background.

GOLDEN RATIO/FIBONACCI SEQUENCE

The golden ratio/ratio of the Fibonacci sequence is an irrational number (1+√5) / 2, approximately equal to 1.618. It can be traced back to Euclid, being one of the most popular compositions for masterpieces. Encyclopedia Britannica defines the golden ratio as: "the ratio of a line segment cut into two pieces of different lengths such that the ratio of the whole segment to that of the longer segment is equal to the ratio of the longer segment to the shorter segment." Often called the "divine proportion," you can find it frequently in nature, such as in petals of flowers, sunflower seeds, snail shells and galaxies. The Fibonacci sequence is defined as "each number being the sum of the preceding two numbers." This mathematical formula was discovered by Acharya Pingala, an ancient Indian mathematician and poet, who termed this formula *mātrāmeru*. It was later popularized in the West by Fibonacci, who called the answer to this equation "Phi," after the 21st letter of the Greek alphabet. Phi is an irrational number (1.61803...), and while the golden ratio isn't the same as Phi, it's very close. When adding a quarter circle to each rectangle in the golden ratio, the curved lines form the Fibonacci spiral. Place focal points and leading lines across the golden ratio to bring harmony to the piece and to fluidly draw your viewer's eye across the painting.

GESTALT PRINCIPLES OF DESIGN

Lastly, the Gestalt principles of design is a list of design concepts developed in the 1920s that focuses on six principles: symmetry, proximity, similarity, continuity, closure and connectedness. We will be focusing on five of these principles, as we have already defined symmetry. Some designers use different terminology for these principles, so this is a very interesting topic to research if you'd like to learn more about good design in general!

1. The principle of proximity simply means that items grouped together are perceived as a whole. Utilizing the design principle of patterns, a pile of rocks all close to each other will automatically be grouped by the human mind into their own shape together.

2. The principle of similarity states that objects that are about the same colors, sizes and shapes will be perceived as a group.

3. The principle of continuity states that our eyes follow straight lines, even if they are broken up by something else.

4. The principle of closure refers to the human mind's tendency to fill in gaps in lines to complete a shape or picture.

5. Lastly, connectedness is pretty self-explanatory: Our minds group elements that are connected to each other.

You can utilize any of these principles to create a more striking composition; I often use the principle of closure in my pencil sketches and digital paintings.

PROMPT: PRACTICE FIVE COMPOSITIONS

Take the same subject matter and sketch out the five types of composition. Reflect on the following: Which composition do you prefer? Do you usually gravitate toward one specific composition? How can you be mindful of your composition in future pieces?

For the first thumbnail, compose your subject with a classic symmetrical composition. While this is the most basic composition type, it can be bold and graphic. The figure shines as the focal point of the piece, and there is a graphic silhouette that separates her from the background. While the figure is delicate and feminine, we see her at her broadest, shoulders back and face forward, her eyes holding the viewer's gaze. This creates an intimate moment and shows the character's power and confidence.

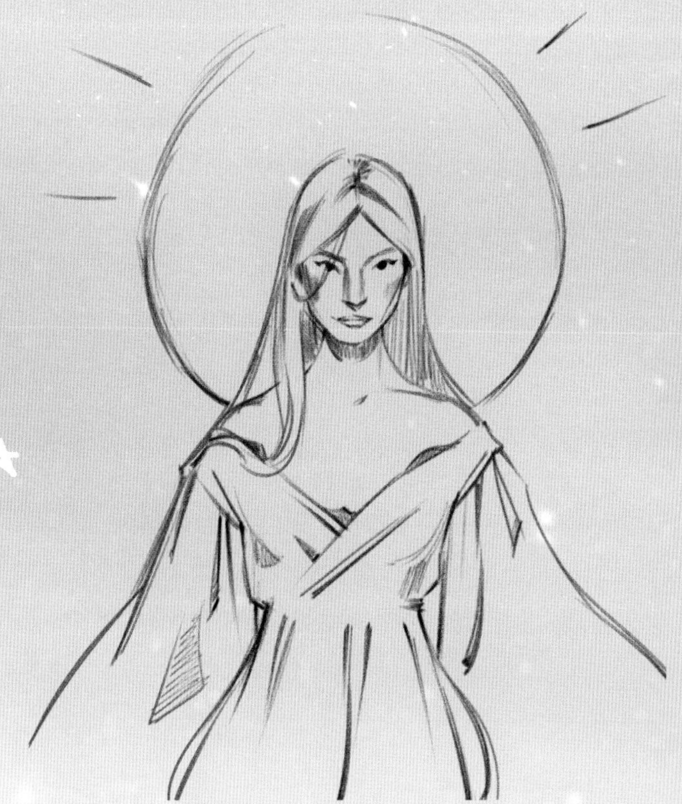

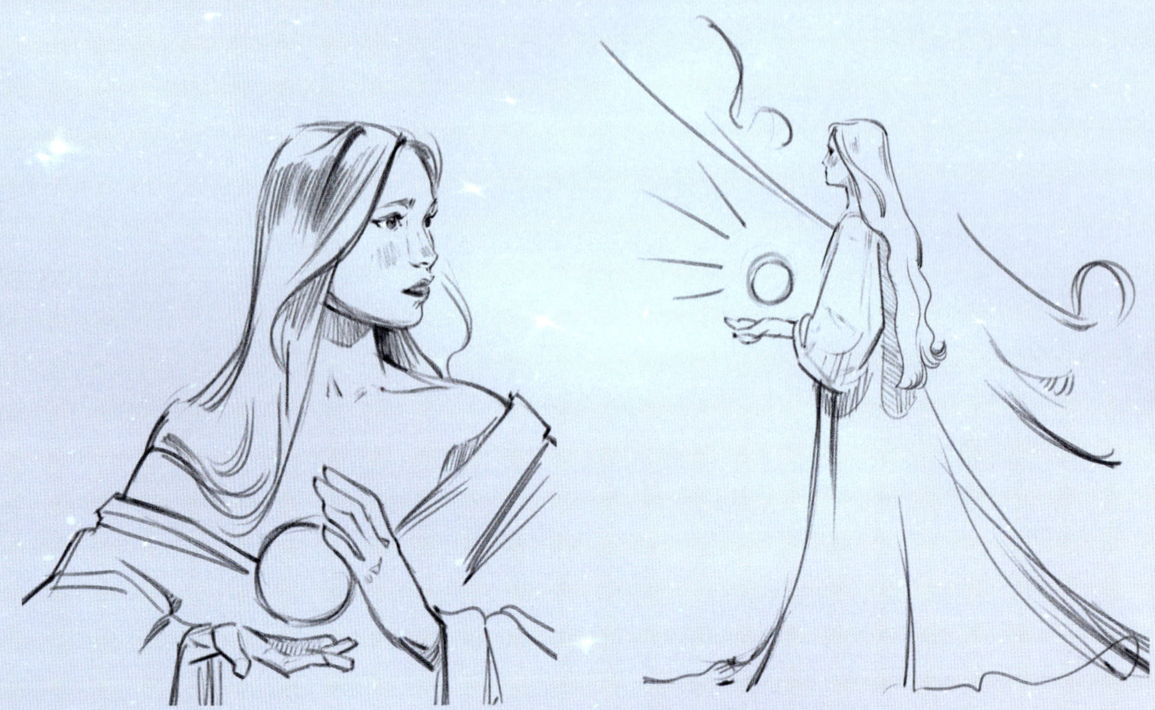

For the second composition, use the rule of thirds. While the first composition showed the subject as strong and large, the turned angle of the head, elongated neck and sweeping hair of this sketch portray the subject in a more delicate fashion. The image is pleasantly broken up by the negative space behind her head, and the far-off gaze makes the viewer wonder what she is looking at or thinking about. The overall feeling of the first piece is dominance, while this second thumbnail is more romantic.

This third thumbnail establishes the subject in her setting by using figure-ground as the composition. The flow of her gown and train brings the eyes toward the ground on which she's standing. Similar to the first composition, this image is more graphic, but the side profile of the figure creates a more dynamic storyline.

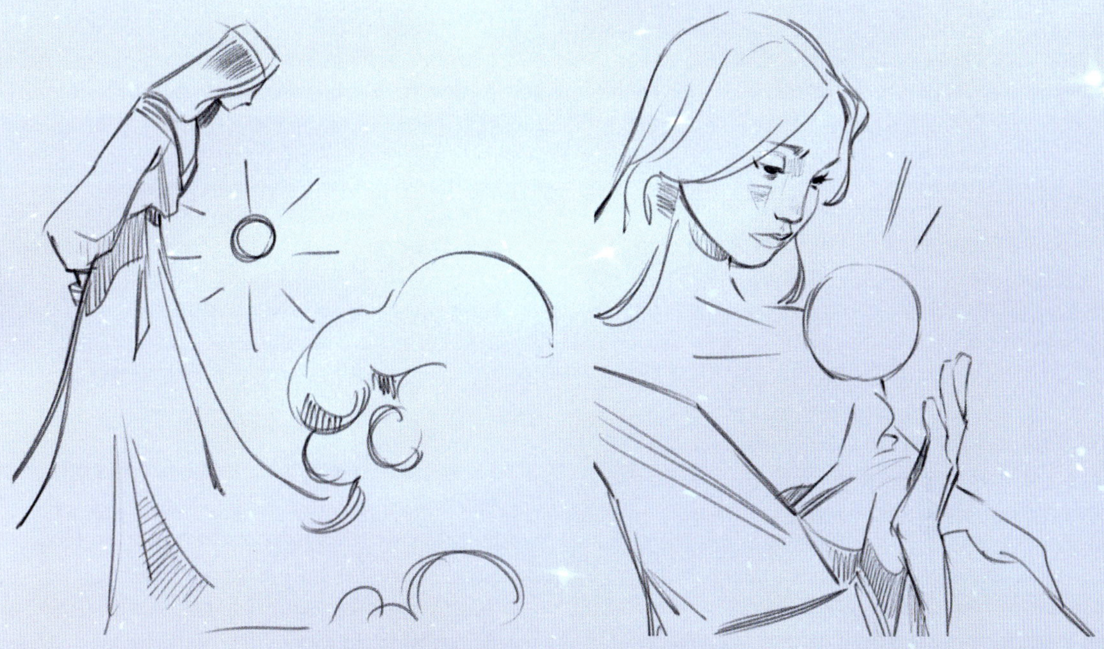

The fourth thumbnail shows the golden ratio in practice. The placement of the figure, sun and clouds creates circular movement and energy within the piece, which is satisfying yet intriguing. A successful composition will keep the viewer's eyes floating around the piece. This is done by the intentional placement of important elements. Overall, the composition helps convey stillness and nostalgia in this piece.

This last thumbnail incorporates elements of Gestalt principles and the rule of thirds. The way that the face, sun and hand are lined up in a diagonal across the piece creates movement and drags the viewer's gaze from the subject's eyes to her hand. The face and hand are placed on thirds, while the sun is in the center of the piece. This composition is calm but keeps the viewer's eyes moving, mimicking the subject's curious look at the sun.

BRAINSTORMING

Like other creative media, the painting process begins with brainstorming. I highly recommend that you write and draw everything with a physical pencil on paper. There is something very important about physically connecting a thought to a tangible piece of paper; especially with so much media and art trapped on computers, tablets and phones, it is good both for your eyes and for your brain to step away and exercise with traditional tools. You can see that some of the thumbnail sketches shown in this book are pencil sketches instead of digital. When beginning this brainstorming process, there are several places to start. Here are a few things to consider when brainstorming.

1. What mood would you like to evoke with your piece? This is a relatively esoteric idea and doesn't require you to come up with a subject matter just yet. Do you want to portray your current emotions, or would you like to share a message? Think about a form of media that emotionally impacted you; what mood did it have? What colors and elements helped it achieve that emotion?

2. Is there a specific composition you would like to paint? Would you like to focus on symmetry, negative space or maximalism?

3. Is there a key element that you would like to build the painting around? Maybe a specific dress, striking eyes, a drink or an animal? If you have one specific element that you want to highlight, you can build the rest of the painting up around it to complement it.

4. Think about a subject matter that you are struggling with and want to improve on. If you are unsure what to paint, it might be a good moment to step back and consider taking some time to study and understand how to paint that particular subject matter.

5. Is there a subject that you've never painted before and that intrigues you?

6. Try to interpret and come up with a symbolic painting for a song, poem, short story, book, photo or piece of media that inspired you. I love to take inspiration from classical literature and historical period dramas.

7. Look at the posts you've saved recently on your Instagram, Pinterest or other social media platform. Is there a common theme in the subject matter, colors or execution? If so, you might have just found a theme that you are inspired by and want to replicate.

8. Try automatic writing. Start with a word and then don't stop writing; an automatic writing list can help you find ideas and themes that are buried deeper inside your subconscious and haven't surfaced yet. It could look like "purple, fairy, book, sparkle, brunette, black, green, forest, enchanted, barefoot, water, drowning, bubbles, void, Ophelia, falling." It makes no sense, but it can inspire you!

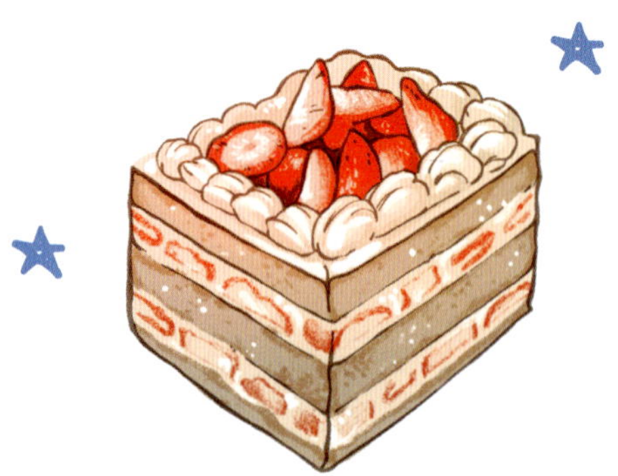

Thumbnail Sketches

Now that you have some concepts in mind, you can start fleshing them out into thumbnail sketches. Thumbnail sketches are small, rough drawings that help you figure out the composition of your subject matter. Drawing these small sketches will save you the time of detailing a larger sketch and then realizing you don't enjoy the overall composition, pose or tone of the piece. The best way to start a thumbnail sketch is to draw a box representing whatever canvas or aspect ratio you will be using, place your base character according to the proper composition you want and then add elements around them. After you have your first thumbnail and composition, draw out a couple iterations of this same subject matter, with different poses, compositions, angles, lighting scenarios and supporting elements.

While you may sometimes love the very first thumbnail and composition you created, often pushing yourself to think outside of the box will help you come up with a more striking and unique idea. For variety in the thumbnails, sketch out both portraits and full-body pieces. Even if you have a clear understanding of what you want the piece to look like, it doesn't hurt to conceptualize how the piece would look with unique or varied compositions. You might think a portrait composition will be the most effective but realize you can portray the theme and mood of the piece better with a full-length shot. If you are struggling with creating good thumbnails, set a one- or two-minute timer per thumbnail to help you make decisive marks. Not every thumbnail needs to be presentable; however, you might find the spark of a good idea in a messy sketch.

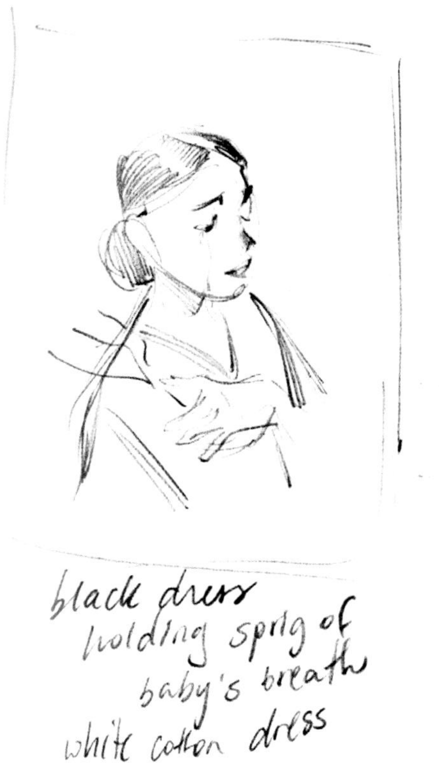

Since I often sketch as ideas come to me, I make note of the colors I envision to ensure I don't forget them later.

Personally, I think about a concept for the painting I want to create next as I am doing busywork or chores during the day. I often get an idea that I absolutely love when I'm away from my computer or sketchbook, and I've found that carrying a small notebook where I can jot down the general thumbnail and elements of my idea is the best way for me to remember it. I often will write down the mood of the piece, what key colors I want in it, if the character has a particular facial expression or angle I want to highlight. I will write down any backstory I think of. I love having these small sketches as inspiration for times when I sit down to create a painting but don't really know what I want to create.

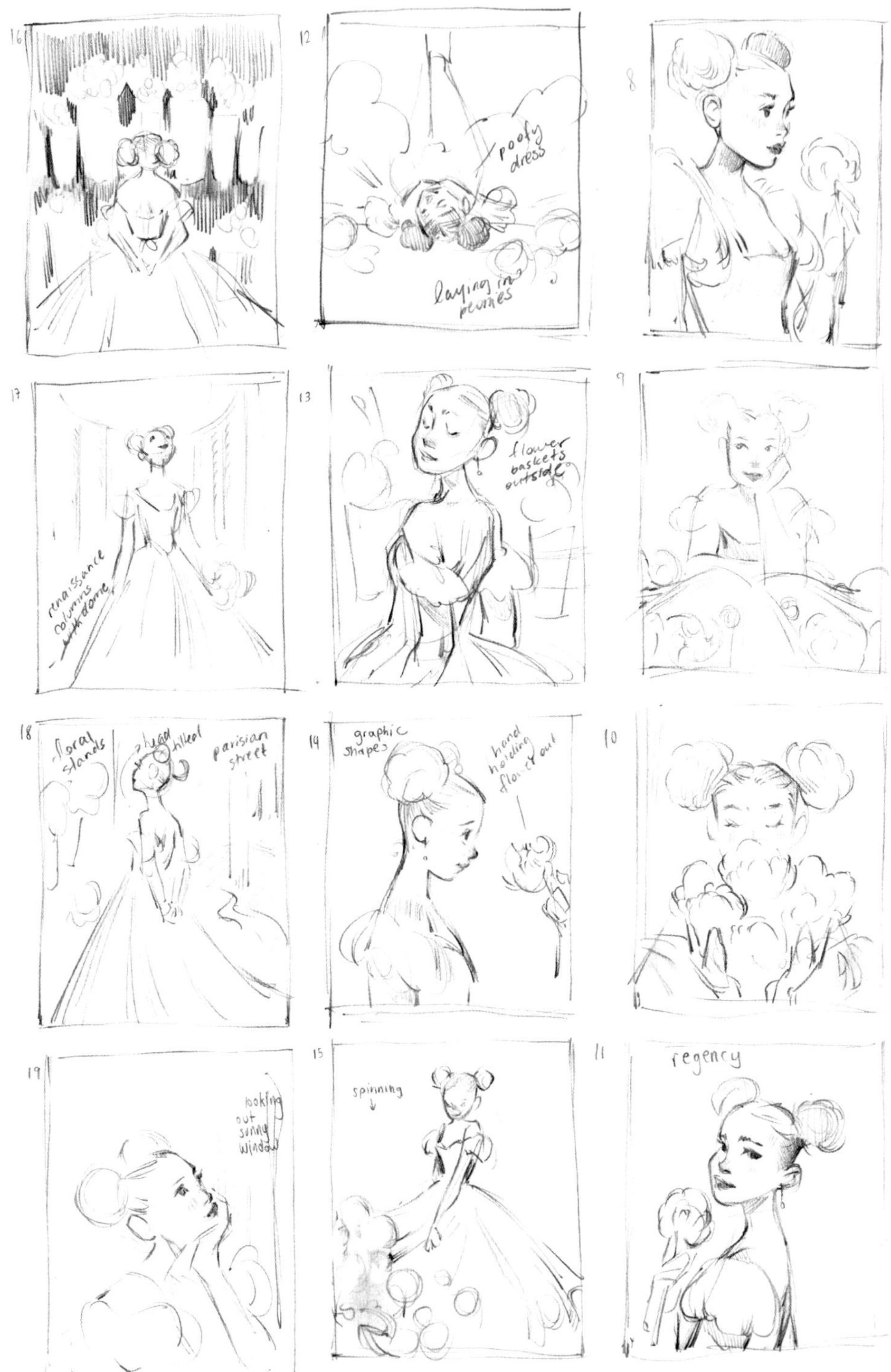

There are endless possibilities for composition with the same subject matter and color palette. Creating multiple thumbnails can ignite your creativity!

PROMPT: CREATE 25 THUMBNAIL SKETCHES

Use the brainstorming section and come up with a prompt for yourself. Draw 25 thumbnails for that painting; think of different poses, angles and elements.

Do you find yourself drawn to unconventional compositions or more classic ones? Do you prefer creating close-up portraits or full-body poses? How significant are backgrounds when planning your thumbnails? Answering these questions can give you insight into what you generally enjoy painting and help you discover your own art style. Try to have your sketches be as varied as possible; this will help you to come out of your comfort zone and to think of something outside of the box.

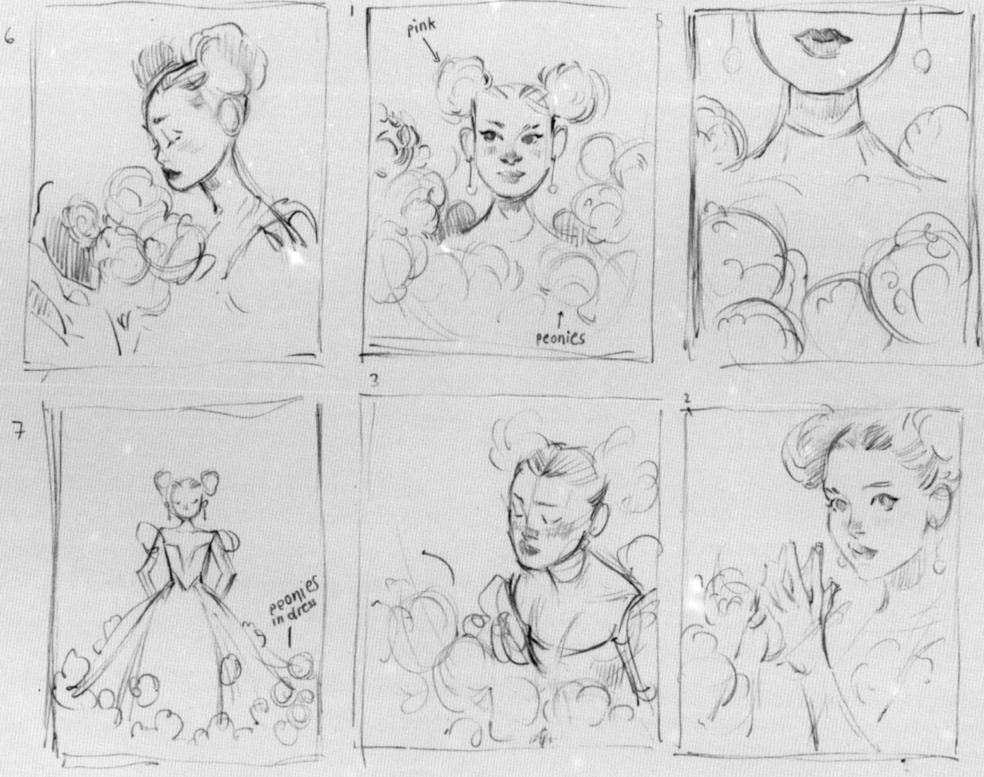

I number my thumbnails in the order I create them, but since I'm left-handed, the sequence can look a little strange.

SKETCHING

Once you have come up with a thumbnail you are happy with, it's time to transfer it to your canvas. Choose the best iteration of your brainstormed concept, set up your file and make a new layer above the blank white one. Using the Soft Airbrush (see page 17 for brushes), select either a bright color, such as a magenta, cyan blue or lime green, for the sketch if you want to create a colorful piece (see Composition, page 88, for more on colors), or a muted or natural color, like a warm dark brown or dusty rose, if you want an organic, subdued color palette.

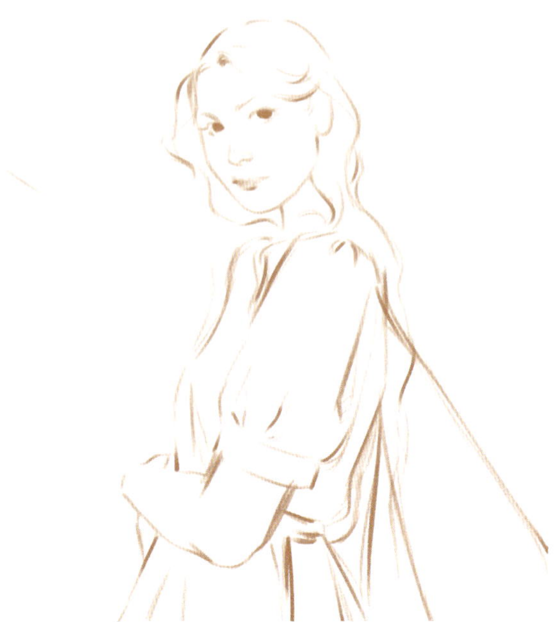

The sketching process is crucial to creating a final image you're satisfied with, so take your time refining your thumbnail drawing into a clean sketch.

Begin sketching out your thumbnail onto your canvas. Don't focus on details, but rather the major shapes and composition of your subject matter; this is your rough sketch. Use the Soft Airbrush for your sketching to more easily blend the sketch layer into the base colors, and to create an easy shadow color around the edges of your subject when you move to rendering your piece. However, if you want a textured look, feel free to use more of a textured brush for the base sketch.

Once you have the proper composition and general shapes and angles down, move to the tight sketch. Turn the opacity of the rough sketch to 50% and start a new layer on top of it; using the same Soft Airbrush but with a darker value and smaller size, start defining the features, hair and other elements in your piece. This step in the process is so important to getting your composition and anatomy exactly how you want it. If you are unhappy with your sketch, it will be much harder to fix later in the painting process. The best-case scenario is that the painting process is prolonged trying to fix the anatomy or composition of the sketch, and the worst-case scenario is that you will give up on the piece after hours of work. Don't take a shortcut; it is both important to improve your drawing abilities and to set a good framework for the rest of the piece. If you are uncomfortable drawing from imagination, use a reference and study the shapes and silhouette of the model.

During the sketching process, I like to lightly map out where the contour, shadows, blush and highlights go with the Soft Airbrush at either a low opacity or soft pressure. Blocking these shapes in will help you set the base colors down. If you are focused on hyper-realistically laying down all the details in this sketch layer, scale back and try to look at the reference as a bunch of shapes within shapes. Simplify each feature and add detail to it after you have the base shape laid down.

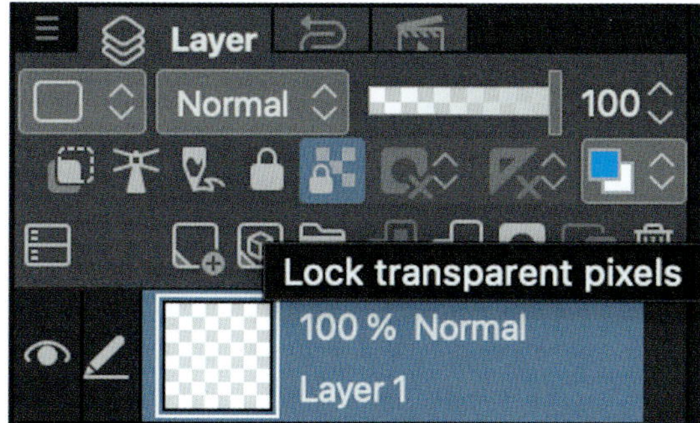

Lock the transparency of your layer, so you can solely target your line art.

Once you have both sketch layers completed and ready for color, feel free to delete the rough sketch layer if it is distracting. A useful tool to change the color of your line art is "Lock Transparent Pixels," the checkered box found in the "Layers" panel in Clip Studio Paint. You can "Alpha Lock" a layer in Procreate by going to your "Layers" tab and clicking on the layer that you'd like to modify; a pop-up will appear with "Alpha Lock" as one of the options. Alpha Lock will lock any of the transparent parts of a layer, leaving only the areas painted in as editable. I will usually use Alpha Lock on both layers and change the color of the line art to something that matches the color palette of the piece. Use a brighter color if you want the tones and shadows of the piece to be more vibrant, and use a warmer brown if you want the piece to be muted and natural. Set both of the layers on Multiply so that they can blend into the base colors later on.

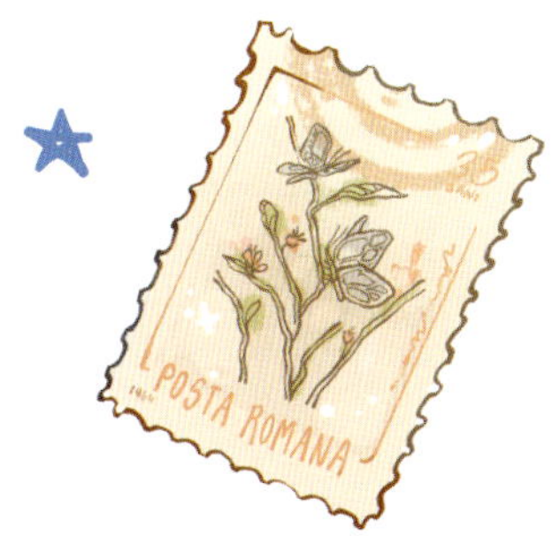

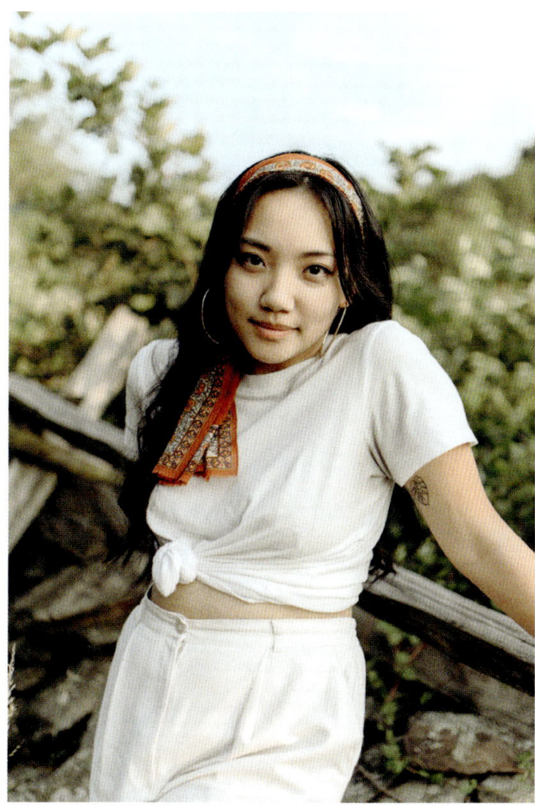

Finding References

Find reference photos on royalty-free websites like Unsplash or take your own reference photos. Copyright laws on using licensed photography as reference for original art are relatively dubious, so it is always safer to use royalty-free imagery when creating your work, especially if you would like to sell the original and/or prints. Taking your own reference photos can also help you obtain the perfect reference instead of being confined to splicing multiple references together to come up with your desired pose. You can ask your friends if they would like to model for you or take photos of yourself using a self-timer. You can even video record yourself in the pose to get the most range of references possible.

PROJECT 8: CREATE A FULL-SIZE SKETCH

Choose one of the thumbnails you drew in the prompt on page 99 and create your main sketch. Make sure to focus on composition and getting the anatomy and angles correct. Come up with a detailed framework for the painting process.

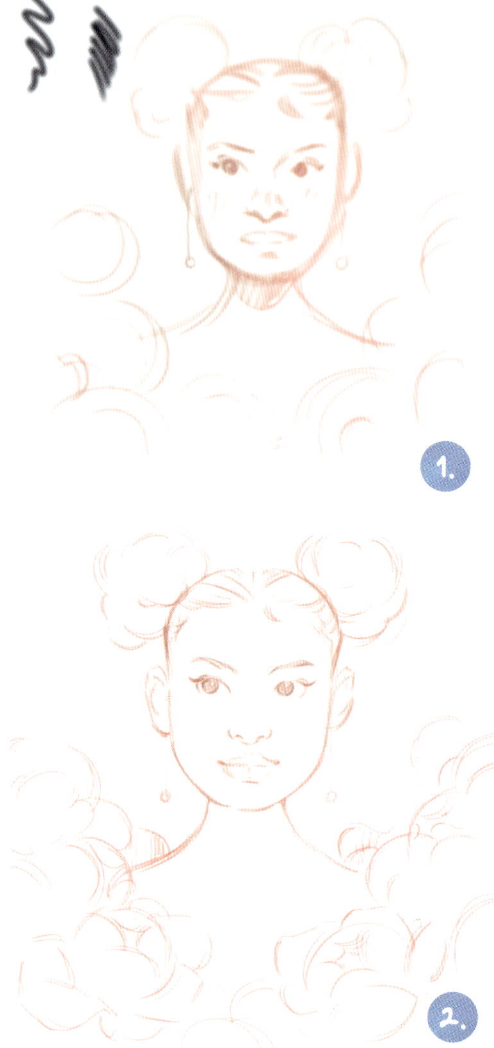

1. Create a canvas of 4 x 5 inches (10 x 13 cm) at 300 dpi (see page 16 for canvas sizing). After setting the base layer to a background color of your choice, create a new Multiply layer for your sketch. Using the Soft Airbrush (see page 17 for brushes), map out the general shape of your subject and composition. Use a large brush to lay down your linework. Use soft circular shapes to map out the placement of the head, hair and flowers. Use general shapes, like lines, ovals and curves, to test out where the facial features will lay on the face, but don't detail these areas yet. Set this layer's opacity between 20% to 40%.

2. Add a new layer (see Layers, page 18) over the rough sketch. Use a tighter, darker brush to map out the details of your subject, such as eyes, noses, lips and hands. (For how to sketch each, see pages 35, 56, 46 and 72.) If you're struggling to draw smooth, long lines, remember this tip: It's easier to draw the beginning and end points of a line and connect them than it is to just draw the line. Think of these as vector points along a curve, or a connect-the-dots page. This is useful for properly proportioning features on the face, like the symmetry of the eyes or the shape of the lips and mouth. Darken the line in areas that you know are pointed away from the viewer or in areas that are going to be shaded. For example, the corners of the eyes will be slightly darker than the rounded middle portion of the eyelids; this conveys curvature.

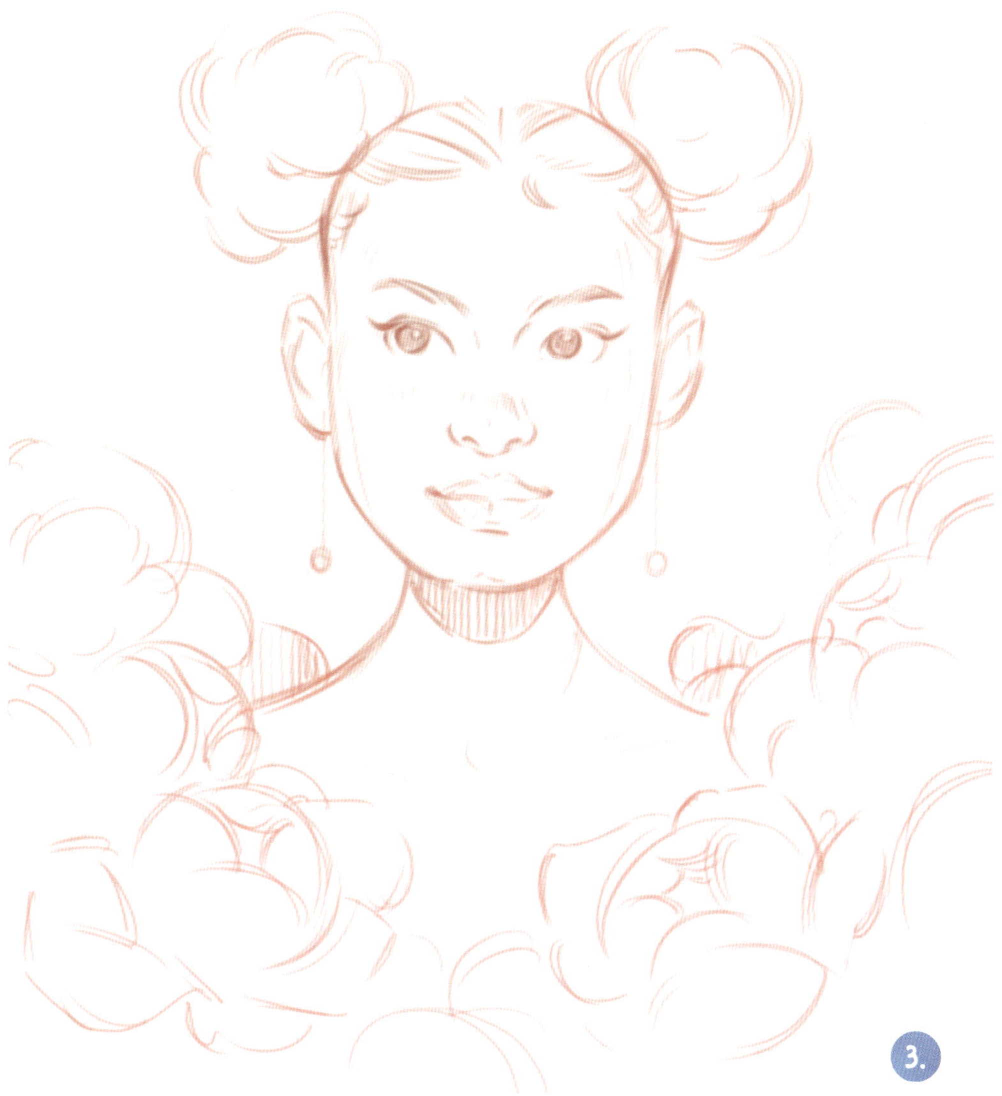

3. Lightly draw outlines of the general shape of shadows and highlights. Considering values as larger blocks of color can help blending later on. Use a thin, light line to shade these areas. Detail areas like the inner brow bone, lower eyelids, corners of the mouth, shadow under the lip and shadow under the chin since those areas give the face a 3D shape and definition. Define the shadows on the peonies so that you have a guideline for where you'll color block later. If you're not used to adding complex shading to your paintings, try outlining where you know shading should go.

COLOR THEORY FOR DIGITAL ART

The digital painting color wheel is different than the traditional color wheel; traditional artists use subtractive primaries (red, yellow and blue) that will eventually mix into a solid black. Since digital artists are working with pixels, color mixing works a little differently. Color mixing with an RGB palette is made up of the additive primaries red, green and blue. Therefore, the color wheel is not comprehensive of values (page 112) but rather only represents hues. Saturation and value are set independently from the hue wheel.

Note: A hue refers to the main color family on the spectrum. A value indicates how light or dark a color of the same hue appears.

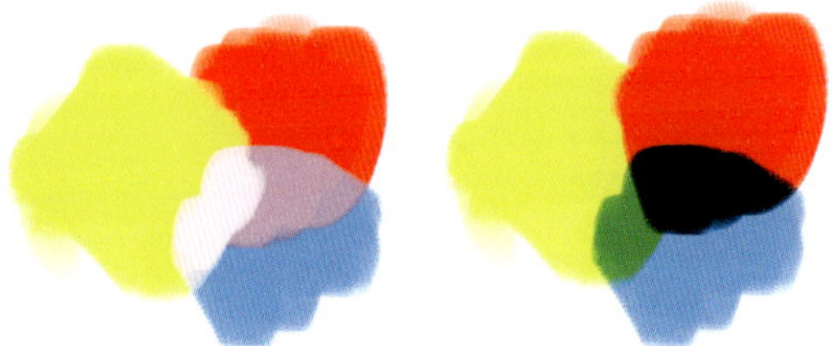

The colors on the left are additive primaries, while the colors on the right are subtractive primaries.

Traditional Color Theory

There are a few basic rules to color theory. While you won't be utilizing the traditional color wheel in a digital program, traditional color theory is still applicable to your use of colors and is therefore important to understand.

In a traditional color wheel, the **primary colors** are blue, red and yellow, while the **secondary colors** are purple, orange and green. Some great color palettes you can incorporate into your work are complementary colors, triadic colors and analogous colors.

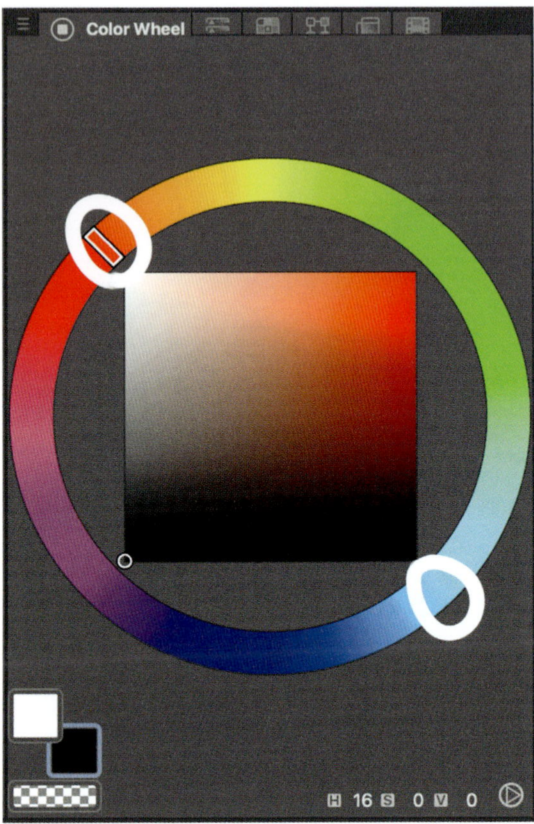

Complementary colors are on opposite ends of the color wheel.

Complementary colors are colors on the opposite ends of the color wheel that contrast well together. Examples are blue and orange, red and green, and purple and yellow. One way to incorporate complementary colors into your pieces is into the brightest highlights. If you have a primarily cool-toned palette, add a warm-toned highlight to add contrast. While this isn't realistic, I enjoy the creative liberty of playing with colors.

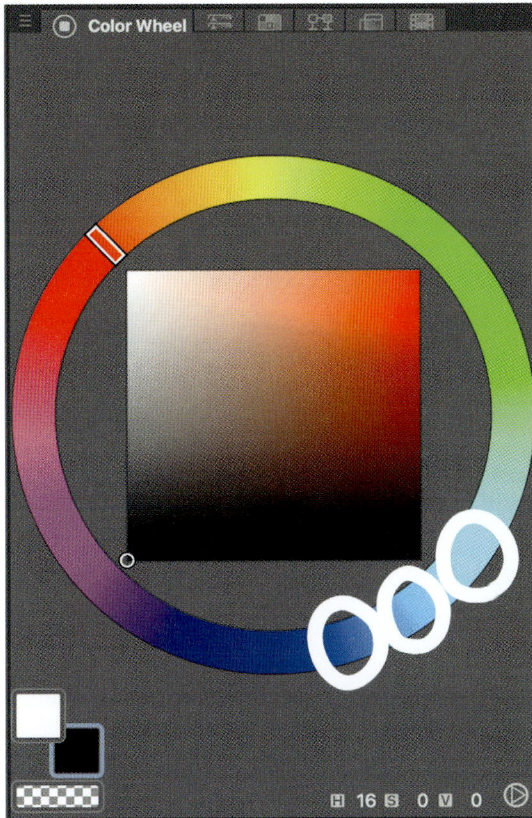

Analogous color schemes are made up of three hues that are adjacent to each other on the color wheel.

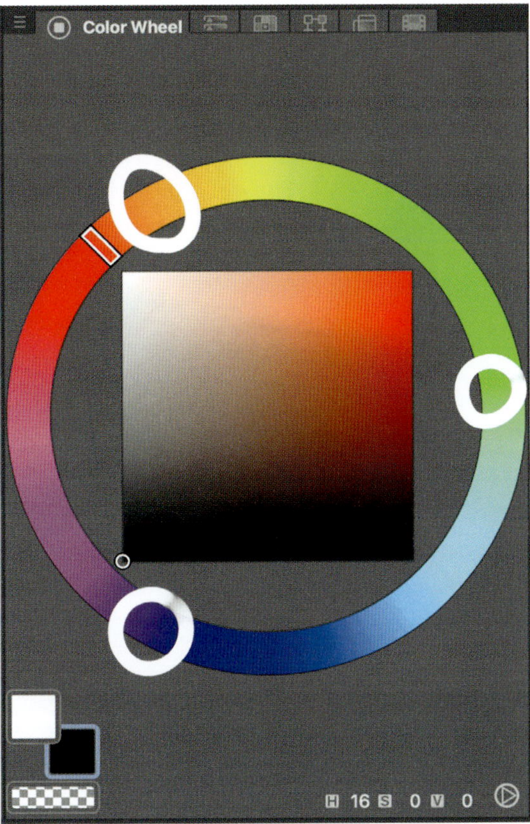

Triadic color schemes use three colors evenly spaced out on the color wheel.

Analogous color schemes consist of three hues next to each other on the color wheel: primary, secondary and tertiary. Tertiary colors are made by mixing primary and secondary colors together, creating yellow-orange, red-orange, red-purple, blue-purple, blue-green and yellow-green. For example, an analogous color scheme could utilize the colors yellow, yellow-orange and orange. This color scheme is almost monochromatic, but with subtle tonal shifts that are striking in their simplicity.

Triadic colors are three colors evenly spaced out on the color wheel. You can use primary, secondary or tertiary colors to create a striking piece with contrasting colors. An example of this color scheme would be purple, green and orange. Many triadic color schemes are bright and retro.

Creating Emotion with Colors

Colors can be used to communicate mood; red can symbolize anger or passion, both very strong emotions. Pastel colors can be peaceful, bright and happy. Jewel tones, such as emerald green or dark navy, can express maturity or elegance. You're not confined to what colors traditionally evoke, but you can

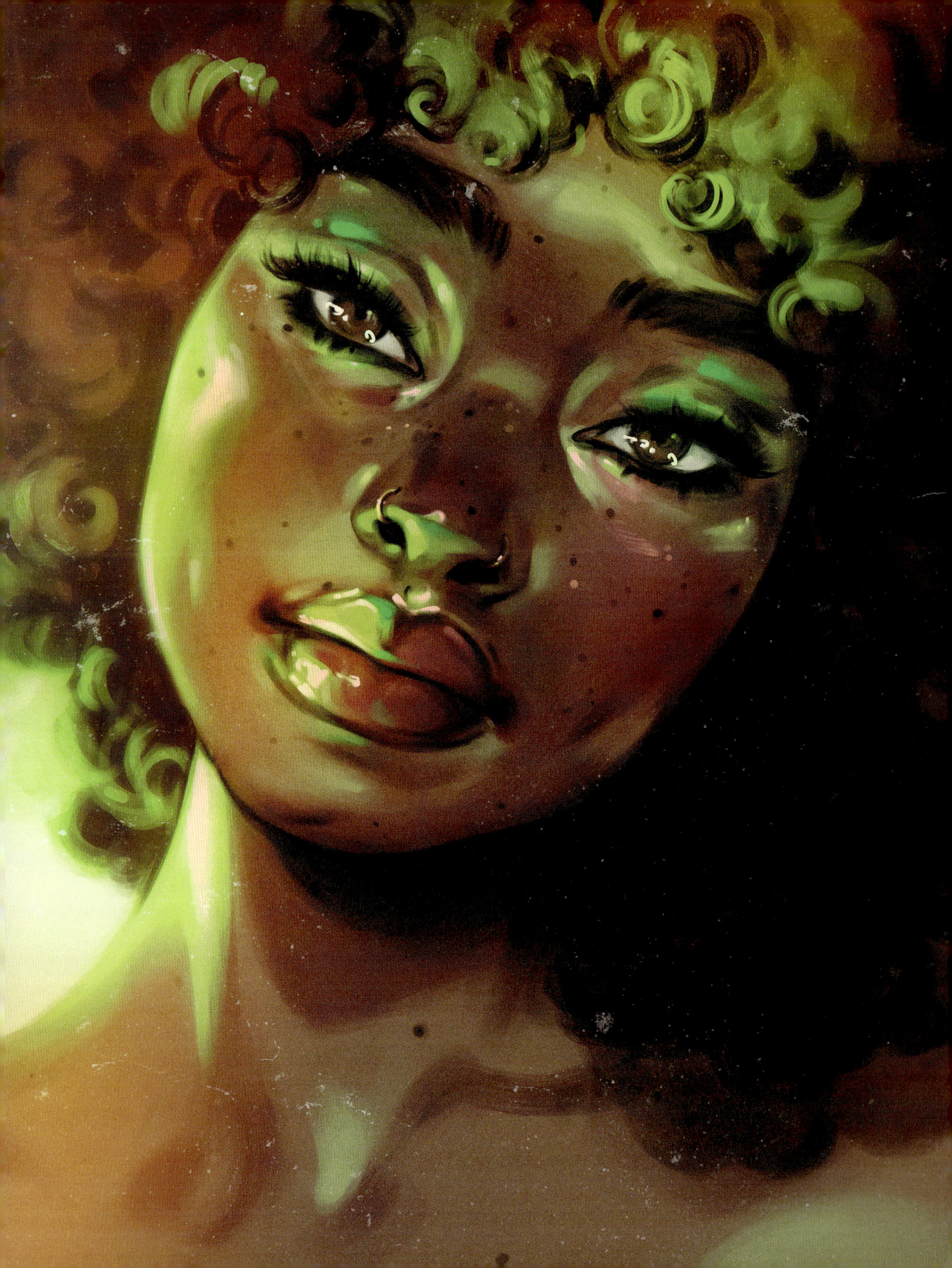

use these concepts to your advantage when telling a story. Additionally, you can use color as a juxtaposed element in relation to your subject matter. Using a color that is the opposite mood of your subject can be a fun take on color theory. For example, you can paint a creepy-looking girl with a pastel color palette. Since you are breaking color theory application, the end result could be unsettling (which is exactly the look that you might want).

Color as the Focal Point

You can also make color the full focus of your piece, leaving the subject matter secondary. You don't have to be confined to the feelings that color usually evokes, or you can use the color traditionally to tell a story. Creating a monochromatic painting can be visually unique, especially if you've never tried it out before. Having to incorporate the same tone into every part of the painting can further help you understand color, tonal shifts and values. Color blocking is a great way to introduce a bright color in a graphic way. Painting a strong silhouette in a bright color can make that element stand out against the environment.

I recommend rarely, if ever, painting with true blacks or whites. These are both extreme colors that are not naturally seen in nature. The petals of a daisy will not be a true white, but rather have undertones of blues and yellows. If warm light hits the petals, they can even have an orange or pink tone. The atmosphere and light that bounces off every object slightly changes the color of that object's hue, which gives you a good opportunity to add interesting tones to your palette. Seeing what undertones you can add to a true black or white will give your piece an organic look. Working with these undertones will help you regularly incorporate subtle tonal variations into your pieces and give you a greater understanding of color.

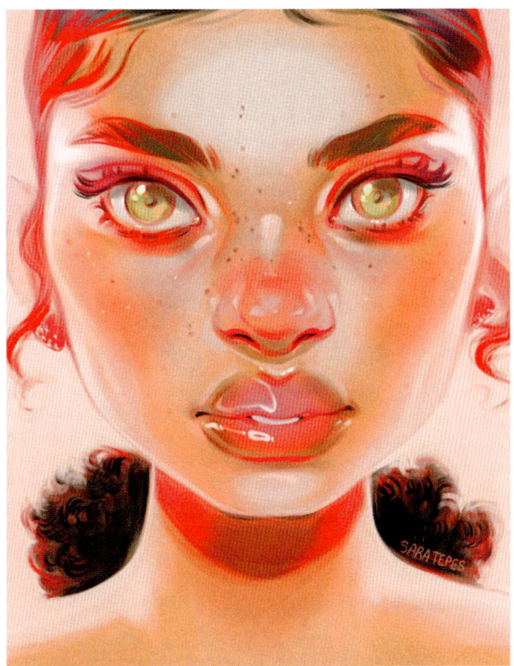

Focusing on color produces a striking result and can enhance your understanding of color use in future paintings.

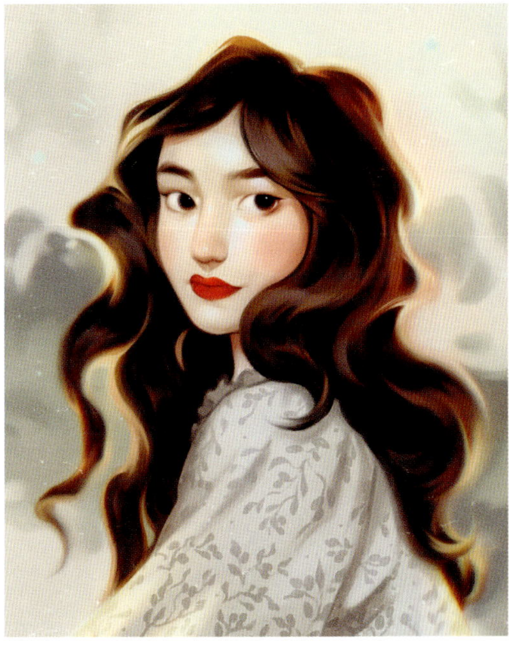

You can achieve great contrast without using true whites or true blacks.

PROJECT 9: PAINT YOUR SKETCH

Choose a color palette (page 17) and paint the sketch you created in Project 8 (page 102). When choosing colors for the shadows and highlights, vary the hue slightly instead of just changing the value of the color. As you paint this project, reflect: What mood does your piece translate? Have you broken any rules? What did you learn? Write down any tricks you've discovered for future reference.

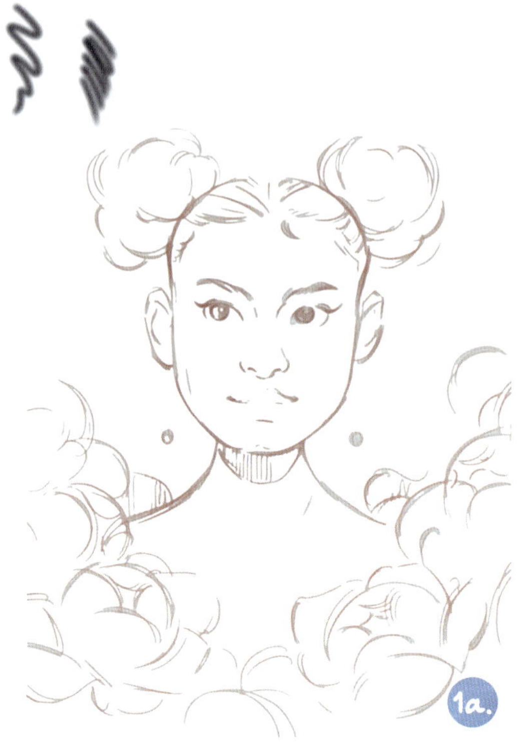

1a.

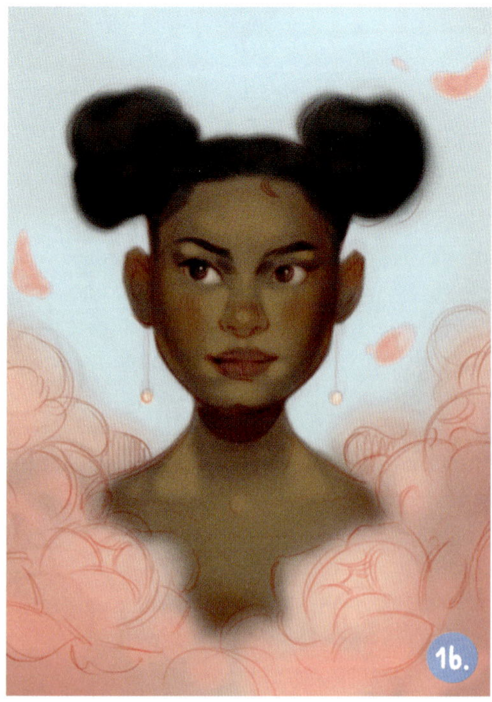

1b.

1. With a fluffy Airbrush (see page 17 for brushes), paint the base colors under the sketch layers; use the color palette of your choice to position the colors on the piece. Think of placing your colors in large blocks to add graphic interest to your painting and to create visual dynamism. Place your highlights and shadows with the same fluffy brush; the soft gradients will make the piece easier to render.

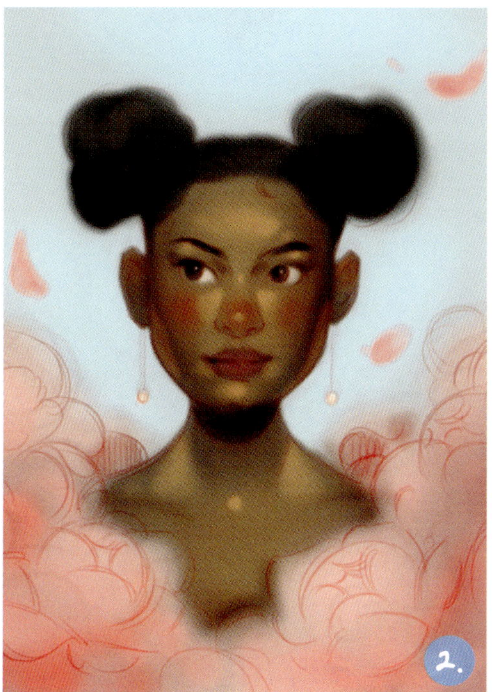

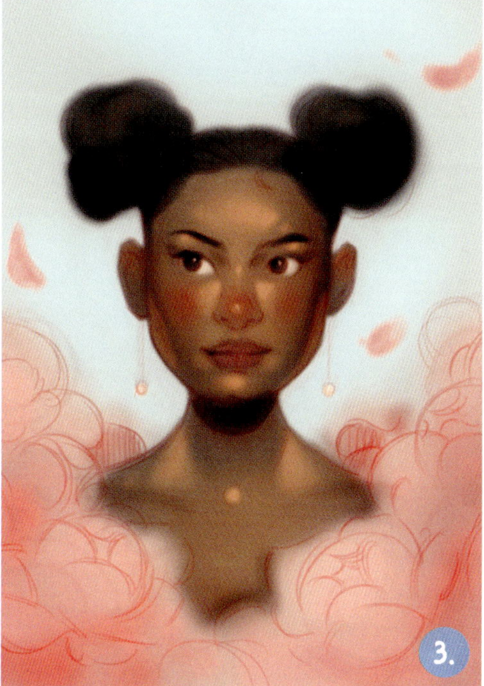

2. Use a Curves adjustment to bring brightness and life into your colors. Curves will create contrast between the values of your piece and bring cohesion to the color palette. I skewed the colors to a warmer tone for my own painting.

3. Turn a new layer into an Overlay layer and use your fluffy Airbrush to add any brightness, additional color, vignette or saturation to your painting. This step will ensure that, as you render, you will be color picking from the exact colors you want on your piece. Use as many adjustment layers as you need to come to a color palette that you are pleased with before you begin rendering.

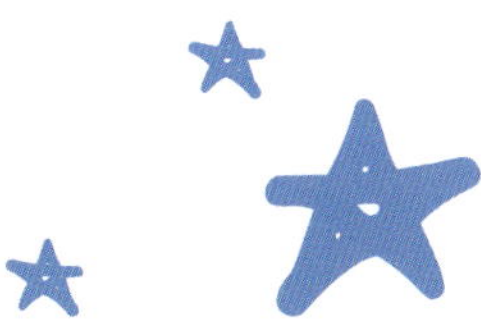

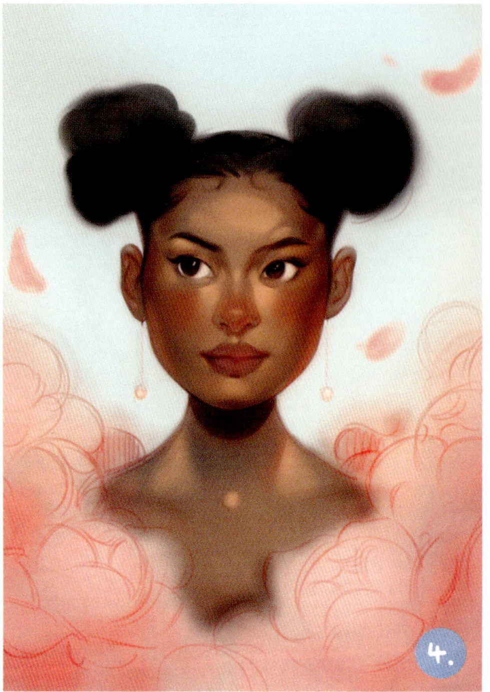

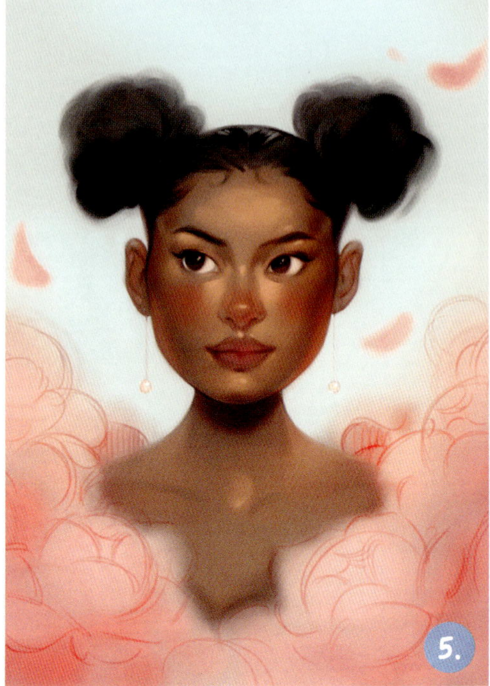

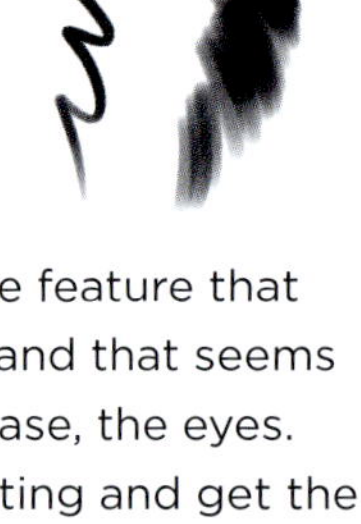

4. On a new layer, use your Oil brush to begin rendering the piece (see page 17 for more on brushes). Start with the feature that is most important to you and that seems most challenging: in my case, the eyes. This will anchor your painting and get the most daunting part of the process out of the way for you. The rest of the rendering should be seamless if you have a good sketch layer. Use your Eyedropper when rendering to pick from the colors you already laid down in the previous steps.

5. Once you have finished most of the rendering on the face, move on to the hair, neck, shoulders and ears. Use heavy pressure on your Oil brush with the background color to create crisp lines around the contours of the face and neck. Use firm, smooth lines to show the taut hair being pulled into the buns, and soft circular motions to create her fluffy hair buns.

6. On a new layer, begin rendering the flowers around the subject; use the Eyedropper to pick from the base colors and use a variety of soft and hard brushstrokes to create texture in the flower petals. Use light pressure as you paint the farther flowers, mixing the pink color with the blue of the background to create a fuzzy, blurred look.

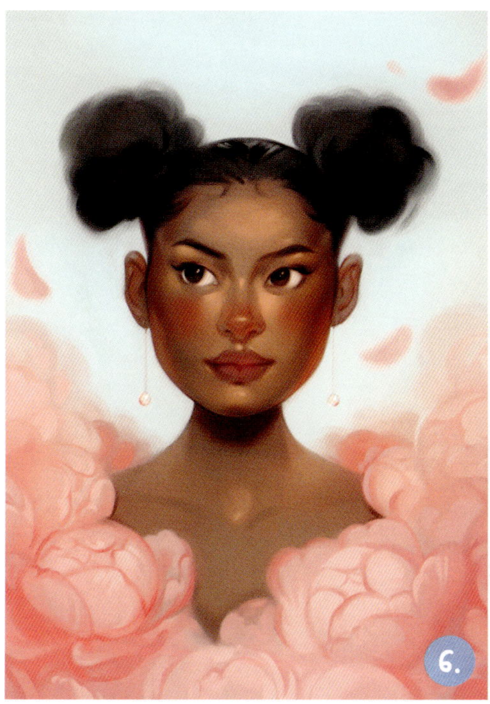

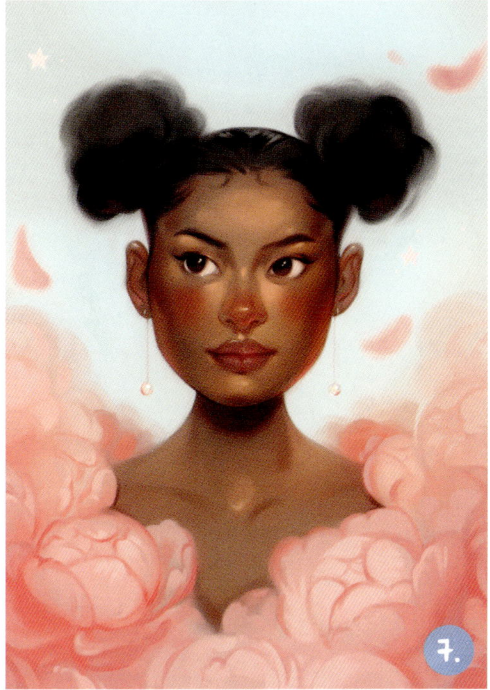

7. Add highlights and sharp details to your piece; use a bright pastel pink to add glossy accents to the eyes, nose, lips, ears and earrings. I add my signature stars and glows at this stage and step back to survey the piece as a whole. Does it need any more rendering or finishing touches?

8. Use Adjustment layers to edit the colors of your painting (see page 152 for final touches). These adjustments add contrast and depth to the hair color, a unified pinkish glow to the piece and crispness in the colors and sharpness.

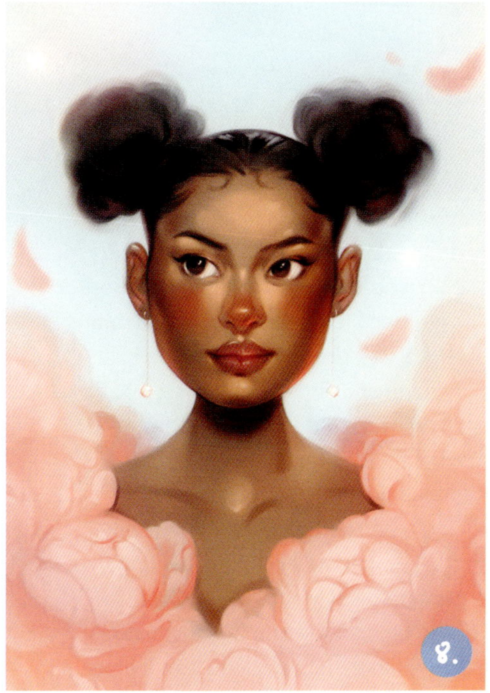

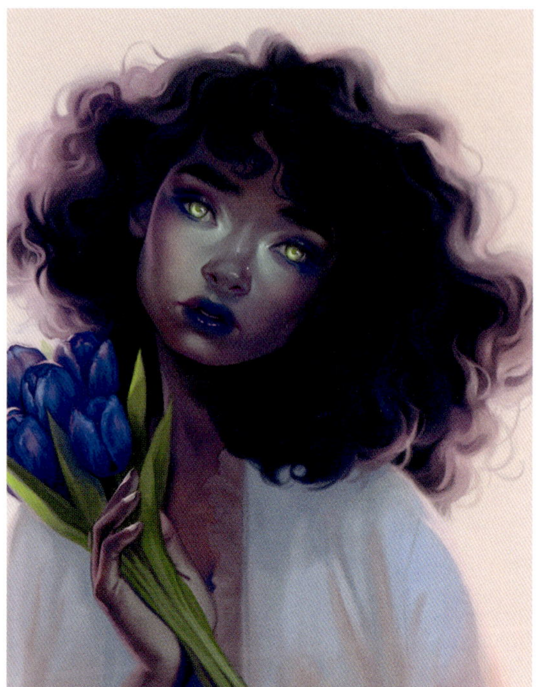

Select colors with varying values to establish contrast between areas you want to recede and those you want to highlight as the focal point.

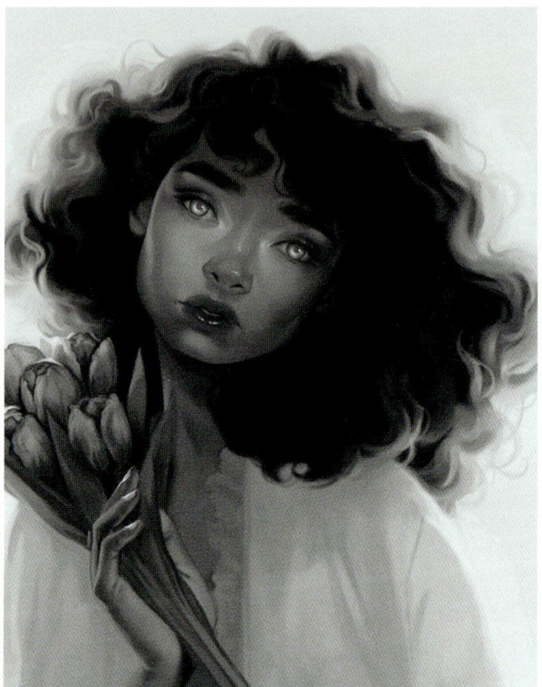

Are you surprised at the values of the piece when color is removed?

VALUES

A good painting must have application of color theory and a strong understanding of values. A value is the lightness or darkness of a color; a baby blue would have a lighter value, while an ocean blue would have a darker value. To begin understanding values, turn any reference photo you are using to gray scale. Are you surprised by the values of the colors and tones? Sometimes, separating color and value and just focusing on value makes the two concepts easier to learn and master. If you are struggling with the colors of your pieces, try painting in gray scale and then adding color later using adjustment layers. This will help you focus on getting the correct values, and once you're comfortable, you can begin to incorporate color, knowing which values should be in different areas.

A beginner mistake I see often is only using light values when painting. Using darker colors can be intimidating to beginners, but I recommend starting with a midtone value, one that's roughly 50% between white and black, as the base for your painting. One reason I recommend this is because you will have much more control over the details that you can put down in your piece; the brighter your piece, the fewer opportunities you will have to add subtle highlight variations. The contrast between the midtone of your piece and the highlight tone will not be high enough, creating a bright and flat result. This often looks as if your subject is flooded with light from all directions. If you are worried your piece will be too dark in the end, you can always easily brighten up a piece using a Curves adjustment layer (page 18), but it is much more difficult to darken a piece after

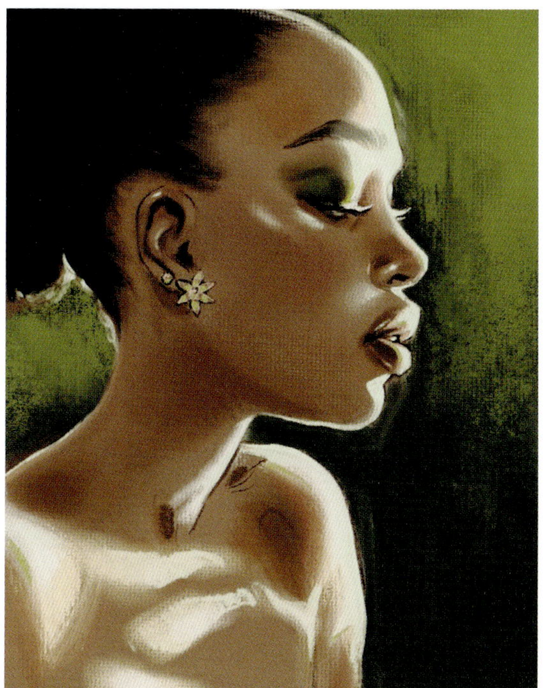

The rim lighting along the subject's silhouette contrasts sharply with the deep green background.

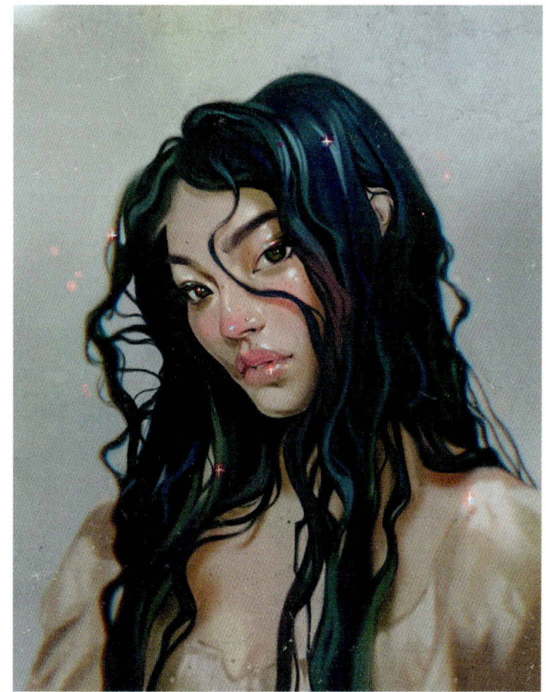

The dark, muted hair around the subject's face draws attention to her brighter and more vibrant features.

you've finished painting it. Again, stay away from using a true white and black in your piece. If you absolutely want the contrast, add those tones as finishing touches. Keeping either a true white or black in the color palette of your painting will distort how you interpret the rest of the values in your piece, so only add them intentionally.

Remembering composition, bright values draw attention to the eye while darker values recede into the painting. Utilize this concept to create flow in your painting. You can always brighten or darken areas in your painting using the Multiply, Soft Light or Overlay Adjustment layers (page 21), so focus on using mostly midtones in your piece. When in doubt, color pick values from your reference to build up an understanding of how your eye interprets values.

PROJECT 10: PAINT A PORTRAIT USING ONLY GRAYSCALE VALUES

Painting in grayscale is a good opportunity to learn and understand values without being daunted by color. You can either color pick from your reference photo or stick to mainly mid-tones. As you practice this technique, try to focus on adding proper shadows and highlights to your piece. Feel free to add bright highlights or dark shadows at the end of the painting process.

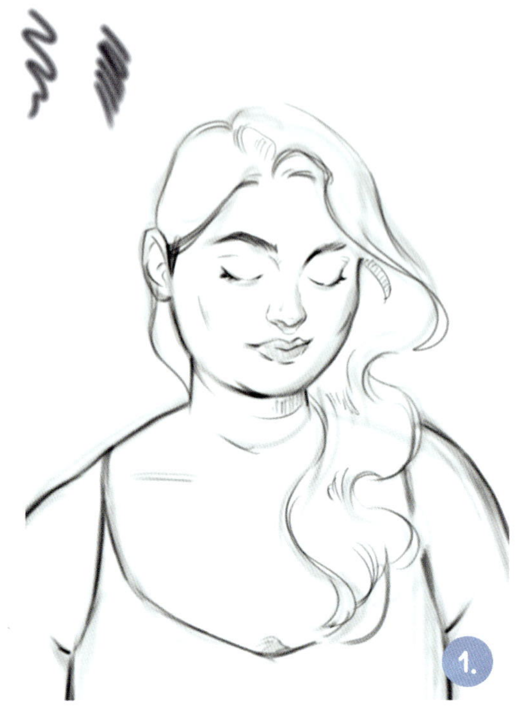

1. Create a canvas of 4 x 5 inches (10 x 13 cm) at 300 dpi (see page 16 for canvas sizing). After setting the base layer to a background color of your choice, create a new Multiply layer for your sketch. With the Soft Airbrush (see page 17 for brushes), use the same steps as you did for the previous project on page 108. Start with a loose rough sketch that blocks in the main shapes, then add a tightened sketch on a new layer. Use thin, faded lines to block in the general shapes of the shadows and highlights. Set this layer's opacity between 20% to 40%.

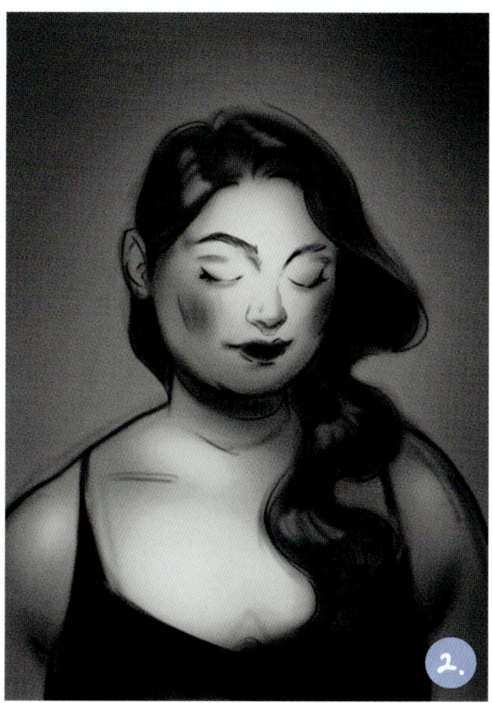

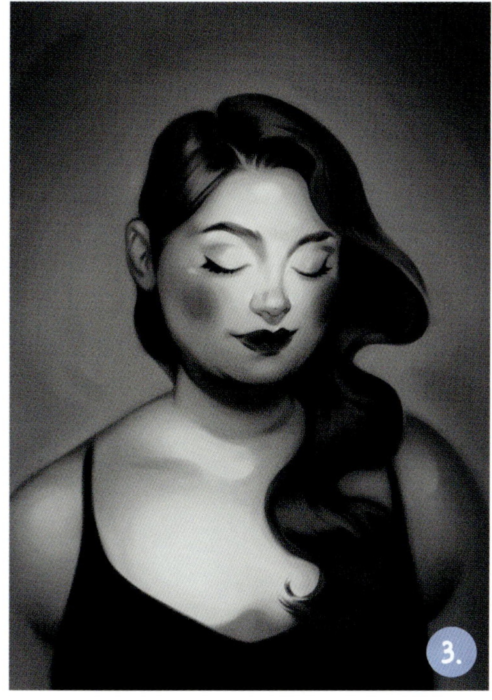

2. Add your base values under the sketch layer. Depending on the look you're going for, you can opt for contrast in your piece by choosing a darker background tone with a lighter-toned subject, or a bright background with a darker-toned subject. Stick to midtones to begin with; you can still add contrast while staying in the boundaries of midtones. I personally love the lighting of old Hollywood portraits, so I referenced that lighting model for this painting. A dark, moody background helps the lighted subject pop out. The diffused lighting casts prominent shadows from the eyelashes and lips, while the cheekbones are strongly contoured. Wait to add the bright highlights to the image until later stages, but for now, use an Airbrush to smooth out the shading and base values.

3. Begin rendering your painting by right-clicking on any layer and selecting "Merge visible into new layer." Using the Oil brush (see page 17 for brushes), blend the values of the sketch with those of the base values. Lighten the opacity of the sketch layer if you feel that it's over-powering, but often, the sketch blends in well with the values placed. When rendering, avoid adding texture to the chin, since it often can look rough and masculine, but I like adding extra definition to the nose and cheeks.

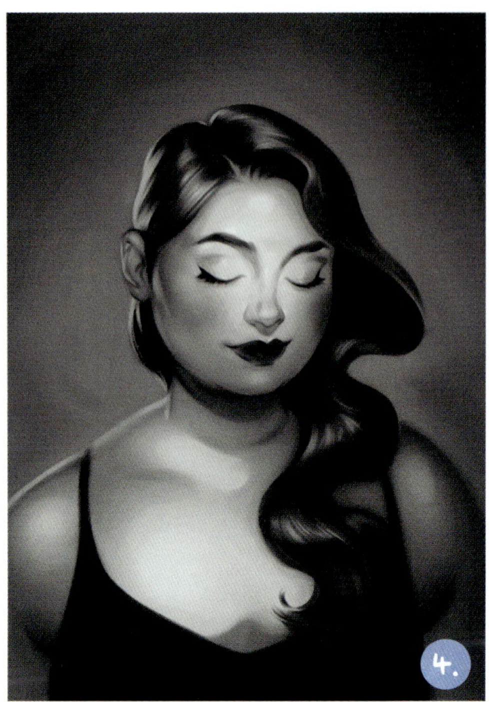

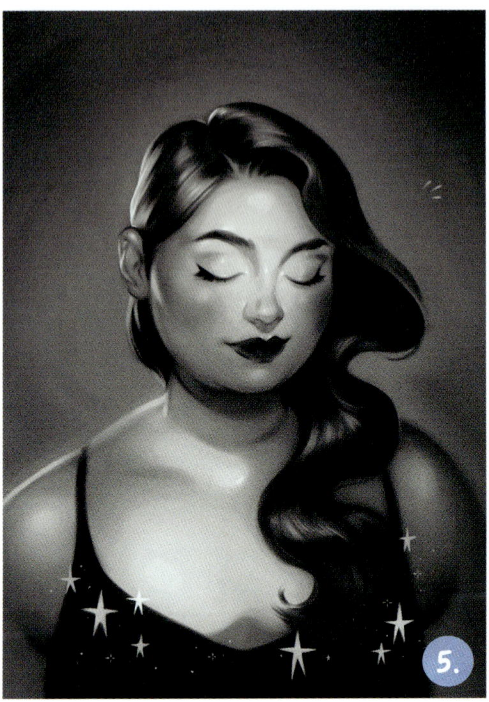

4. Once you like the level of detail you've achieved, add bright highlights and dark shadows to your painting. Adding them after you flesh out your painting will add contrast to the overall piece. Save the sharp white highlights on the eyes, cheekbones, nose and lips until last. This will help you preserve the true value of the skin; if you add the bright highlights in the beginning, you will often end up blending them into the base values and lightening up the overall tone of the piece. Use a charcoal or true black for the lashes, but also for any areas in heavy shadow, like the nape of the neck. Be sparing with the blacks and whites that you add to the piece; any bright white will instantly draw the viewer's eye, while anything in deep shadow will recede into the background.

5. Use a Curves adjustment (see page 18 for adjustment layers) to lighten or darken your piece, and then use the Soft Airbrush on an Overlay or Soft Light layer to add any gradient highlights or shading to your piece. I like using Curves to adjust the contrast in a piece and to play with varied looks. Experimenting with blown-out or subdued values can take your painting in a new direction. For this piece, try to get the values to look as soft and creamy as the inspiration photos of old Hollywood portraits. On a new layer, use the Oil brush to add glimmering stars on top of the dark dress. This is a cute take on a glamorous, glittery dress.

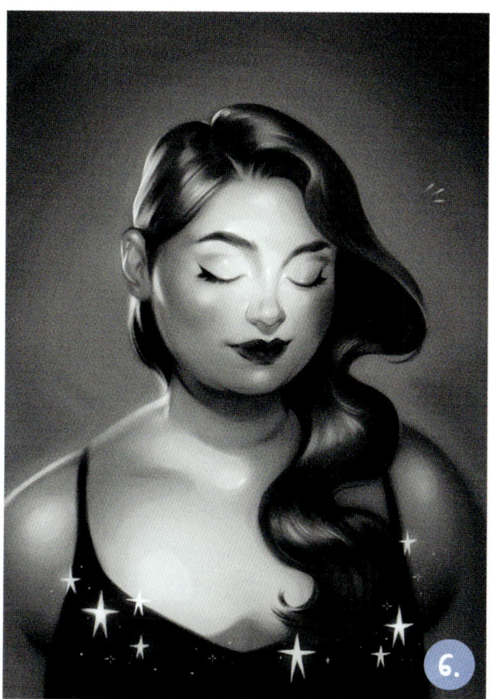

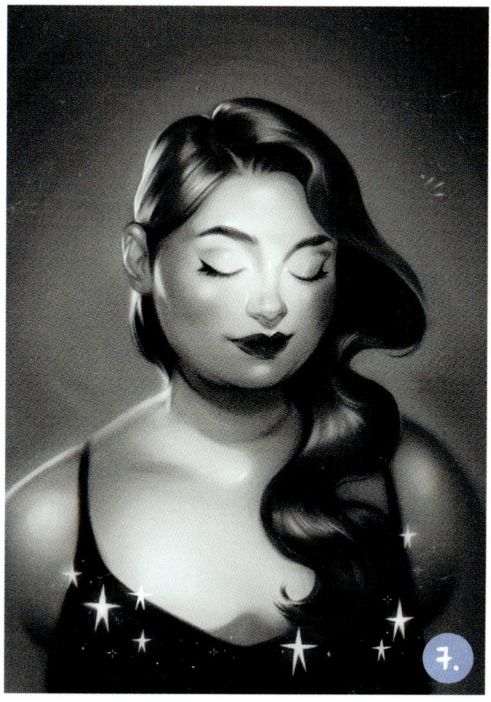

6. You can add any final touches or details to your painting (see page 152 for more on finishing touches). Because you put thought into your layers and brushstrokes, the final piece should have depth in the values and shading. Add extra details in any areas that you want to be sharp and glossy, like the highlights on the eyes, as well as adding noise and sharpening to complete the image.

7. Diffuse some of the details on the fringe of the painting by either using a circular motion blur or an airbrush to tap over any details that you want to be blurry. I feel that this creates a dreamy effect and keeps the piece from being too technically perfect.

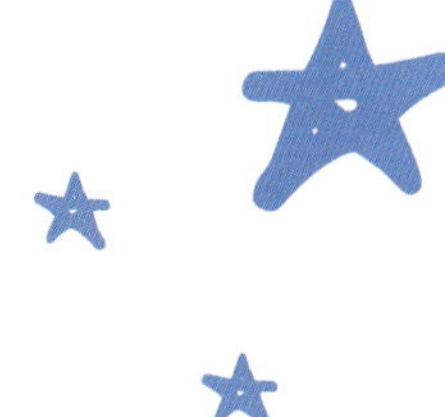

Adding Color to Grayscale Paintings

The process for adding color to grayscale paintings will not replace learning and understanding how to use color and value at the same time, but it can help you polish up and complete a piece. It can also help you try out different color schemes on your painting without wasting much time or energy. I would recommend trying this out if you're a beginner or undecided on your color palettes in general. I used to paint this way for a couple of years until I finally learned how to effectively paint with colors.

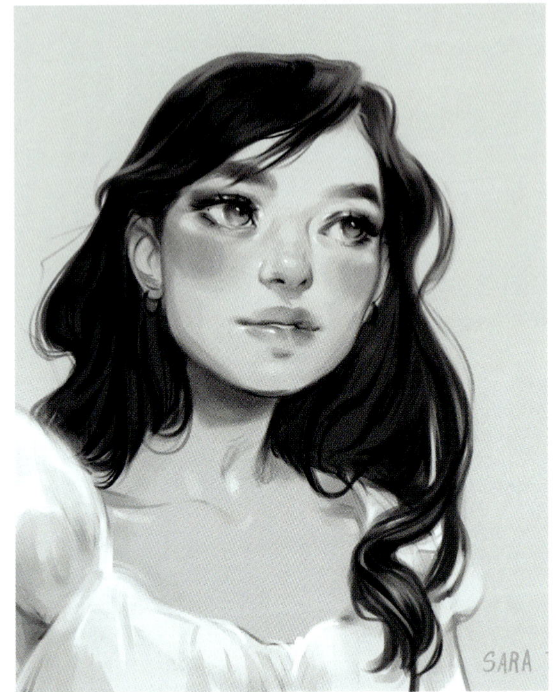

You should utilize a combination of adjustment layers to build up a variety of colors and hues in your piece. You can generally start off with the Soft Airbrush and an Overlay layer to lay down the base colors, then stack a couple of Soft Light layers over top to add subtle variations of hues in the skin, hair and clothing. Add color shifts to shadows in order to give them more visual interest. Once you are happy with the colors, add a new layer on top of everything (on a normal mode) and paint in some extra details by color picking from the canvas. Paint bright highlights with pastel undertones in order to tie the piece together, as well as a Curves adjustment layer to further edit the values and colors, unifying the piece.

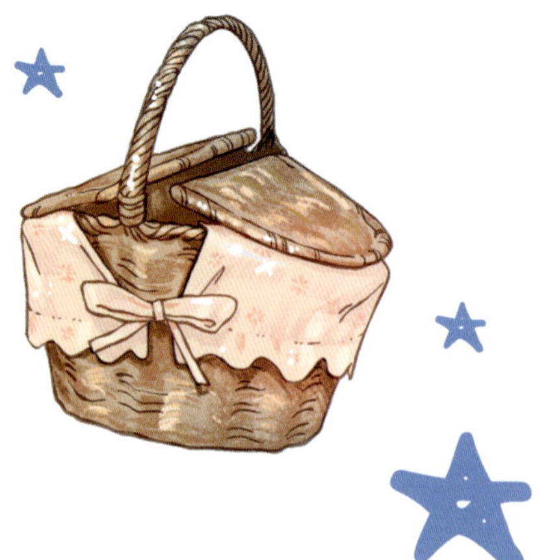

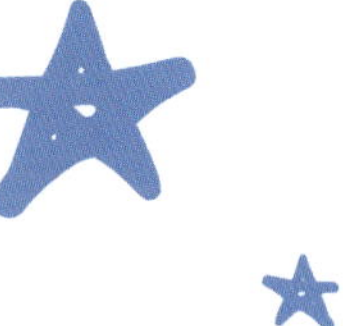

PROJECT 11: ADD COLOR TO YOUR GRAYSCALE PAINTING

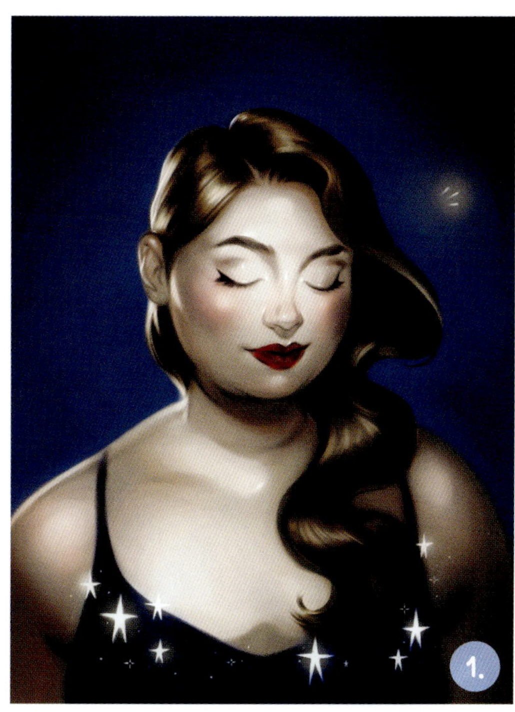

Use an assortment of adjustment layers to add color to your grayscale painting from Project 10 (page 114). Feel free to experiment with the color palette. Once you've laid all the colors down, add a new layer over top and paint in some added details to tie everything in.

1. Use a Soft Airbrush (see page 17 for brushes) and an Overlay layer (see page 18 for adjustment layers) to lay down your base colors. The colors will be pale and desaturated: the navy, ruby red and silver tones I want in the final piece look more slate gray, muted maroon and midtone gray. This piece reminds me of dark blue crushed velvet. Contrast the pale figure with deep jewel tones in the piece: A midnight blue background contrasted by a bright red bottled lip and the magical silver glistens in the stars of the dress. If you don't have a clear direction for the color palette of the piece, use this step to experiment with different color palettes until something fits perfectly. In this case, I had a clear vision based on my inspiration and notes I jotted for the thumbnails.

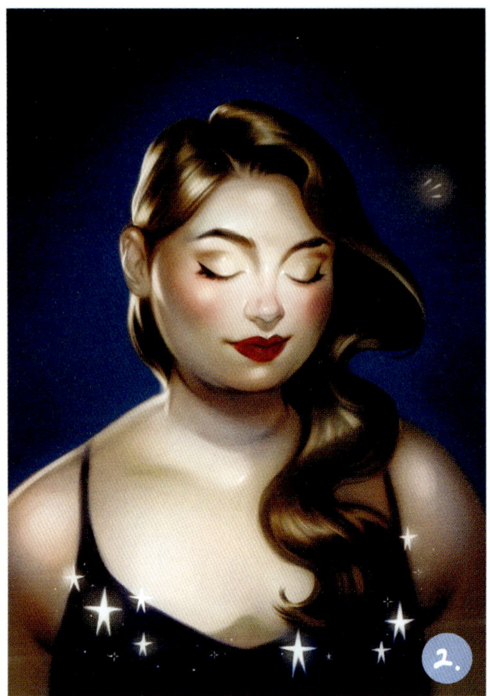

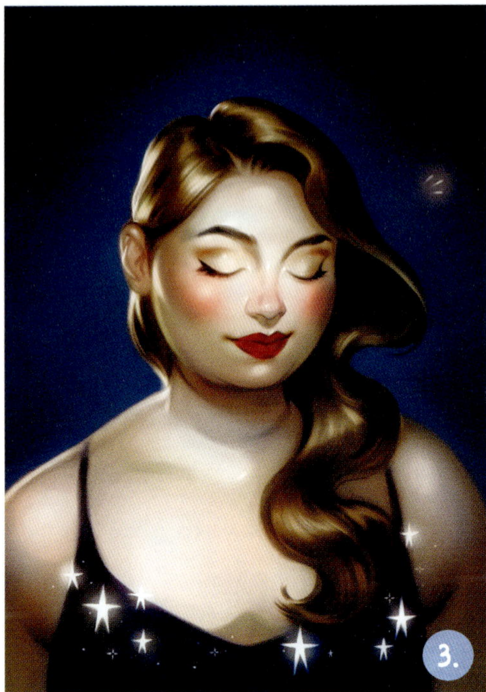

2. Add a new Soft Light layer and begin adding varied hues and colors to your subject. This is where you can deepen the colors and add saturation to the piece. Add hints of greens, purples, blues and pinks to the skin to add dimension and translucency.

3. Repeat adding adjustment layers as many times as you need to achieve the saturation and colors you want. By this point, you might have lost some of the subtle details you added to your grayscale piece. Since these adjustment layers are subtle, build up the subtle hues of the skin, as well as shadows. You can also play around with different stylistic choices, like adding heavy blush or heavier gradient shadows.

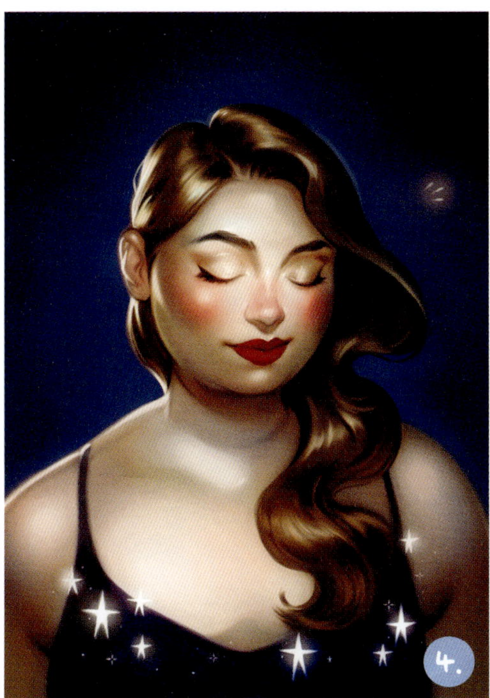

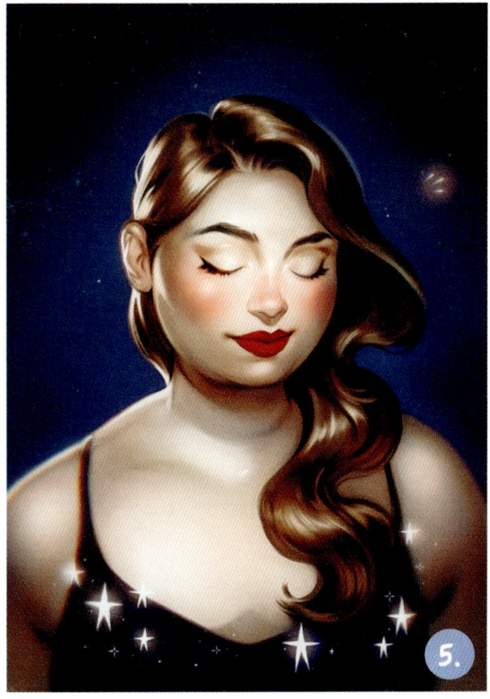

4. Add a Curves adjustment layer if you want to add more contrast and depth to the painting (see page 18 on layers). Tweak each of the Curves until you land on a color palette that you like. This is a good way to experiment with warmer or cooler tones in your pieces without sacrificing a lot of time detailing a color palette you don't love. This will also help you learn more about cohesive color palettes; the process is similar to color grading a photograph.

5. On a new layer on top of the rest, use the Oil brush to add bright highlights, dark shadows and details that you want to accentuate. The adjustment layers will smooth out some of the more nuanced details, so go back in with a detailed brush and bring back some of the finer marks that were lost. Add any finishing details like flyaway hairs, beauty marks, freckles and any glittery highlights you want in the final piece. The idea is that you're adding crisp marks on top of the smooth, blended subject matter and drawing the eye to these small details. Use this last step to double-check anything that you might have missed.

BRUSHSTROKES

The pressure of your marks will influence both the mood and feel of your piece, as well as have an effect on your body's well-being. If you have bad posture and press hard on your tablet, you're going to develop more back and wrist pain than might be necessary. It's important to be strategic with the pressure of your marks; if you consistently want the look of bold brushstrokes without the physical toll it will take on your body, adjust your tablet's sensitivity setting to allow you to apply lighter pressure for the same effect. Open your pen tablet's driver to adjust this setting.

Pen pressure will affect the size and/or opacity of your brush. You will have to play around with different settings to find out what type of brush you like best, but I have personally found that I don't like brushes with changes in pressure size unless I'm working on inked line art (which I am very rarely working on). I prefer manually changing the size of the brush with shortcuts. This gives me more control over my marks and their opacity.

The type of mark you put down will affect the overall tone of your piece. If you use heavy pressure and quick, sweeping marks, you will have a rougher impasto effect, which is an effect similar to thick layers of oil paint laid on a canvas with a palette knife. If you use light, circular motions (like I do), you will achieve a softer, blended look. I recommend trying out soft pressure and color picking often to blend your colors. If you use an oil-type brush, you will achieve a painterly look, but it will be diffused and blended. You can incorporate marks like crosshatching or blocky shading to achieve differing levels of detail.

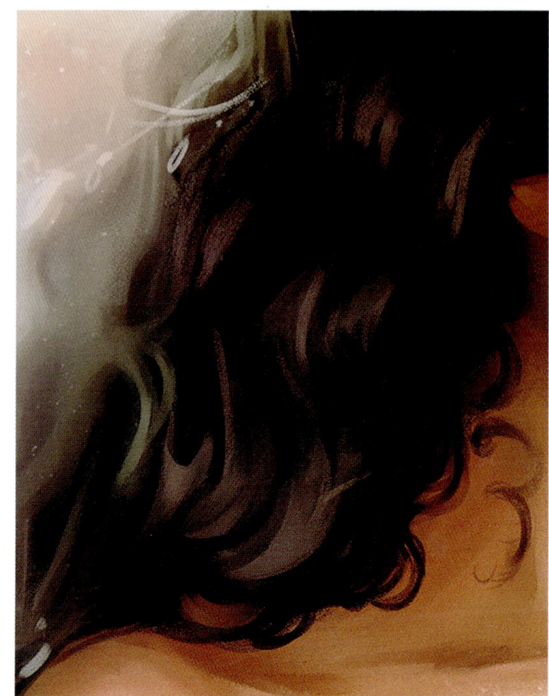

Heavy, textured brushstrokes

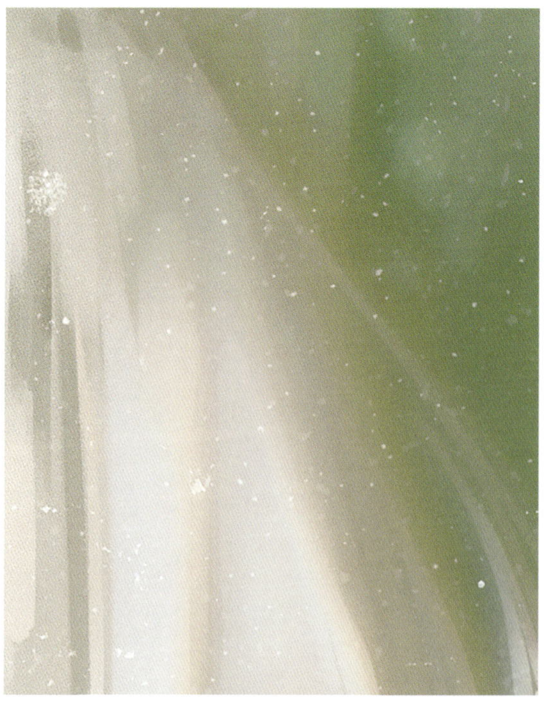

Soft, blurred paint strokes

As the designer of the piece, choose marks that will carry the mood; feel free to go as realistic or impressionistic as you want. When placing marks, remember to draw lines around the curves and contours of the object you are painting. This will help create the illusion of a curved or angled surface; avoid using only vertical or horizontal lines since it will be harder to express volume and curvature. Following are several techniques you can incorporate into your paintings to add style and texture.

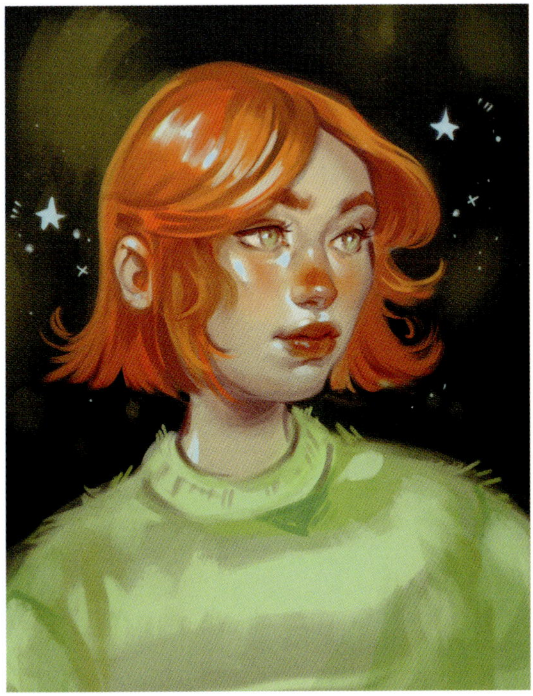

An impasto effect using the Oil brush

Impasto

Use hard and quick marks with a flat oil brush to create a rough, impasto effect. The goal is to keep the piece from looking too blended, so choose colors from the color wheel often and keep color picking and blending to a minimum. If you're unsure of how to incorporate this style, pull up references of impasto painters. Good examples come from the Impressionist time period, since painters began to be more emotive and expressive with their brushstrokes instead of focusing on accuracy.

Crosshatching

Crosshatching can be a great way to practice shading while keeping a piece visually interesting. I usually hatch my pencil sketches, but crosshatching can be a great way create texture and depth in a digital painting. Using a Pencil brush or Oil brush, draw short vertical strokes in the areas where you want to add shading. Then, overlay these strokes with additional short strokes in a perpendicular direction. Use thicker strokes with hard pressure in shaded areas, and keep your marks light in any areas you want to bring forward to the viewer's attention.

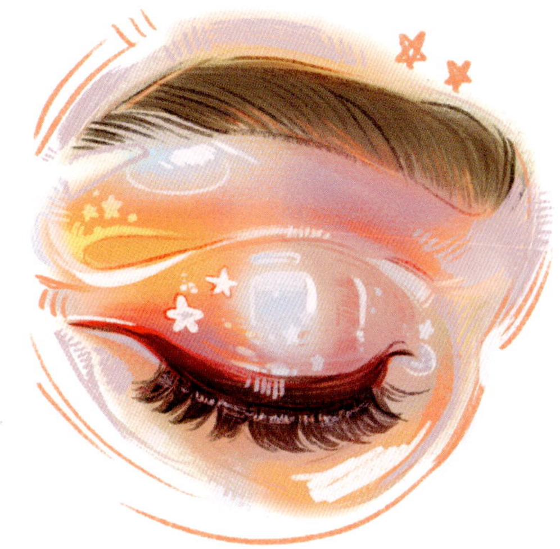

Using hatching and crosshatching to shade with the Pencil brush

Color Blocking

Break your subject down into basic shapes when color blocking. You can simplify a larger shape into three or four smaller shapes: one for the highlights, one for midtones, one for shadows and maybe one for any strong reflected color on the object. This will give you a better idea of how to shade volumes effectively. Color blocking is one of the best ways to learn form and shading. Break down your shape based on a reference, and then break the large shapes down into smaller sections.

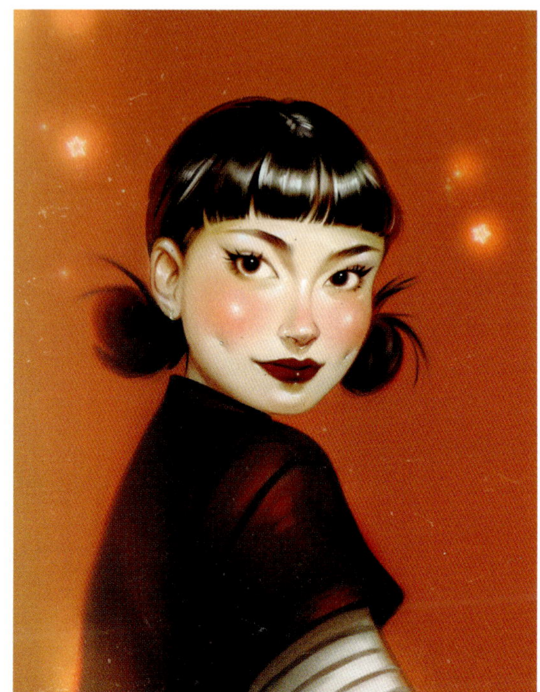

Soft, fluffy look created with the Airbrush

Smooth Shading

Use any airbrush and soft-edged detailing brush to blend your values into a smooth shading style. Color pick often to softly blend everything together. Color pick in the gradient between two contrasted colors and continue to color pick in those middle gradients until you come out with a smooth blend. Add a few hard edges to create definition where needed, but most of the painting should be well-blended and soft.

Mixed Techniques

Use an oil-type brush to create a textured but blended painting that resembles a traditional piece. This is my personal style; I like to use a mixture of airbrushes and soft oil brushes to blend the painting, and then add intentional texture over the blended areas. This is almost a combination between impasto-style painting and the soft-edged airbrush style.

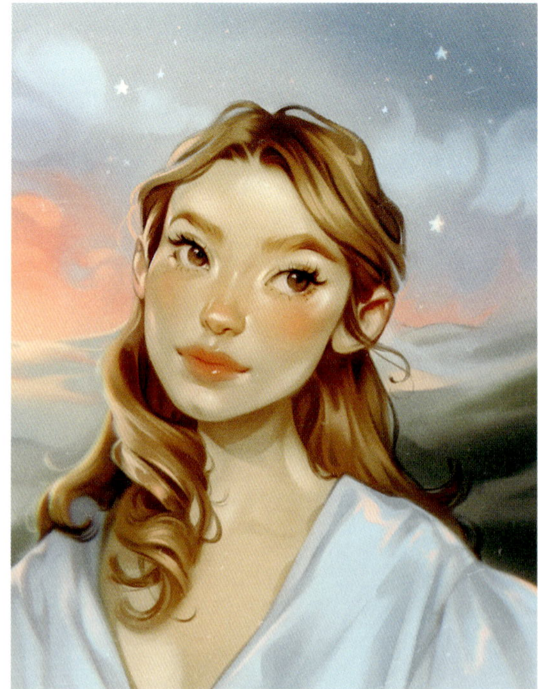

Use the Oil brush to softly blend and build up on the painting.

PROMPT: CREATE A PAINTING WITH DIFFERENT BRUSHSTROKES

For this prompt, choose a simple object, like a mug or a water bottle, and paint it using a variety of different digital brushstroke techniques. Try your hand out at five different styles; you can incorporate impasto, crosshatching, color blocking, smooth shading and so on into your paintings. This will loosen you up and might help you add texture and detail into your next paintings.

Do you find that a particular style comes more naturally to you? Can you blend different techniques to discover your personal style? Are there other techniques not covered here that you'd like to explore?

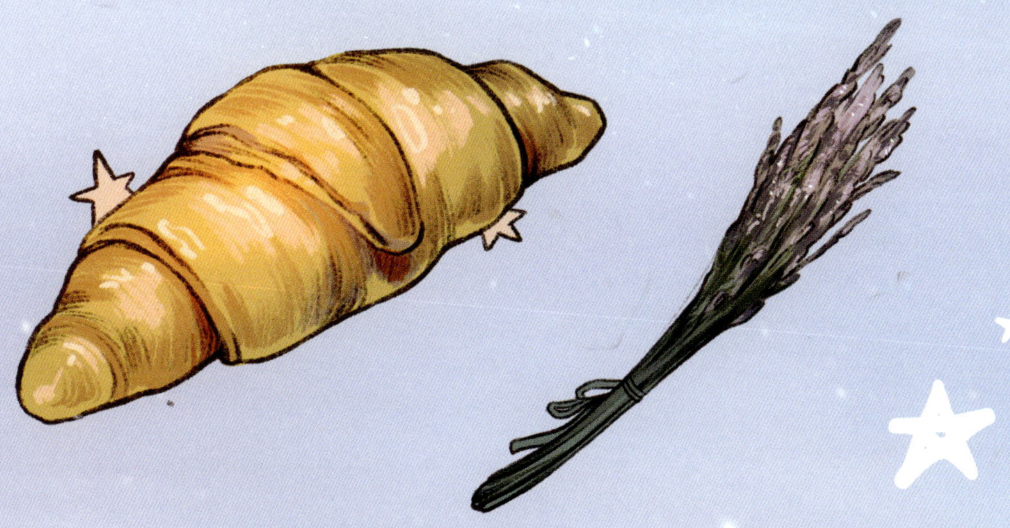

LIGHTING

Mastering lighting will take your painting to the next level, and it might be one of the easiest aspects of painting to learn. Many beginners don't consider setting their character in an environment affected by lighting, therefore creating flat images. Learning how light bounces off a subject from various directions can help you learn facial anatomy more easily.

Think about the look you're going for; are you wanting to paint a serene and calm piece or one that carries intense emotion? Depending on the look and environment you're placing your subject in, you will paint either direct or indirect lighting.

Direct lighting is harsh and unfiltered. It casts stark and unflattering shadows on your subject and is often not the appropriate lighting scenario for a calm painting. The exception to this would be if you set your character in a sunny or golden hour setting. While there will be harsh shadows as they are directly hit by the sun, you can darken the highlights and lighten up those shadows to paint them in warm and saturated tones. Essentially, you would be removing much of the contrast that would be found in the original lighting scenario. Those same shadows would be much more dramatic if they were deepened rather than lightened, such as in direct studio lighting. Use direct lighting if you want your subject to look dramatic, tense, angry or showcase another intense emotion.

You can utilize indirect or diffused lighting for a much more even and calm look to your piece. Your model can be in the shade outside, backlit by the sun, indoors or under diffused studio lights; indirect lighting is much more flattering and peaceful. The hue of the light hitting your model will be different in each of these scenarios, so taking and studying a reference photo will help you understand the shifts in color. For example, if the scene is painted at sunset, don't have the light bouncing off the face be a cool tone: Consider the environment and atmosphere.

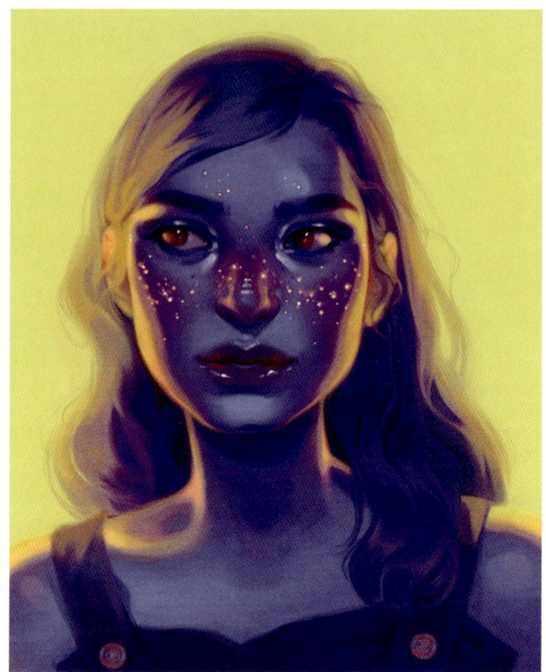

Diffused lighting hitting the face, rim lighting coming from behind

You can always create an artificial lighting setup by altering the colors hitting the face. If you're taking a creative liberty, you don't have to stick to natural lighting and colors. Using the guidelines discussed in the chapter on color theory (page 104), play around with colorful lighting as one of the main swatches from your palette.

Notes: Rim lighting illuminates the edge of a subject to create a halo silhouette.

Chromatic aberration occurs when lenses don't focus correctly, leading to blurred bright colors such as red, blue and purple.

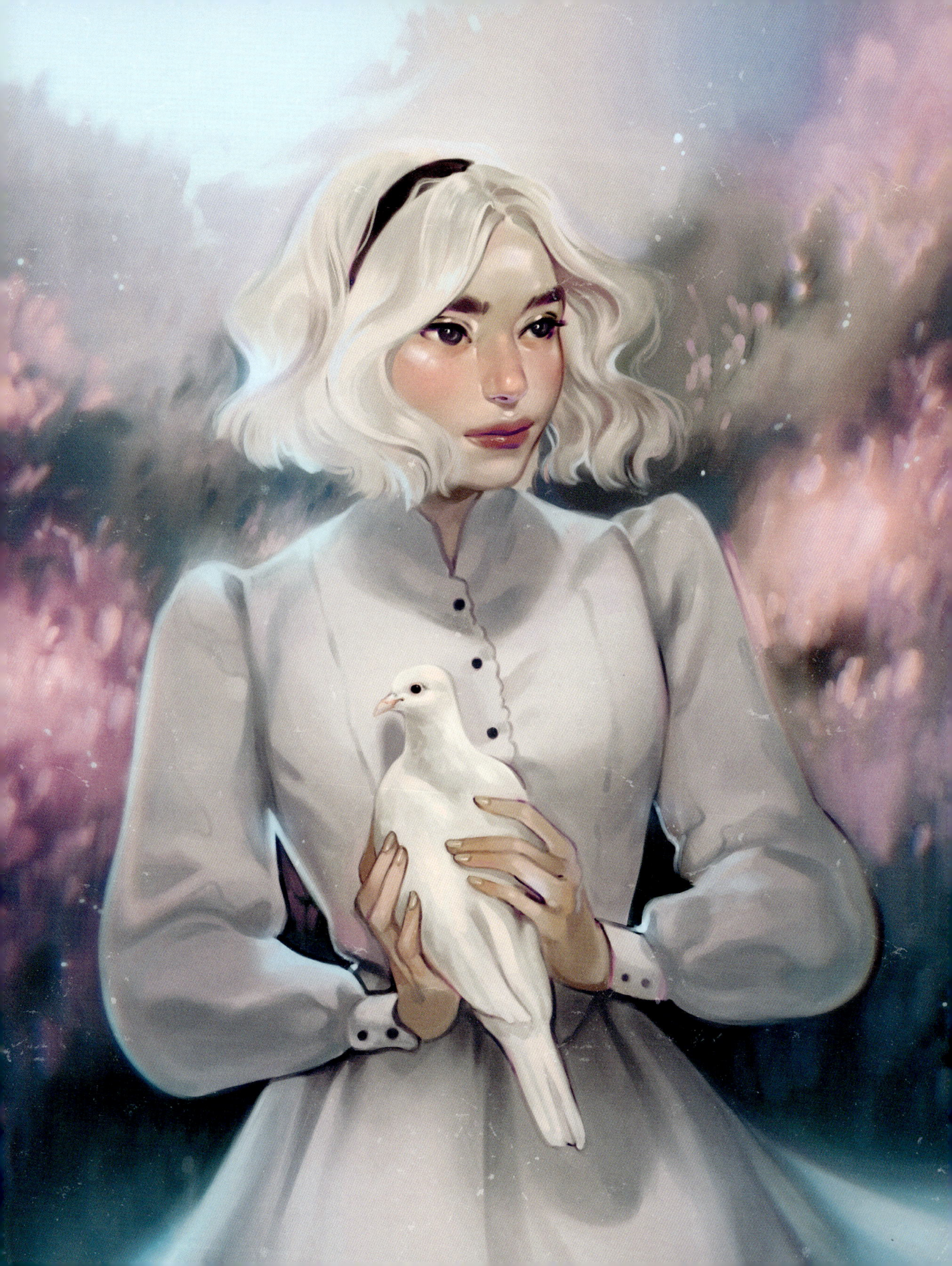

PROJECT 12: CREATE TWO PAINTINGS WITH DIFFERENT LIGHTING

For this project, paint the same subject two ways: one with backlighting and one with direct sun. As you paint, reflect: How do the tones and shadows change based on the position of the sun in relation to their face? What hues are you finding in the shadows and highlights, and how do they differ? Write all these thoughts down for future reference.

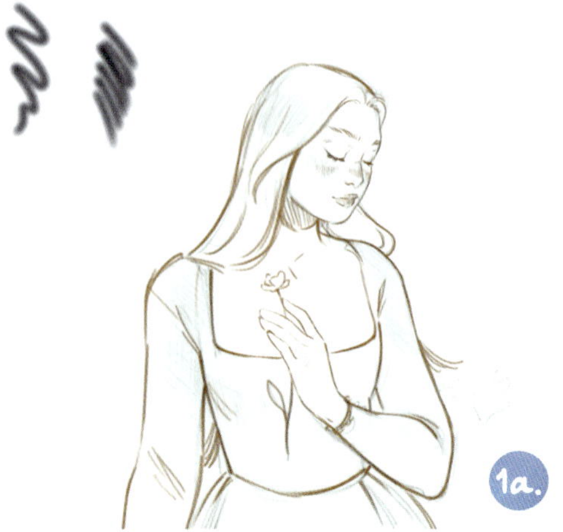

1a.

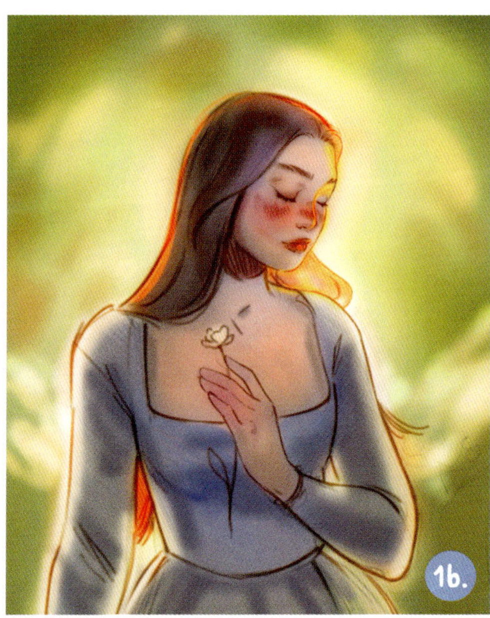

1b.

1. Create a canvas of 4 x 5 inches (10 x 13 cm) at 300 dpi (see page 16 for canvas sizing). Create a new Multiply layer for your sketch. With the Soft Airbrush (see page 17 for brushes), sketch in first your rough lines and then your tight sketches to solidify your composition. Use thin faded lines to block in the general shapes of the shadows and highlights. Set this layer's opacity between 20% to 40%.

Backlit: When adding the base colors to the subject's skin, use soft instead of harsh contrast when placing the shadows and highlights. Since the shaded part of her face is evenly diffused, don't add sharp edges. Create smooth transitions in the values and tones of the face instead of accentuating them with contrast. Because the rim lighting will be harsh and bright, the sharp lines of the highlights will help separate the subject from their background, making your painting pop. Use slightly cooler tones on the faces of backlit models, and then use bright warm colors in the backlighting. Opt for pinks, purples and hints of blue across the shadows.

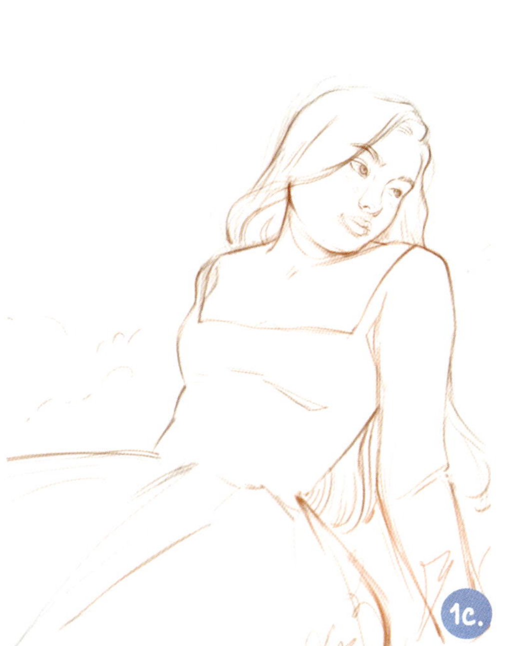

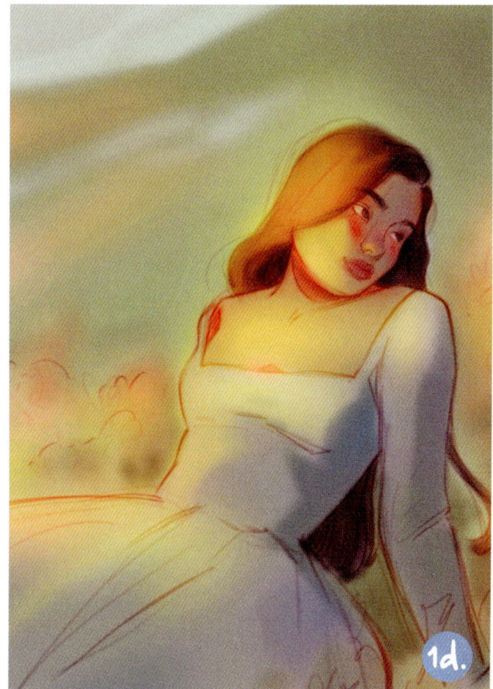

Direct Light: The subject will have harsh shadows and highlights across the face. It's easier to simplify the face into blocks of color, and then add details later in the process. When painting, you can opt for a harsh contrast in the shadows and highlights for a hot, stressful look, or you can use similar shades between the highlights and shadows while maintaining the harsh lines created by the shadows. Use less contrasted colors to mimic golden hour; this creates a glowing and cozy look in a painting rather than a harsh one. A good comparison of the techniques is to compare an unedited photo taken on a professional camera to an iPhone photo of the same subject facing the sun; somehow, iPhone photos always manage to create a glowing, even look that is flattering across all skin tones. A professional camera will capture a much more contrasted image that will need editing to lower the harshness. Use warm tones across the face, adding the most subtle hints of purple or blue in the harsh shadows to create some dimension in the painting.

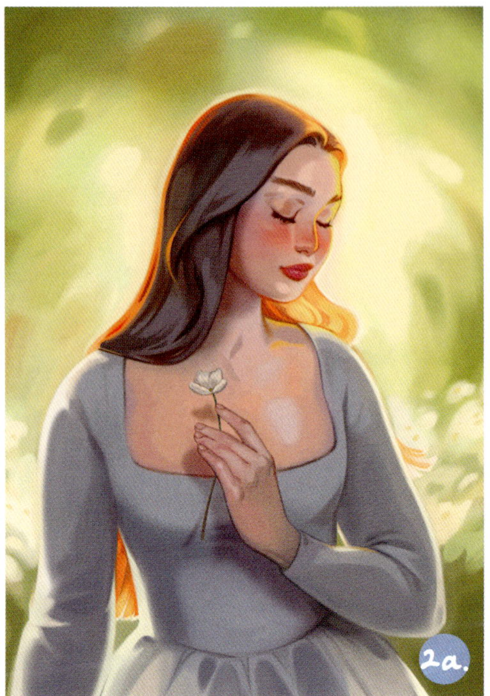

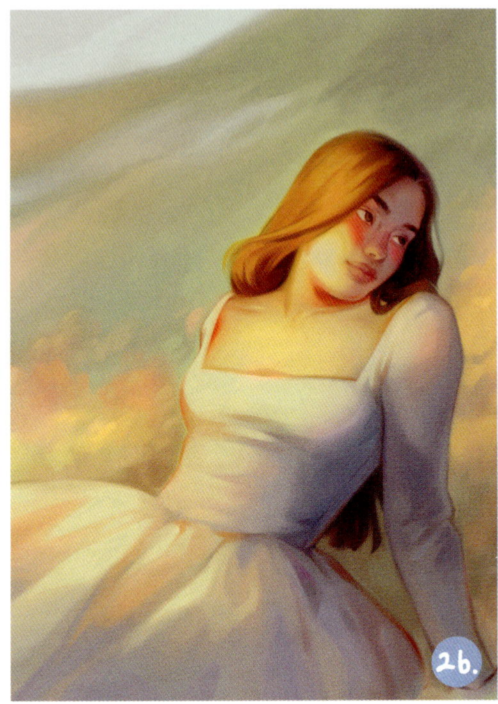

2. Once you've laid the base colors on your sketch, it's time to refine and add details.

Backlit: As you begin adding details to the face, hair and body, consider how you can add energy to the piece. Small details like adding thin brushstrokes of neon colors across the edge of the backlight can look like the chromatic aberration of a photo, making your painting more lifelike and interesting. Refrain from using too bright of highlights on the shaded portion of your painting; instead, use thin washes of muted pastels to add dimension to the face. Lavender, burnt orange, moss green and dusty rose are great examples of colors to easily integrate into the shadows without creating too much contrast. The goal is to create a pop of contrast with the bright backlight, and to keep the rest of the shaded portion relatively deep in tone.

Direct Light: Add small pops of bright colors in the shadows and highlights to bring life and energy into your piece. For example, if you're painting sunlit skin, add small pops of orange, pink and red to the skin to add interest. Add cooler tones like greens, indigos and teals to the shadows for more saturation. Use more saturated tones for bright images like this one; color is easy to play with in this lighting situation, so add a variety to the piece.

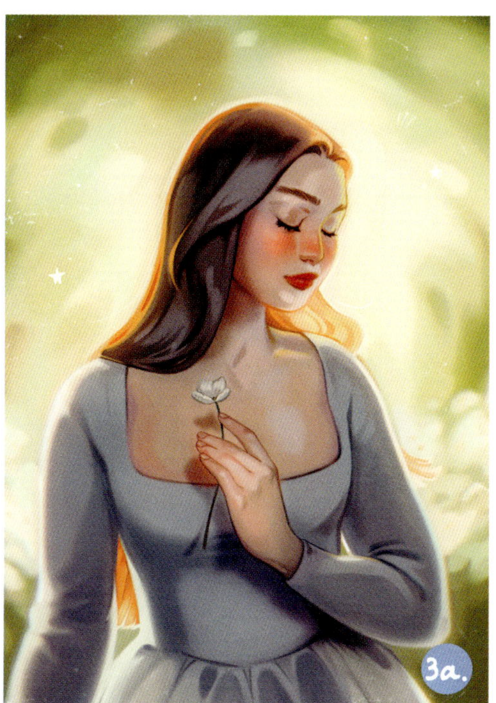

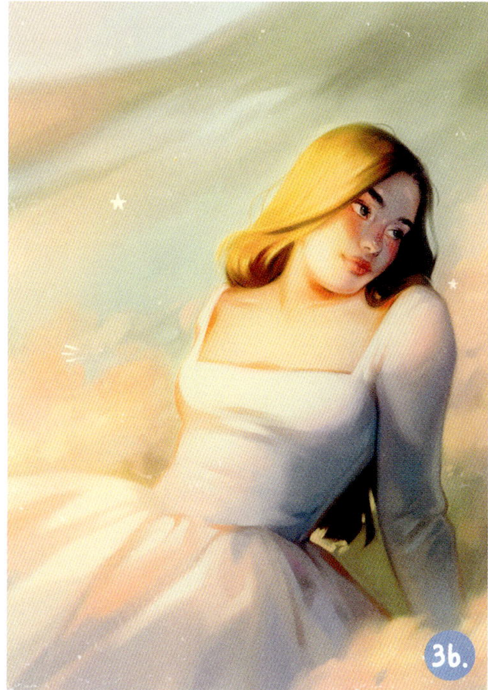

3. Add any highlights, adjustment layers and final details to make your pieces pop in their environments (see page 152 for more on adding final details).

Look at your final pieces and observe what tones you ended up using in each piece. How will you apply these concepts to your next paintings? There is a clear difference of mood and tone in the two final pieces. While I love both, I think it's cool to see how I implemented various tones and saturations into each piece to effectively communicate the feel. The backlit image is dreamier, while the direct lighting looks more playful and brighter.

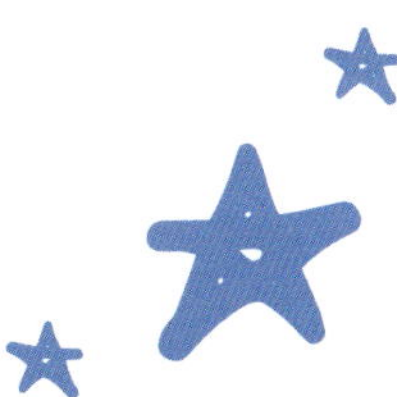

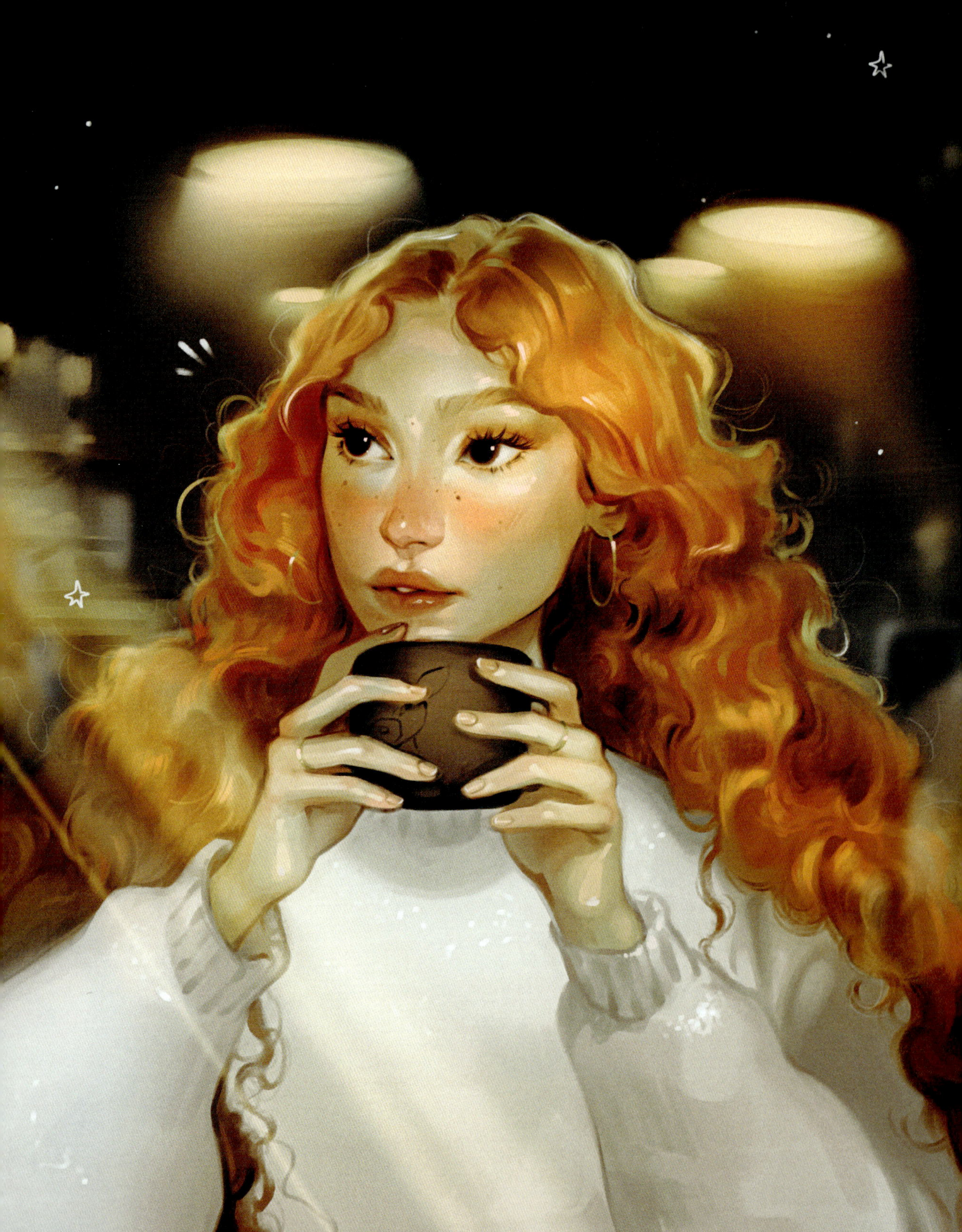

Chapter 4

REFINING YOUR TECHNIQUE

Now that you have a grasp of the basics—drawing facial features, creating strong compositions, sketching and rendering with color and lighting—it's time to explore additional concepts that will refine your technique. In this chapter, you'll learn how to paint different fabric textures, props and details, and how to use your own reference photos to inspire fantastic paintings.

FABRIC

Painting your subject's clothes can seem like a less exciting task than painting the face, but there is truly endless freedom in the brushstrokes and textures you can create when painting fabric. Since there is no one way that all fabric folds, wrinkles or moves, you have creative freedom to decide how you want to highlight your subject through their clothing. We will be looking at how to paint draping fabric, tight and loose garments and accent details.

Adding texture to your piece by painting different fabrics will add life and interest to your work. The materials and colors that you choose for your subject can carry a mood or tell a story; if your character is wearing thick velvet with a brocade pattern, you're probably letting the viewer know that your subject is wearing an expensive garment. You can dress your subject up or down depending on the scene and mood of your piece, but I personally recommend taking extra time to purposefully think up an outfit that adds texture to your piece. Organza is going to have a different texture than a jean jacket, so consider the overall feel and message that you want to communicate and choose a clothing item that will complement your idea.

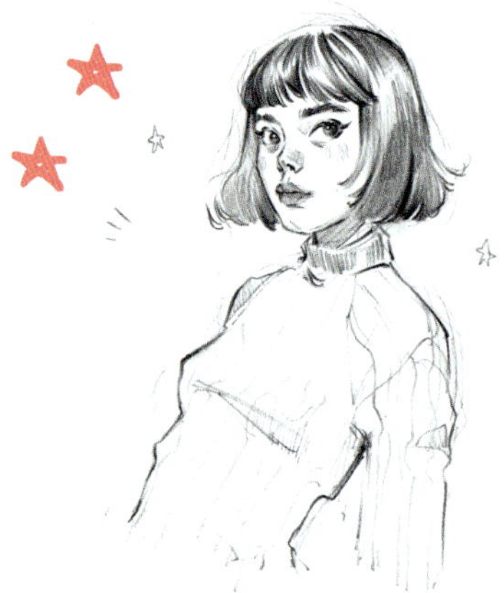

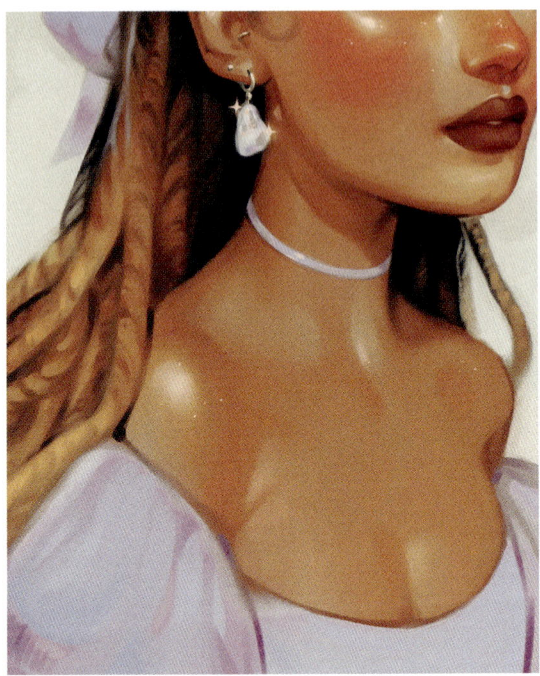

The fabric for the dress is opaque and thick.

Draping

Just like hair, the thickness and texture of fabric will indicate how gravity affects it and how the material will move and crease. Natural fabrics like cotton and linen will fold and wrinkle easily around the joints of the body. A thick cotton, like a jean jacket, would have fewer and thicker folds around the joints, while a cotton T-shirt would have multiple thinner wrinkles and creases. Use bolder lines and details when painting a stiff fabric like that of a jean jacket. A lightweight fabric like organza or tulle could be sewn to stick up and be puffy. When painting a tulle skirt, layer your brushstrokes to create a soft and fluffy effect.

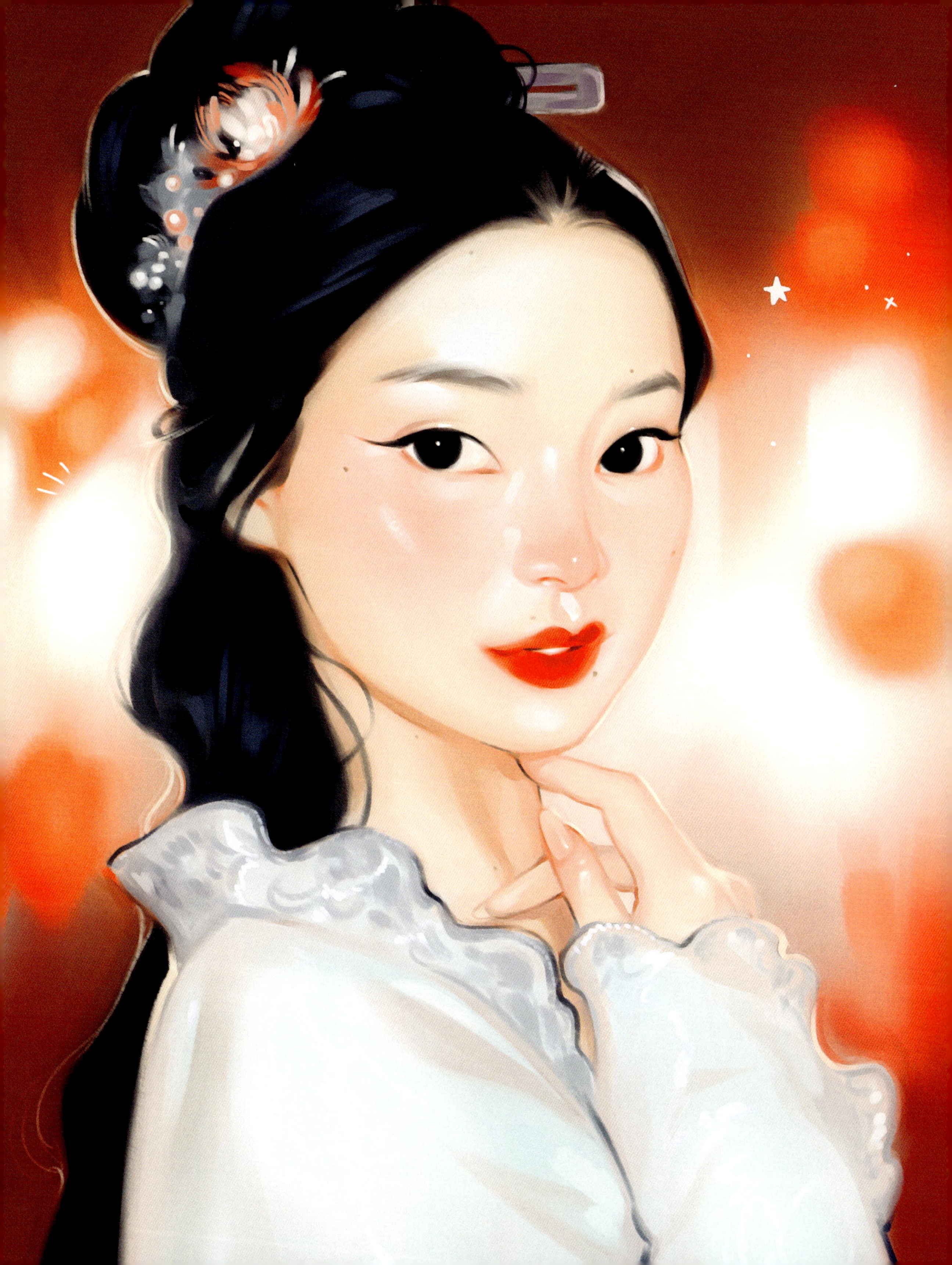

PROMPT: PAINT FIVE SKETCHES OF TEXTURED CLOTHING

Pick five reference photos of models wearing differently textured clothing, such as a flowy dress or stiff denim, and paint each individual texture. Write down your strengths and weaknesses, as well as any pointers for the future.

What brushstrokes are you using to paint your piece and create the proper details? How challenging is it to paint varying opacities in fabrics? Do the wrinkles in the fabric change based on its texture and thickness? Do you have the patience to incorporate texture or patterns into clothing?

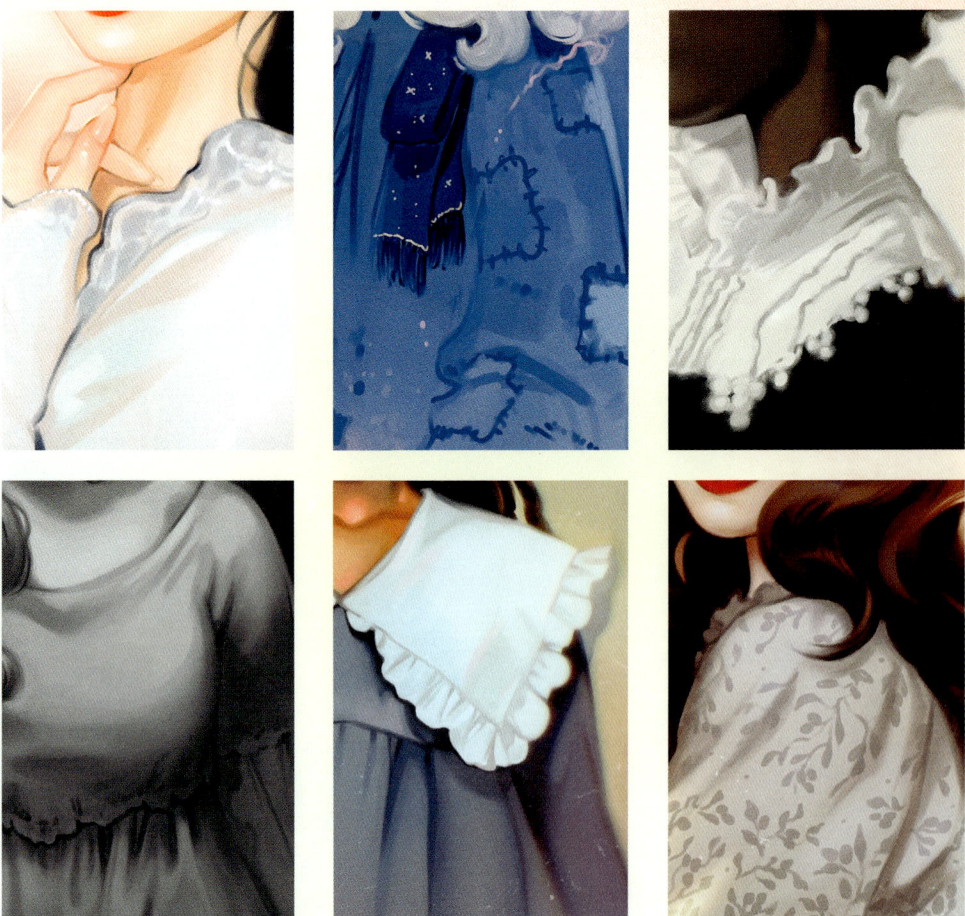

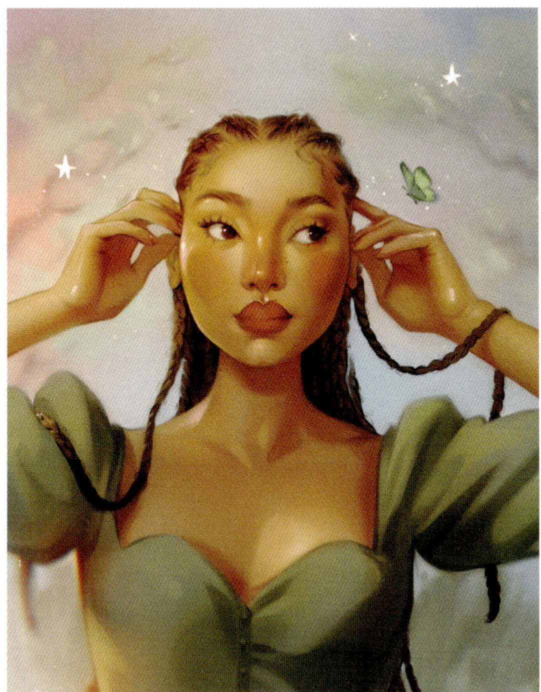

Notice how the fabric stretches around the arms as they're raised.

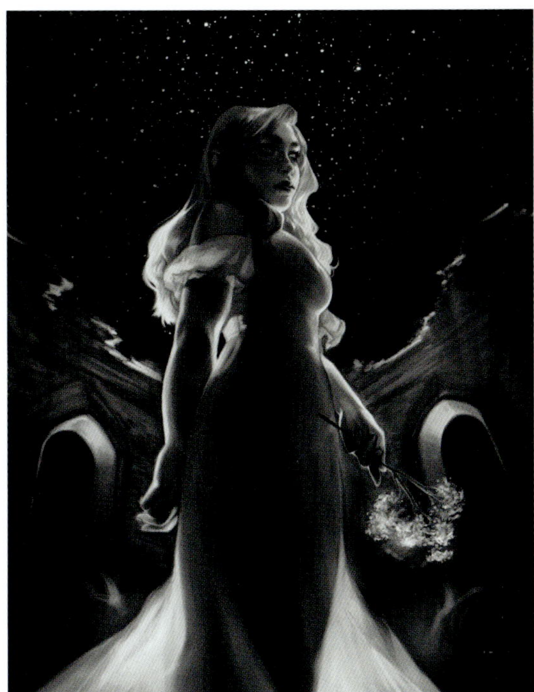

The sheer fabric allows light to filter through.

Tight Versus Loose Clothing

When painting tight clothing, the garment will wrinkle around the curves and joints of the body. Without adding these creases, the garment will look like it has been spray-painted on. You can add a realistic touch by adding loose folds around where the garment might not be perfectly fitted to your subject's figure. Tighter fabrics will also have thinner, tighter wrinkles than loose clothing will.

Loose clothing will drape over the figure of your subject instead of clinging to them and often have looser folds and wrinkles. As the artist, choose garments that will be balanced for your subject; if your subject is wearing a tight top, give them loose pants or vice versa. This comes down to your personal style and what you want to communicate in your artwork, but make intentional decisions with your subject's outfit choices.

A combination of tight and loose clothing can add an interesting textural component; a tight corset with a loose blouse underneath can add a lot of texture to a piece with contrasting fabrics and structures.

PROJECT 13: PAINT A CHARACTER WEARING A FLOWY DRESS

Keep your marks soft and rounded, with the goal of relaying both transparency and depth to the fabric. After you're finished, ask yourself: Did you face any challenges in this painting process? Write down what was successful in your piece and what you need to practice more.

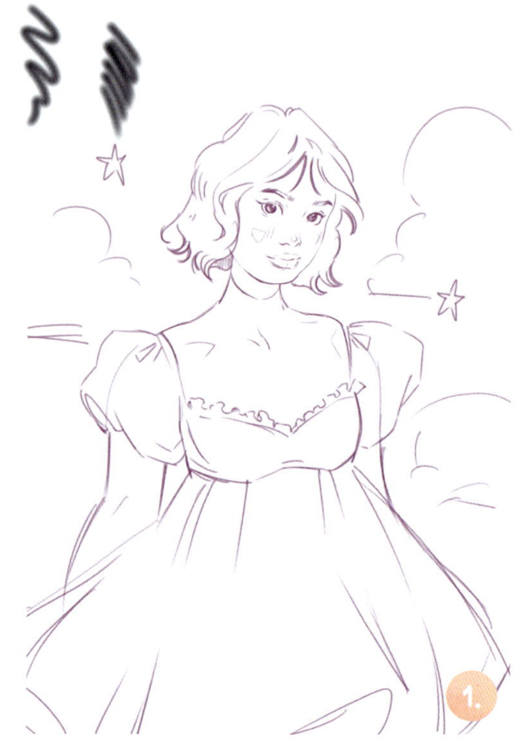

1. Create a canvas of 4 x 5 inches (10 x 13 cm) at 300 dpi (see page 16 for canvas sizing). After setting the base layer to a background color of your choice, create a new Multiply layer for your sketch. With the Soft Airbrush (see page 17 for brushes), start with the base sketch. Make sure to tighten your lines up so that the composition is clearly defined. Use the shapes of the clothing to tell a story; I love to create pieces where the clothing defies gravity. The rounded shapes of the dress are soft and ethereal and take up most of the frame, making it the focal point of the piece. Set this layer's opacity between 20% to 40%.

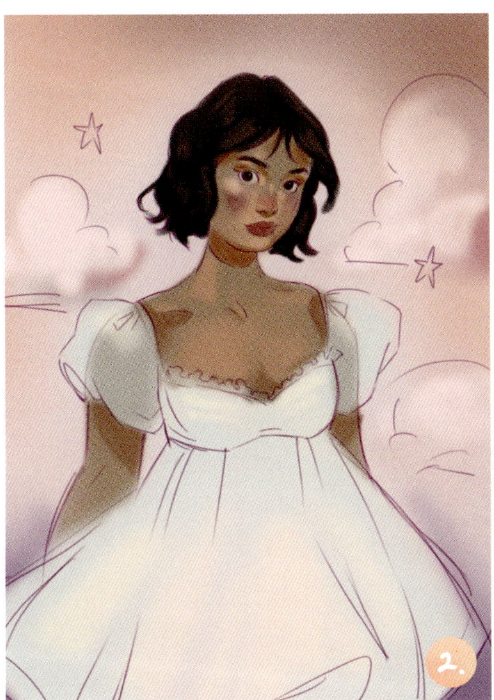

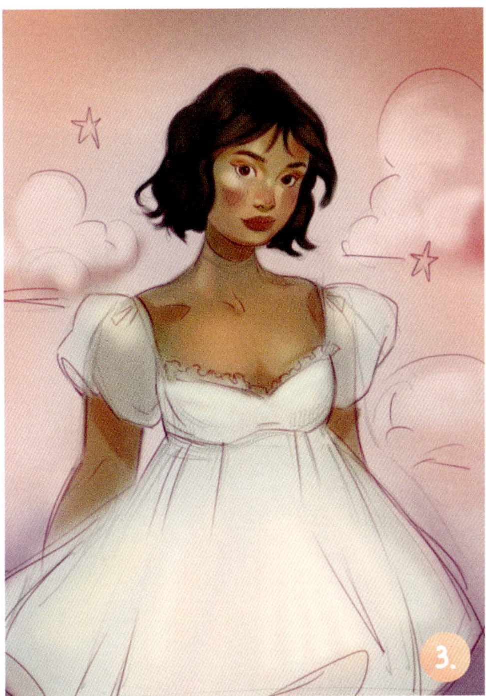

2. On a layer under your sketch, use the Soft Airbrush and add the base colors. For areas that indicate transparency, like the arms underneath the puffy sleeves, I block in the skin in the same way I do the face. Using light pressure with my brush, I choose my sleeve color and gently block in the tone to let some of the skin peek through the sleeves.

3. Add any adjustment layers needed to unify the tones in the piece (see page 18 for adjustment layers). Using the Soft Airbrush on a Soft Light layer, create a vignette around the edges of the painting with the center of the portrait brightened up.

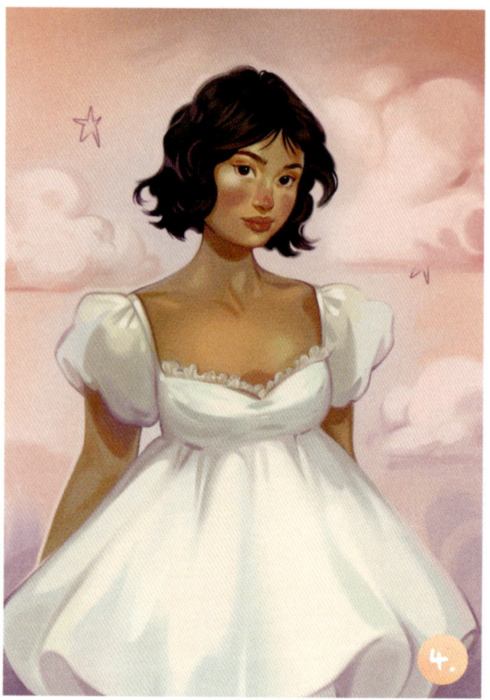

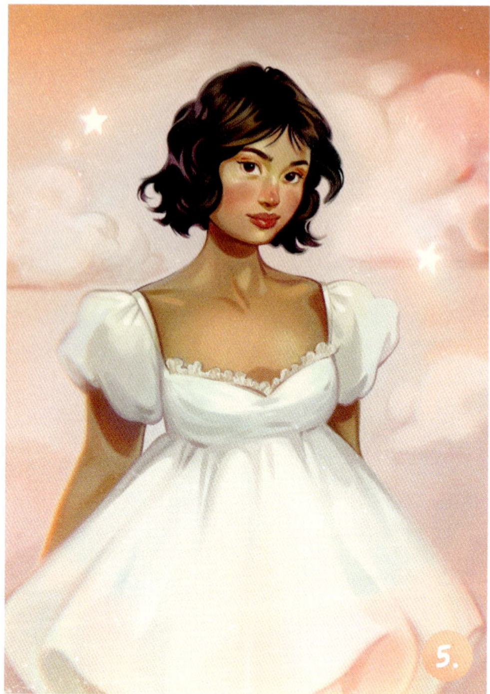

4. Right-click on any layer, select "Merge visible into new layer" and begin rendering your piece using the Oil brush. Use light pressure when painting lower transparency, creating the illusion of flowy layers of fabric. Grab a mirror and observe the way your own clothing folds around your joints and body. Can you incorporate any of these folds into your painting? I paint both my subject's hair and dress flowing in the same direction, making it look like a breeze has just flown past her.

5. Add adjustment layers to unify the colors of the piece, as well as final touches, such as highlights, glows, stars and halos (see page 152 for more on final touches). These small and sharp details perfectly pull the piece together and give the viewer even more to look at and admire.

Details

Many garments have small wrinkles and folds around the seams, and painting those details will add character to your piece. A quick way to add interest to a plain garment is by adding ribbing, a hem to the collar, a folded-over collar, a lettuce-edge hem, ruching, ruffles or embroidery. You can suggest sewn seams by looking at your own clothes and observing how fabric drapes and folds where it's been sewn.

You can also indicate shine in your fabric by using higher-contrast light and dark tones as you're painting folds of the fabric. Using low-contrast shades will portray a regular, matte fabric, while high contrast can be used to detail leather, polyester, latex, organza, etc. Use the sheerness of the fabric to add depth to your piece; if you're painting a sheer top, use light strokes to suggest what is on underneath. You can always paint the base shape and values of a garment without added details, and then add a pattern to it using adjustment layers. The way to convincingly paint a pattern on fabric with folds is to vary the angle and size of the pattern in a consistent manner. Adding a suggestion of the pattern to a fold is a better idea than placing that pattern directly onto the fold and not distorting it with the fabric.

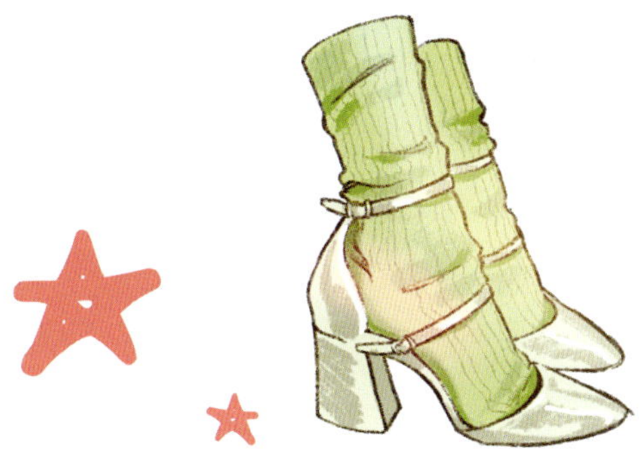

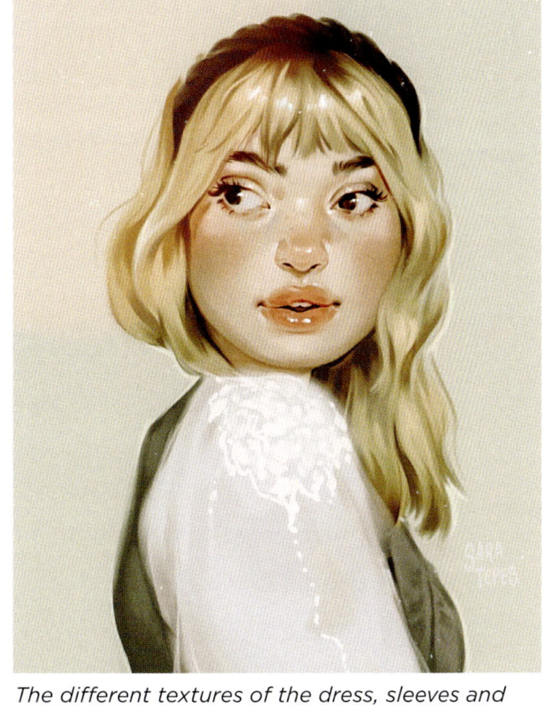

The different textures of the dress, sleeves and headband add dimension to the piece.

Choose colors that will complement the palette of the piece and will make sense in their environment. If you're painting a dark-themed piece, don't add a neon clothing item, unless you are deliberately creating contrast and emphasis in your piece through the character's clothing choices. Choose the colors of your fabrics and garments to match up with, or thoughtfully and intentionally contrast, your color palette.

PROJECT 14: PAINT A CHARACTER WEARING INTRICATELY PATTERNED CLOTHING

If you like, make the piece of textured clothing the focal point of the piece. After you've finished, think on the following: Did you have the patience to work through the intricate details of the fabrics? What would you do differently next time? Write down your experience and what you learned.

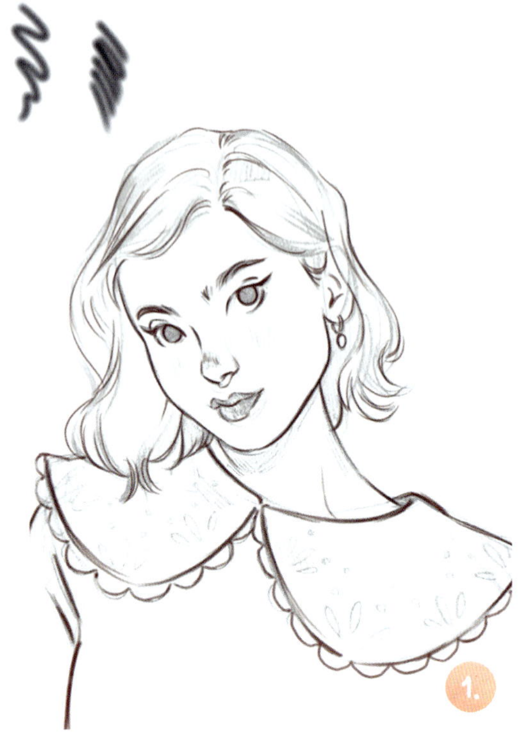

1. Create a canvas of 4 x 5 inches (10 x 13 cm) at 300 dpi (see page 16 for canvas sizing). After setting the base layer to a background color of your choice, create a new Multiply layer for your sketch. With the Soft Airbrush (see page 17 for brushes), start off with the base sketch. Make sure to tighten your lines up so that the composition is clearly defined. Draw in the basic shapes that the eyelets will take, knowing that you will render these shapes in Step 4. Set this layer's opacity between 20% to 40%.

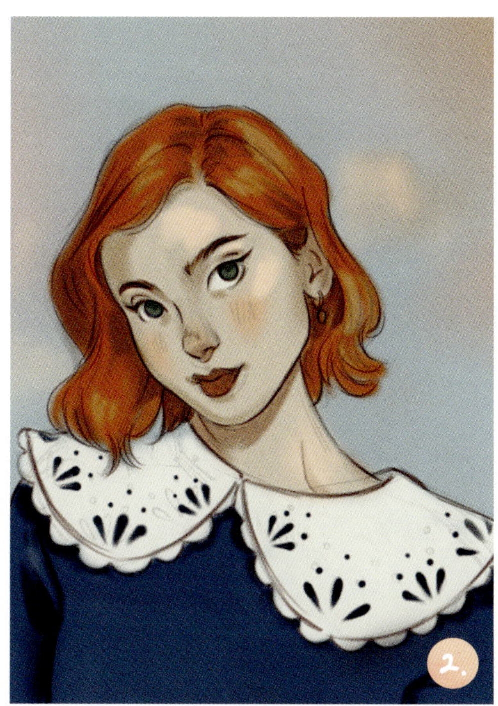

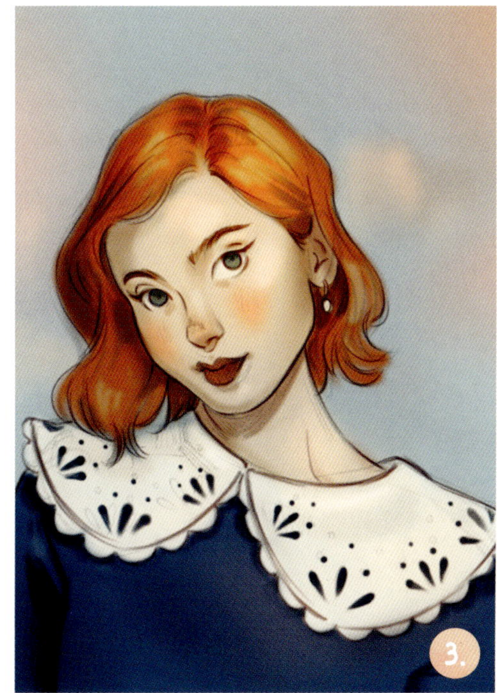

2. On a new layer underneath your sketch, add the base colors. Since the focus of this piece is on the texture of the eyelets on the subject's blouse, I kept the background muted to contrast with the light collar and skin tone.

3. Add adjustment layers to bring warmth and brightness to the subject's face and hair (see page 18 for adjustment layers). Use golden tones across the highlights and warm gray tones across the shadows on the side of the face and collar.

4. Right-click on any layer, select "Merge visible into new layer" and begin rendering your piece using the Oil brush. Render the shapes of the face, hair and blouse, color picking between the tones you place on the canvas to create unity in the painting.

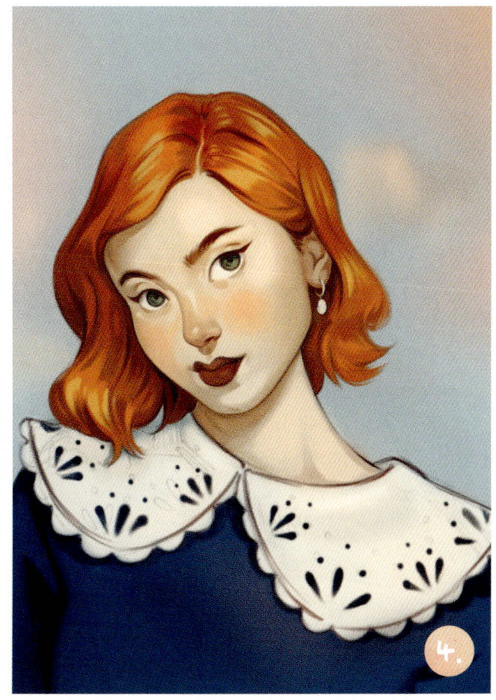

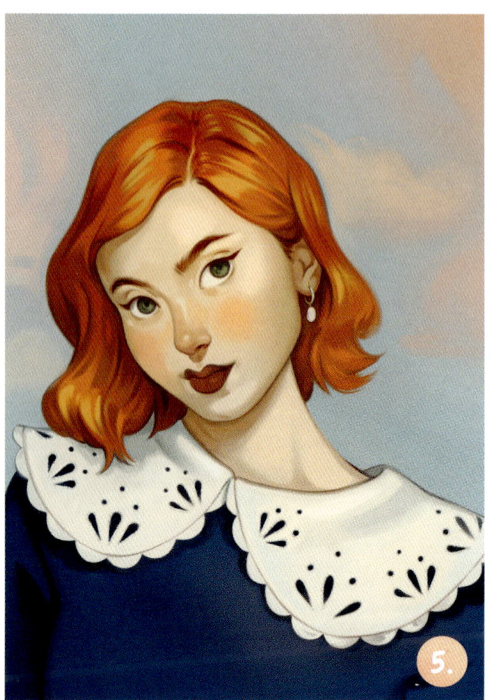

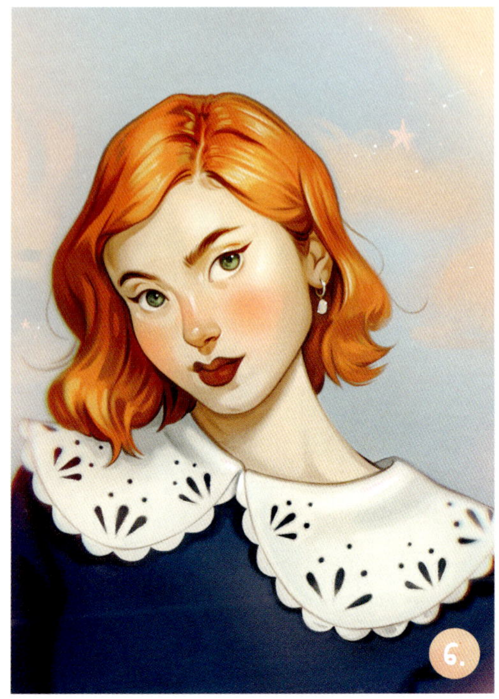

5. Add any patterns or details to the top of the fabric. Stripes, polka dots and embroidery may seem like daunting elements to add; remember the mass and volume of your subject, and paint the patterns and details based on the basic rounded forms underneath all the details. The eyelets wrap around the Peter Pan collar, and the scalloped details are shadowed by the collar they are sewn to. Take a reference photo of patterned and draped fabric if you have a hard time visualizing how the pattern would move across fabric.

6. Add adjustment layers to unify the shadows, highlights and colors of the piece. Add any final touches, like glows or stars to the painting to polish it. (See page 152 for more on adding final details.)

PROPS & BACKGROUNDS

Once you've completed painting your subject and their clothing, it's time to tackle the additional touches of props and backgrounds. Adding props is a good way to keep the viewer's eyes engaged with the painting, as well as adding story and strengthening themes in the piece. You can choose to paint either a simple or complex background depending on how detailed you want the final image to be; next, we will cover which props and backgrounds will work well with your desired end goal.

Props

Props can be crucial in conveying your desired emotion or message; they add interest and added detail to a piece and will take it to the next level. You can use props in your paintings to give your subject something to do or hold. When deciding on what props you want to incorporate, try to find or take reference photos of that object in the correct angle. If your subject's hand is wrapped around it, take photos of your own hand holding that object. If you don't have that option, hold something with a similar shape and position your fingers the way you want them to appear in your final painting. Hard objects like cups or books will be slightly more difficult to draw correctly, so start off with an accurate sketch, color block the basic shapes and work down to the details. You can add weathering to the surfaces of your props like chips, scratches or dirt to add further dimension.

Painting Backgrounds

When planning out a portrait, you must decide whether you want a simple or complex background. Most of the time, I like to paint simple backgrounds with subtle gradients, light leaks, stars, sparkles, dust or other particles floating in the air. To be honest, this choice comes out of my own laziness and restlessness. By the time I've finished painting the skin, hair, clothing and hands, I have no patience to paint a detailed background. However, I think it would be wise to take my own advice and step away from the painting process until I have a little courage built up to finish the piece correctly.

You can decide to add an indication of a background or a detailed one. Adding an indication of a background can have a dreamy, romantic feel. The focus is still primarily on your subject, while the background serves to add depth to the piece. This should not take too long or be too complicated since you can use any soft brush with quick, loose strokes to achieve this effect. I find this to be a good idea when painting scenes with golden hour backlighting, since you can easily add indication of an environment without explicitly painting out every detail. You can

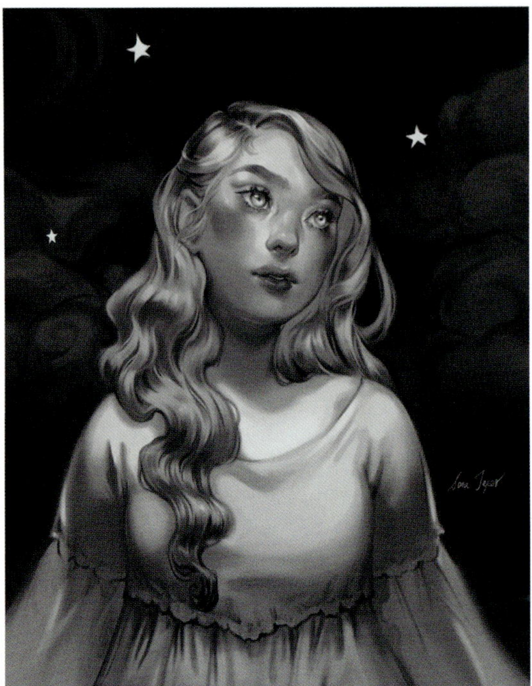

When in doubt, I paint clouds as the background!

paint light streaming through a suggestion of trees instead of explicitly painting every tree trunk, branch and leaf. This is arguably a dreamier and more impressionistic approach to finalizing your painting.

Deciding to paint a detailed background, however, takes more planning. It is important to have your color palette and lighting correctly placed to achieve a realistic effect. The goal when painting a detailed background is to make the subject blend in with their environment. The eyes should flow over the details rather than be caught up on how the foreground and background do not match up. When painting backgrounds, use the concepts discussed in the chapter on composition (page 88).

Whether you want to finish the painting with a minimal or maximal approach, take time to think about what would be most effective in the finished artwork. Color pick often and place the same values and hues around the foreground and background to unify the piece.

Foreground Elements

In both scenarios, you can add foreground elements to take your work to the next level. If your character is out in nature, feel free to add flowers, leaves or grass in the foreground to add depth and dimension to the painting. You can set this foreground painting to a Gaussian blur in order to soften it up and have the artwork look more photographic. When detailing so many portions of a piece, sometimes it's nice for the viewer's eyes to have a break from the details.

Reference Photos for Background Inspiration

When looking for reference photos, feel free to check out a royalty-free website like Unsplash or take your own photos for inspiration. If you live in a particularly beautiful area, take advantage of that and utilize your scenery for reference images. You can take phone photos of mountains, lakes, fields of flowers, the forest or a sunset across the horizon. Keeping a collection of photographs for later paintings can make the brainstorming and ideation process much simpler. If you do take your own photos and love the colors and tones in them, color pick from your photos to learn what colors you like together and how different hues work effectively in different scenes.

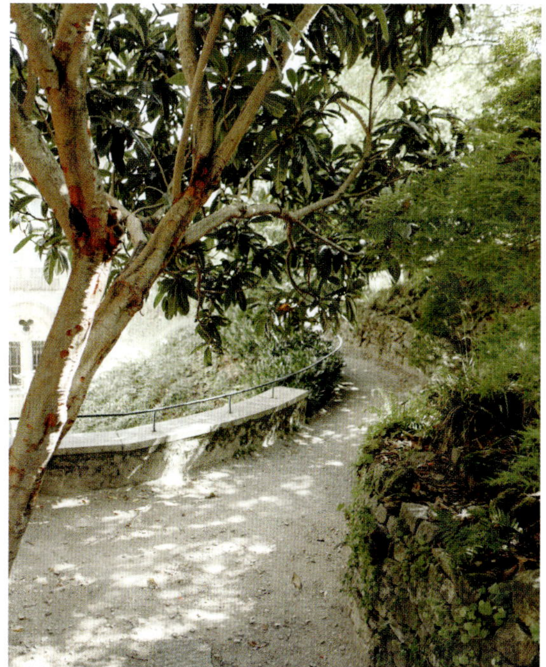

Place the subject in this scene, or use the basic colors to inspire an abstract background.

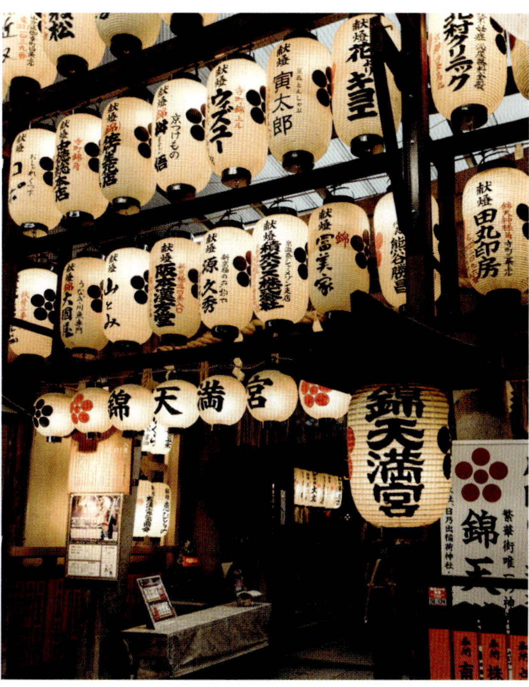

Use the photo to inspire the feeling of your piece or directly refer to it for the background.

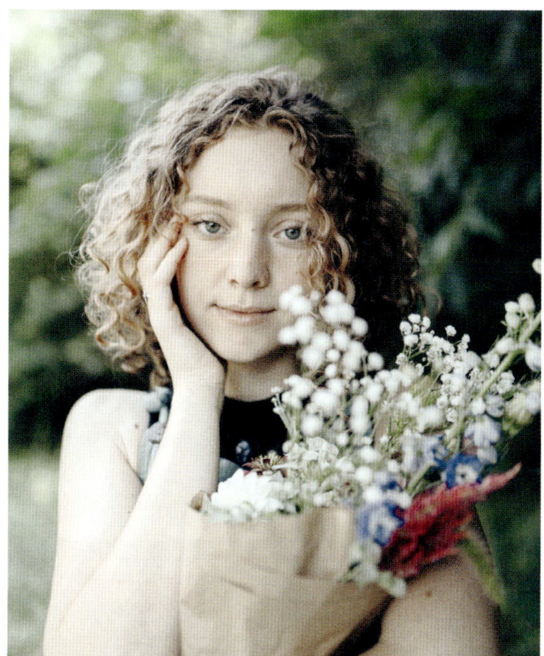

The diffused lighting in the shade adds a creaminess to the painting, while the pops of color from the flowers add colorful texture.

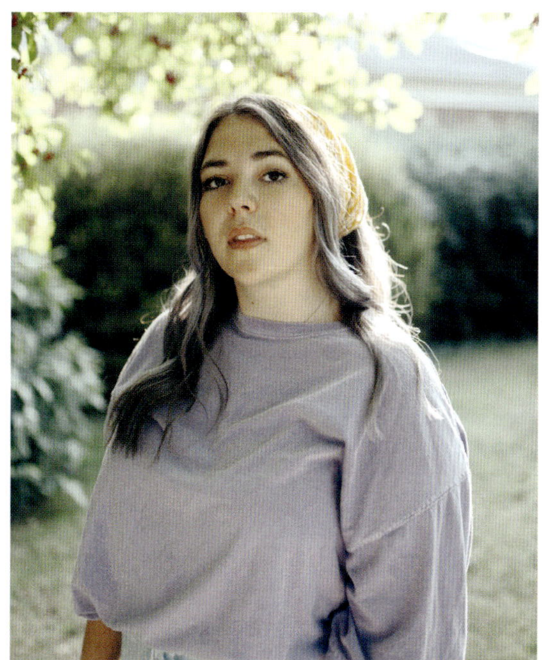

This reference provides a strong example of leading lines in the background, backlighting and fabric texture.

PROJECT 15: PAINT A PORTRAIT WITH A COMPLEX BACKGROUND

You can paint nature, a coffee shop, something surreal or your own totally unique idea. Be patient with the process and jot down what you enjoyed and disliked about the process. If you don't feel like heavy backgrounds incorporate well into your portraits, write down the reason why you think they don't work. If, however, you learn that you love the added detail, write down how you plan to incorporate this design detail into your next pieces.

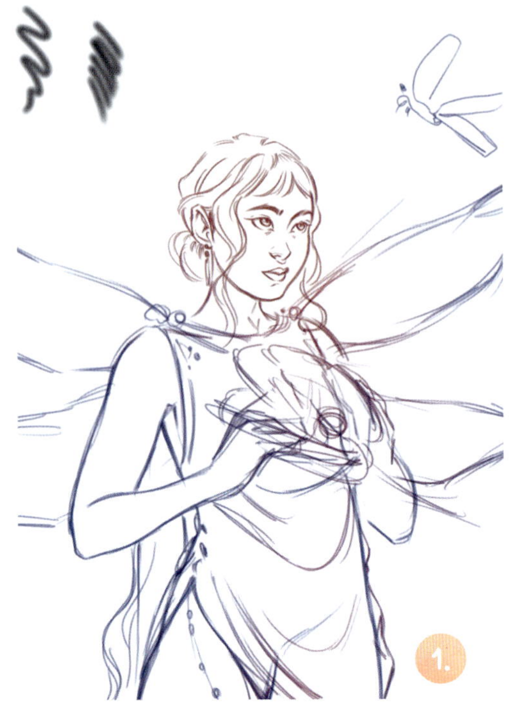

1. Create a canvas of 4 x 5 inches (10 x 13 cm) at 300 dpi (see page 16 for canvas sizing). After setting the base layer to a background color of your choice, create a new Multiply layer for your sketch. With the Soft Airbrush (see page 17 for brushes), start with the base sketch. When deciding to paint a piece with a detailed background, take extra time on your initial sketch layer to decide on a balanced composition. When dealing with a busy image, it's important to know how to fade unimportant elements into the background while highlighting the key elements. Even though the subject is standing near a river, the background doesn't need to clearly show the riverbed to indicate its presence. Set this layer's opacity between 20% to 40%.

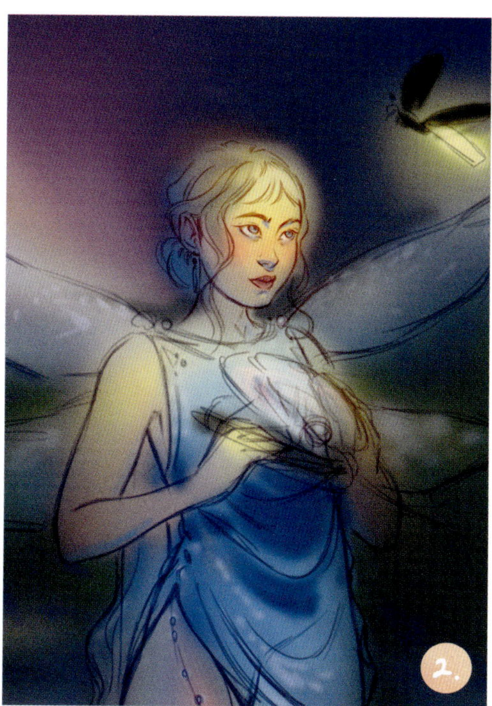

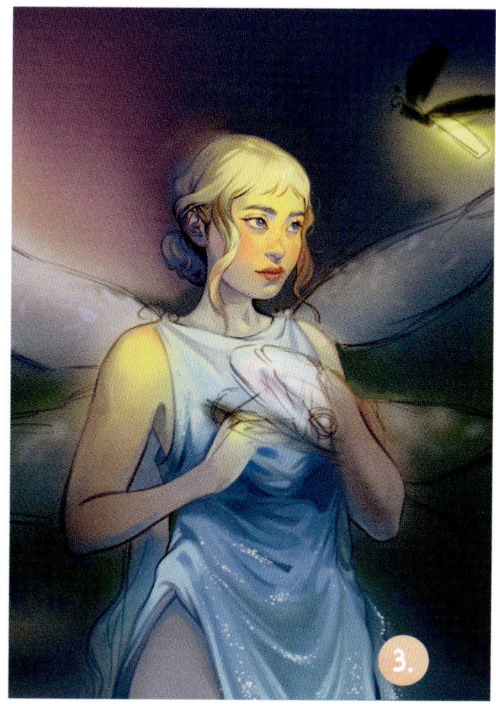

2. On a new layer underneath your sketch, use the Soft Airbrush and place your base colors down; remember the rules of composition and color theory (pages 88 and 104), and utilize the proper values and saturation to bring attention to the main subject and elements while pushing secondary elements into the background. I use a slightly darker, more muted tone for the background elements so that the subject can pop as it is illuminated by the glow of the lightning bug. Use adjustment layers to unify the tones in the painting.

3. Right-click on any layer, select "Merge visible into new layer" and begin rendering your piece using the Oil brush. Work on your character's face and facial expression, as that is the focal point, adding sharp highlights and small details like eyelashes and freckles to grab the viewer's attention. As you're adding details to the background, use light and shadow to draw the viewer's eye across the piece. I don't focus on the background in the first stages of adding detail, but I do keep lighting and color tones in mind as I paint the subject.

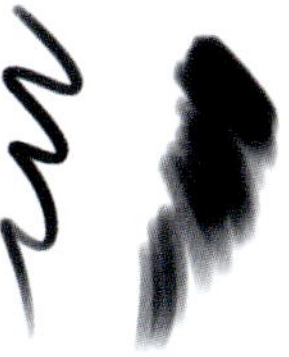

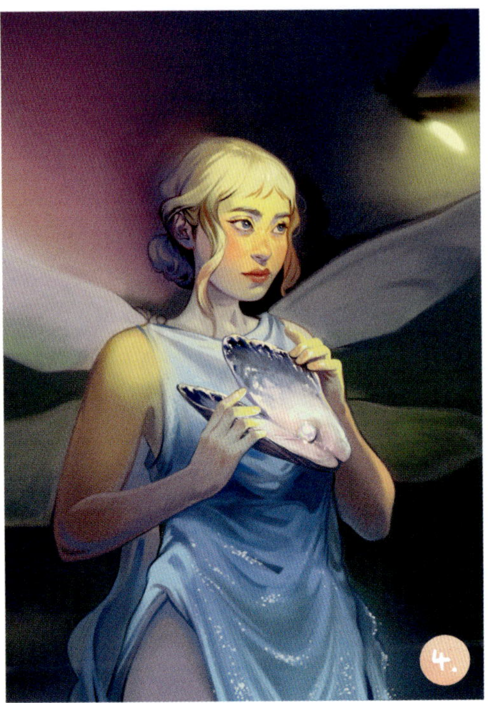

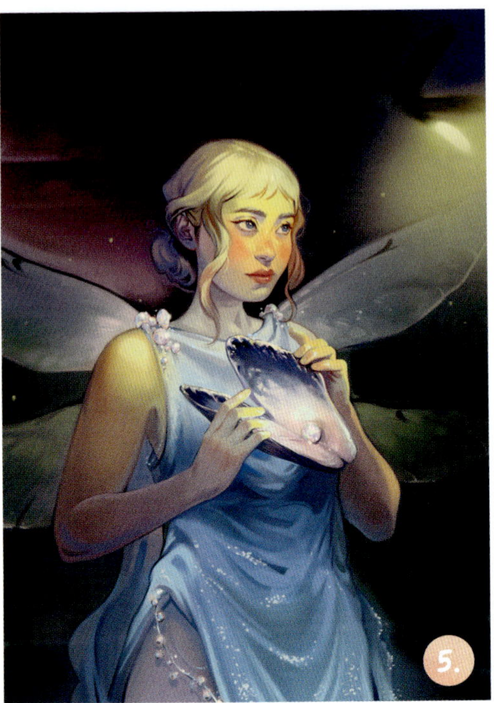

4. Detail the props, background and foreground. Render the pearl and mussel in the fairy's hands, using a variety of pastel tones to create an iridescent effect in the shell. With some of the same tones as the ones in the shell, I render the lightning bug on its own layer; since it is in the foreground, add Gaussian blur to the layer to make the bug slightly out of focus. Once blurred, render it further with the Oil brush if you want to bring back any lost brush texture. The background can also be blurred, or you can use soft pressure to create a soft effect.

5. With the Oil brush, finish detailing the dress, pearls and wings, using a variety of blues, purples, greens and pinks to create a pearlescent effect. Use the Navigator window (see page 14 for program layouts) to check the overall composition and hierarchy of colors and lighting in the painting.

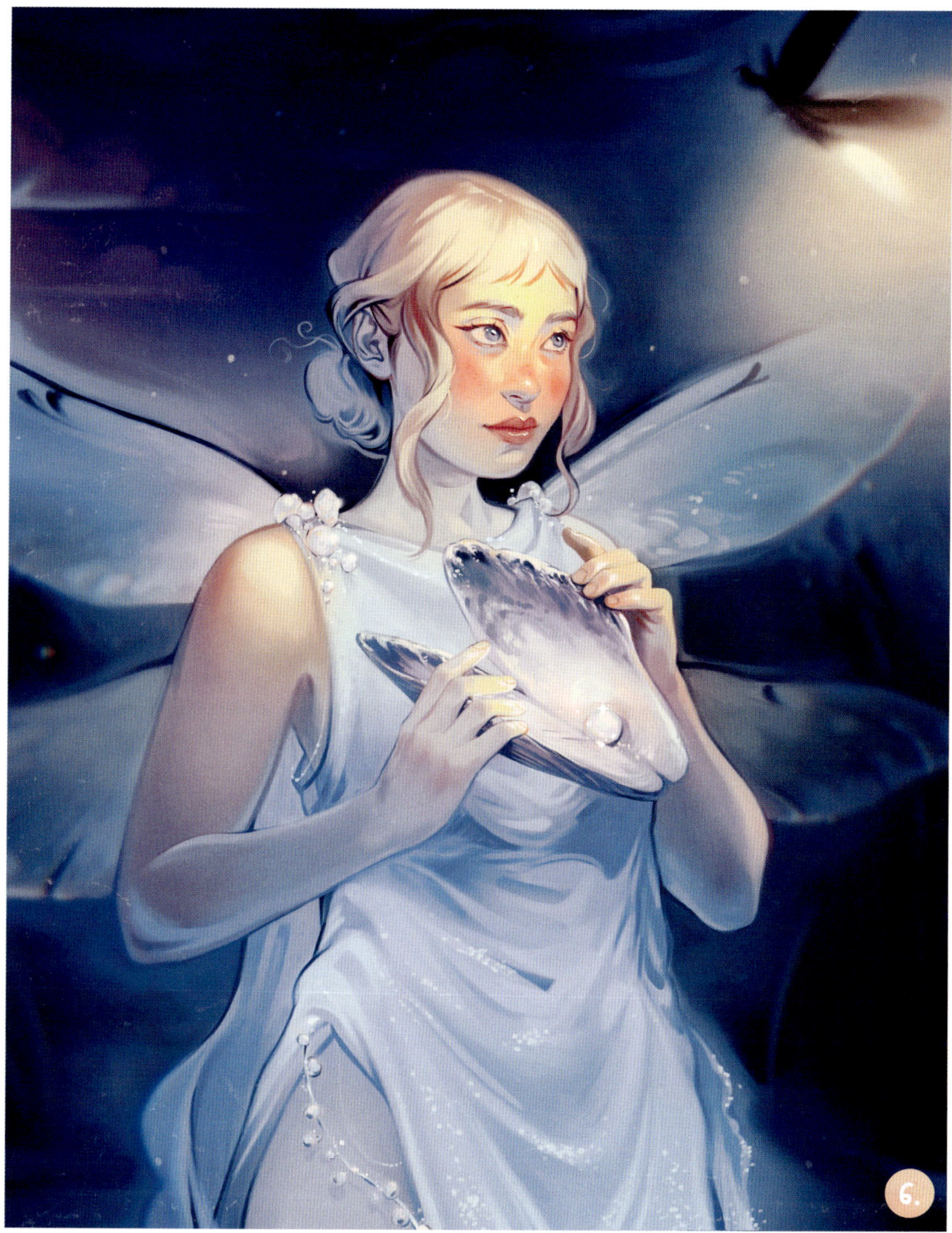

6. Add adjustment layers to add a cohesive touch, blending the background tones more seamlessly together. Gently shade in some darkness around the corners of the piece to emphasize the twilight hour. Add any last details, like the faint glows of distant fireflies and reflections of the warm light on the pearls. (See the next section for more on adding final touches.)

FINISHING TOUCHES

Final touches are necessary to tie all the elements of your painting together. One of the best tricks I learned for leveling up my pieces and being truly proud of the end result was that I could add small details, adjustments and filters to make my paintings pop. I never considered adding photo presets to my paintings since I thought it was "cheating;" in reality, presets were one of the many tools I was offered as an artist working with a digital medium.

Now that you've learned how to ideate, sketch, paint the face, hair and clothing, and add interest through props and backgrounds, it's time to add the finishing touches to your piece, like adjustment layers, light leaks and specks of dust, and sign the final painting.

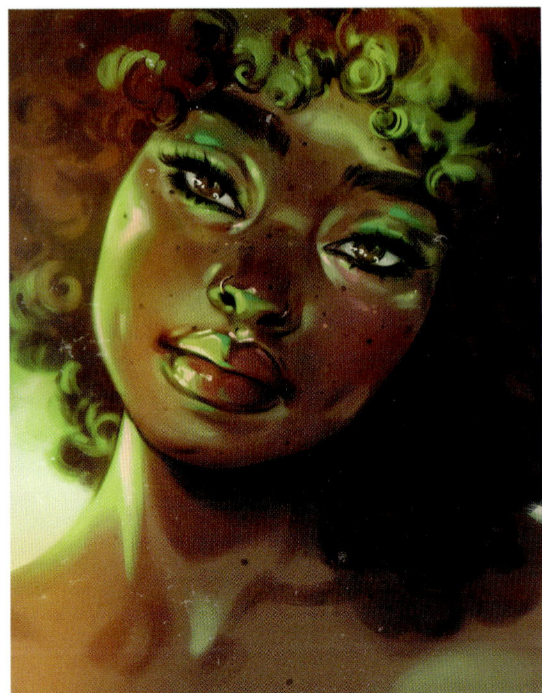

Add finishing touches with small details, such as freckles and colorful glitter around the cheeks and eyes.

Painted Final Touches

On a new layer, use a small detailed brush to start painting in freckles, glitter, sharp highlights, sharp eyelashes, deep and intensified shadows and any added skin texture. I recommend saving these marks until you are satisfied with the rest of your image, since it is important to work on and be pleased with the whole before adding small details. Assess the situation; is your painting too busy or is it missing an element that would push it to the next level? Take a break from the painting process if you want to rush through these marks and come back to the painting with fresh eyes. Take the extra time to work over any areas you rushed.

I love painting small details like little stars, firefly glows or small glossy details. I think that these finishing marks give so much life and vibrancy to your piece. One of the personal touches I add to every painting is hand-drawn five-point stars. I seriously love adding this small signature mark to my paintings; it adds a magical touch! I recommend experimenting and finding a signature mark to add to your pieces.

Adjustments

There are several tools that I use to add character to my paintings; my goal is to achieve a dreamy, film effect. Firstly, I recommend starting with adjustment layers; you can add a Multiply or Soft Light layer to deepen gradients or shadows in your piece, or to add extra vibrancy to the colors. You can also use the Hard Light mode to intensify rim lighting or add light leaks to your piece. After you've played with these modes, you can use a Curves layer to tweak the values and colors in your piece to be more contrasted and unified.

At this part of the process, bring your painting into any photography editing software of your choice to add a photography preset. You can find these for free or for sale online; since I edit in Adobe Lightroom®, I use Lightroom-specific presets. Don't worry too much about the intensity of the filter as long as you like the tones that the filter adds to the piece. I'm only looking to manipulate the colors of the piece and to add grain. Once I've finished these adjustments, I bring the exported file back into my Clip Studio Paint file over the rest of my painted layers and adjust the opacity of the edited Lightroom file until I like the overall tones in the piece. I "Merge visible into new layer" and add a Sharpen filter to accentuate the sharp edges in the piece like the eyelashes, rim lighting and sharp details I placed down. You can rotate through all these steps however works for your own painting process; sometimes, I will go back in and add extra highlights and details to the piece after I've made all these adjustments.

Once you are happy with the tones and sharpness of your painting, it's time to add light leaks and dust scratches. You can make your own textures or light leaks by finding scans of or scanning textured paper or film rolls. There are many free resources online that provide light leaks and textures; download and experiment with these until you find your favorites. You can manually paint in the dust marks or use a blending mode like Hard Light to add a light leak texture to your piece.

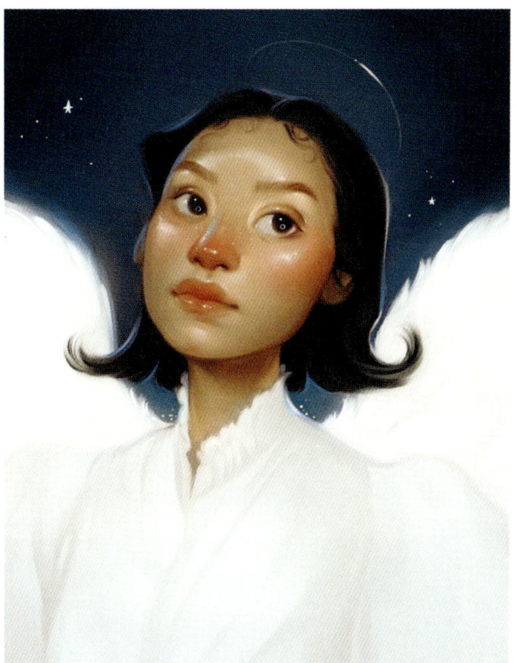

A crisp and clear appearance doesn't necessarily mean a better result. This painting needs an ethereal touch.

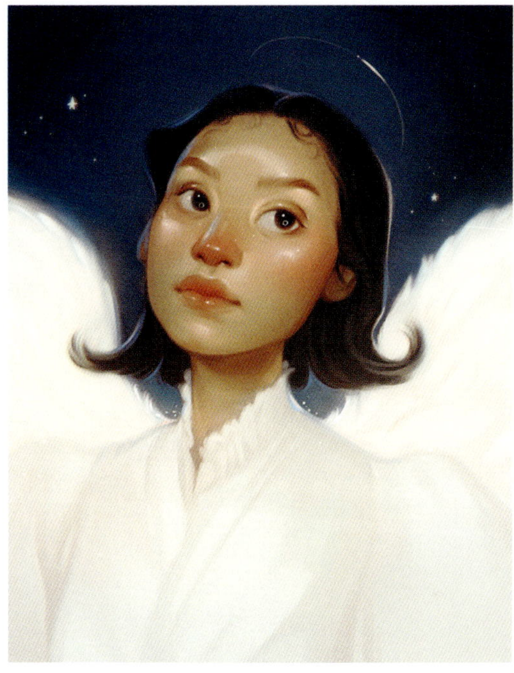

The light leak creates a subtle difference.

PROMPT: ADD ADJUSTMENT LAYERS TO A PAST PAINTING

Take one of the paintings you completed in a past project and add adjustment layers, grain and light leaks to it based on your own tastes. What techniques will you be incorporating into your future paintings?

How do color adjustments enhance your final product? Color pick colors from the finished image; what surprises you, and what can you learn from these colors?

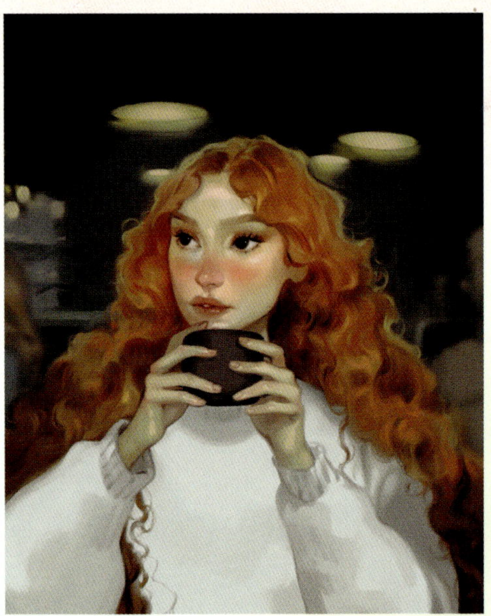

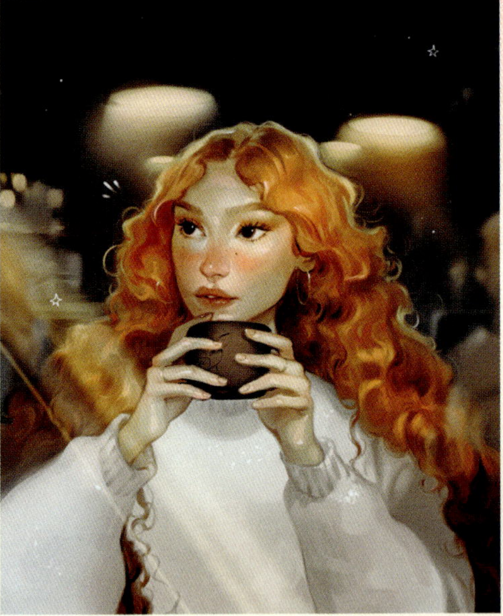

Using Overlay and Soft Light layers, I painted warm golden glows to the hanging lights in the background and a subtle highlight to the face and hair. I used a Hard Light layer to draw diagonal slashes of gold across the top of the canvas to mimic the reflection of a window. I added a Curves adjustment layer to give the shadows a faint indigo tint and to brighten the highlights. Finally, I added freckles, specks of pollen, glitter on the sweater and a few stars to finish the painting.

Signing

Once you have finalized your piece, it's time to add your signature. I usually use a lighter tone found in the piece; you can use your full name, handle or whatever moniker you desire to go by. I recommend saving a duplicate file without your signature in case you would like to create prints and hand sign them. If you are posting to social media, integrate your signature or handle into an area of the piece that is closer to the details or middle of the painting. While reshares and art theft are almost inevitable at this point, it's a good idea to weave your signature and handle into the painting, so that viewers will be able to find your account if your art is reposted without permission or credit.

FINAL THOUGHTS

I hope that you've learned some skills and tricks to digitally paint more easily and efficiently, whether in the ideation process or finishing touches. Don't forget to sketch often and to jot down ideas for paintings when they come to you. Digital painting is such a forgiving and creative medium, and the possibilities for growth are endless. I hope that you continue painting and growing in your journey, and that this book can be a reference to you in the future.

PROMPT: REPAINT YOUR FIRST DIGITAL PAINTING

Mirroring the first prompt in this book (page 27), choose a favorite food to reference for a portrait painting. Using the color palette of the food, brainstorm your composition, sketch out several thumbnails and create a portrait, utilizing the skills you've learned.

How has your process changed since the first prompt? Are there any steps in the painting process that are more streamlined for you?

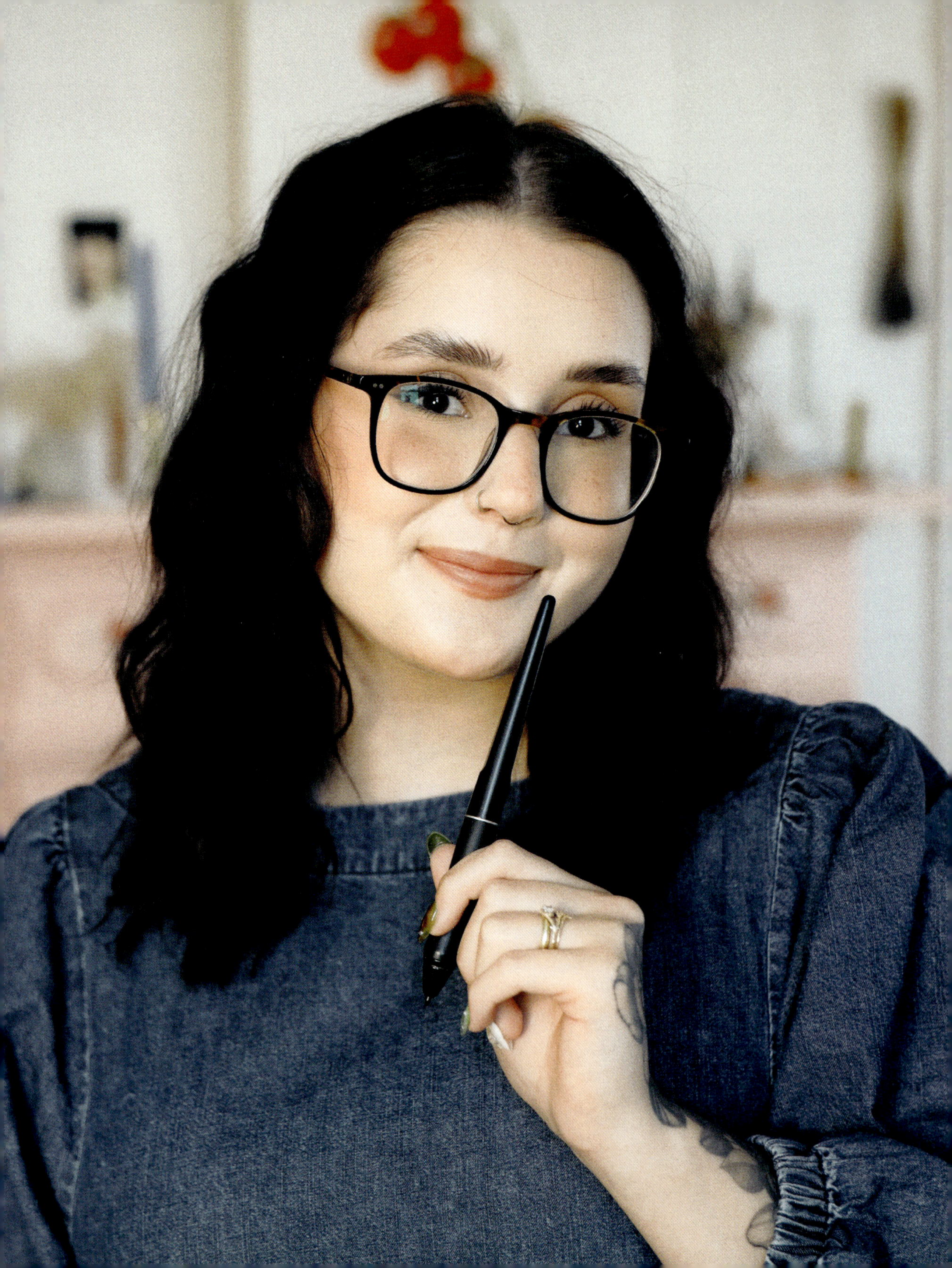

ACKNOWLEDGMENTS

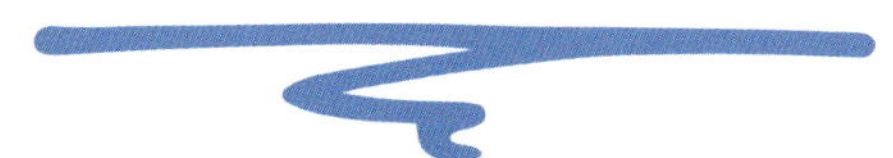

To Zac, for supporting me through this process, staying up with me through the late nights and bringing me so much food. I'm grateful for such a loving and wonderful partner who has encouraged me to achieve my goals.

To my supporters, who have given me the opportunity to make my passion into an actual job.

Lastly, to Page Street Publishing, for being such an understanding and sweet publisher. I appreciate the team that made this book possible!

ABOUT THE AUTHOR

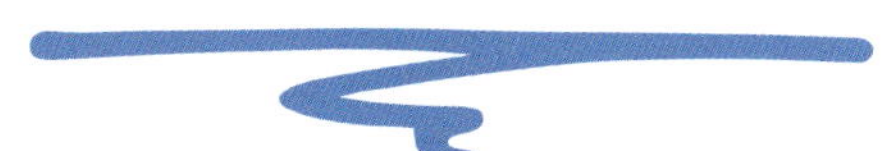

Sara Tepes was born in Romania, but moved to the United States when she was four years old. She has been drawing since she can remember and is a self-taught artist. She has a BS in graphic design and minors in studio arts and photography and lives in Virginia with her husband, Zac, and their three cats: Klaus, Sybil and Priya. You can find her drawing while watching true crime documentaries, cooking with whole heads of garlic and tomatoes or traveling across the world on art retreats with other creative people.

INDEX

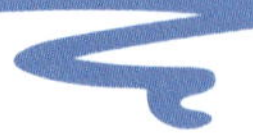